AT HOME WITH
crochet

A LEISURE ARTS PUBLICATION
PRESENTED BY OXMOOR HOUSE

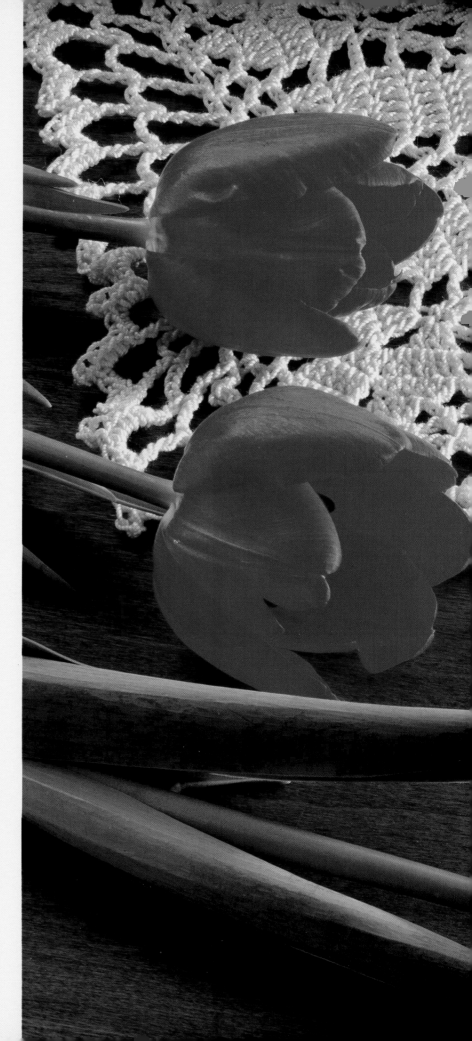

EDITORIAL STAFF

Vice President and Editor-in-Chief:
   Anne Van Wagner Childs
Executive Director: Sandra Graham Case
Executive Editor: Susan Frantz Wiles
Publications Director: Carla Bentley
Creative Art Director: Gloria Bearden
Production Art Director: Melinda Stout

PRODUCTION
Managing Editor: Cathy Hardy
Senior Editor: Teri Sargent
Editorial Assistant: Sarah J. Green

EDITORIAL
Associate Editor: Linda L. Trimble
Senior Editorial Writer: Tammi Williamson Bradley
Editorial Associates: Terri Leming Davidson and
   Robyn Sheffield-Edwards
Copy Editor: Laura Lee Weland

ART
Book/Magazine Art Director: Diane M. Ghegan
Senior Production Artist: M. Katherine Yancey
Photography Stylists: Laura Bushmiaer, Sondra Daniel,
   Karen Smart Hall, Aurora Huston, Emily Minnick,
   and Christina Tiano Myers

BUSINESS STAFF

Publisher: Bruce Akin
Vice President, Finance: Tom Siebenmorgen
Vice President, Retail Sales: Thomas L. Carlisle
Retail Sales Director: Richard Tignor
Vice President, Retail Marketing: Pam Stebbins
Retail Customer Services Director: Margaret Sweetin
Marketing Manager: Russ Barnett
Executive Director of Marketing and Circulation:
   Guy A. Crossley
Circulation Manager: Byron L. Taylor
Print Production Manager: Laura Lockhart
Print Production Coordinator: Nancy Reddick Lister

CROCHET COLLECTION SERIES

Library of Congress Catalog Number: 94-74357
Hardcover ISBN 0-942237-58-7
Softcover ISBN 0-942237-59-5

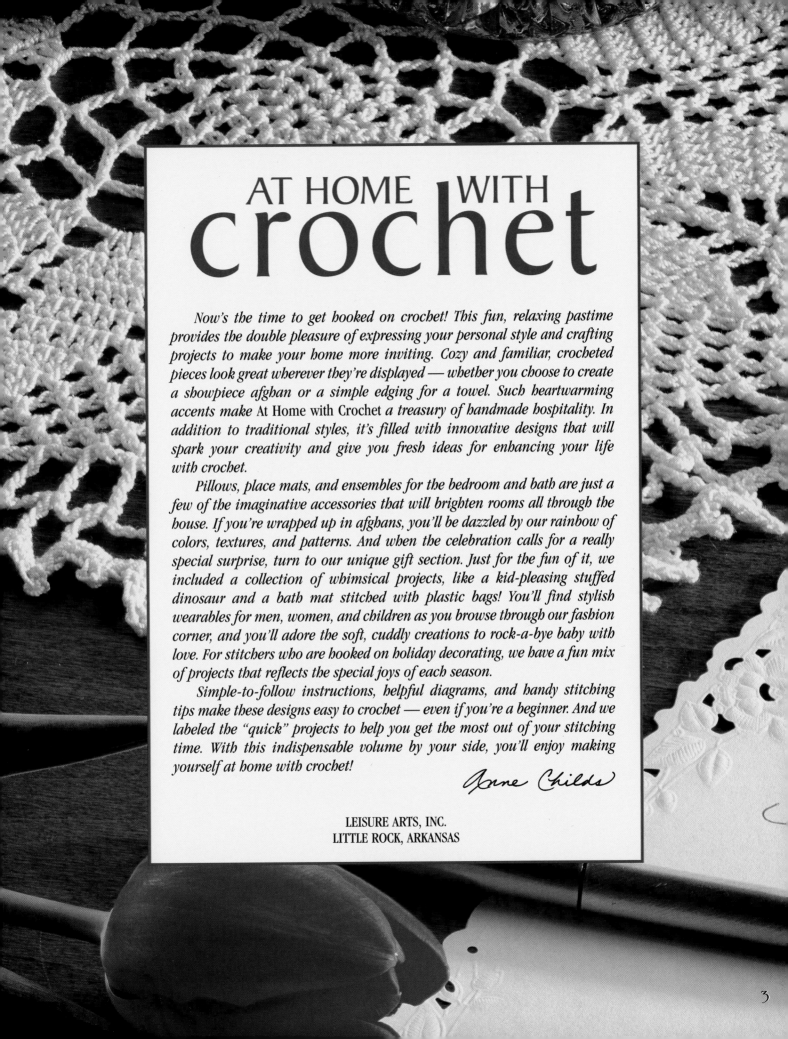

AT HOME WITH
crochet

Now's the time to get hooked on crochet! This fun, relaxing pastime provides the double pleasure of expressing your personal style and crafting projects to make your home more inviting. Cozy and familiar, crocheted pieces look great wherever they're displayed — whether you choose to create a showpiece afghan or a simple edging for a towel. Such heartwarming accents make At Home with Crochet *a treasury of handmade hospitality. In addition to traditional styles, it's filled with innovative designs that will spark your creativity and give you fresh ideas for enhancing your life with crochet.*

Pillows, place mats, and ensembles for the bedroom and bath are just a few of the imaginative accessories that will brighten rooms all through the house. If you're wrapped up in afghans, you'll be dazzled by our rainbow of colors, textures, and patterns. And when the celebration calls for a really special surprise, turn to our unique gift section. Just for the fun of it, we included a collection of whimsical projects, like a kid-pleasing stuffed dinosaur and a bath mat stitched with plastic bags! You'll find stylish wearables for men, women, and children as you browse through our fashion corner, and you'll adore the soft, cuddly creations to rock-a-bye baby with love. For stitchers who are hooked on holiday decorating, we have a fun mix of projects that reflects the special joys of each season.

Simple-to-follow instructions, helpful diagrams, and handy stitching tips make these designs easy to crochet — even if you're a beginner. And we labeled the "quick" projects to help you get the most out of your stitching time. With this indispensable volume by your side, you'll enjoy making yourself at home with crochet!

Anne Childs

LEISURE ARTS, INC.
LITTLE ROCK, ARKANSAS

3

table of contents

wrapped up in afghans

Cozy afghans — especially ones made by hand — are warmers for the body as well as the soul. A snuggly wrap draped across a chair offers an unspoken invitation to "come on in and make yourself at home." The variety of styles in this collection lets you extend the appealing comfort of afghans throughout your home. Whether you prefer traditional elegance, country charm, or bold, innovative looks, these creations will surround you with beauty.

PATCHWORK SAMPLER

The charm of patchwork quilts inspired this colorful sampler, which features four different textured blocks. The squares are individually edged with single crochets and whipstitched together to form the "quilt top." Leaf and vine embroidery enhance the afghan, and a placement diagram makes assembly easy.

Finished Size: Approximately 50" x 64"

MATERIALS
Worsted Weight Yarn, approximately:
    Color A (Teal) - 14 ounces, (400 grams, 880 yards)
    Color B (Gold) - 12 ounces, (340 grams, 755 yards)
    Color C (Maroon) - 15 ounces, (430 grams, 945 yards)
    Color D (Purple) - 12 ounces, (340 grams, 755 yards)
    Color E (Green) - 8 ounces, (230 grams, 505 yards)
Crochet hook, size H (5.00 mm) **or** size needed for gauge
Yarn needle

PATTERN STITCHES
CLUSTER PUFF
YO, insert hook in same st, YO and pull up a loop, YO and draw through 2 loops on hook, skip next sc, YO, insert hook in next sc, YO and pull up a loop even with loop on hook, YO, insert hook in same st, YO and pull up a loop even with loop on hook, YO and draw through all 6 loops on hook.
DECREASE
Pull up a loop in next 2 sc, YO and draw through all 3 loops on hook **(counts as one sc)**.

GAUGE: One Square = 7" x 7"

SQUARE A (Make 16)
With Color A, ch 26 **loosely**.
Row 1 (Right side)**:** Dc in fourth ch from hook and in each ch across: 24 sts.
Row 2: Ch 1, turn; sc in Back Loop Only of each st across **(Fig. 22, page 138)**.
Row 3: Ch 1, turn; working in free loops on previous dc row **(Fig. 23a, page 138)**, slip st in first st, ch 3 **(counts as first dc, now and throughout)**, dc in next dc and in each dc across: 24 dc.
Repeat Rows 2 and 3 until Square measures approximately 6½", ending by working Row 3; do **not** finish off.

Edging: Ch 1, work 22 sc evenly spaced across end of rows; working in free loops of beginning ch **(Fig. 23b, page 138)**, 3 sc in first ch, sc in each ch across to last ch, 3 sc in last ch; work 22 sc evenly spaced across end of rows; working across last row, 3 sc in first dc, sc in each dc across to last dc, 3 sc in last dc; join with slip st to first sc; finish off: 100 sc.

SQUARE B (Make 16)

With Color B, ch 24 **loosely**.

Row 1 (Right side)**:** Sc in second ch from hook and in each ch across: 23 sc.

Note: Loop a short piece of yarn around any stitch to mark last row as **right** side.

Row 2: Ch 2 (**counts as first hdc, now and throughout**), turn; work Cluster Puff, (ch 1, work Cluster Puff) across, hdc in same st as last st: 11 Cluster Puffs.

Row 3: Ch 1, turn; sc in each st across: 23 sc.

Repeat Rows 2 and 3 until Square measures approximately 6½", ending by working Row 3; do **not** finish off.

Edging: Ch 1, work 22 sc evenly spaced across end of rows; working in free loops of beginning ch, 3 sc in first ch, work 22 sc evenly spaced across to last ch, 3 sc in last ch; work 22 sc evenly spaced across end of rows; working across last row, 3 sc in first sc, work 22 sc evenly spaced across to last sc, 3 sc in last sc; join with slip st to first sc, finish off: 100 sc.

SQUARE C (Make 16)

With Color C, ch 26 **loosely**.

Row 1: Sc in second ch from hook and in next 7 chs, (ch 10, sc) 3 times in same ch as last sc, sc in next 10 chs, (ch 10, sc) 3 times in same ch as last sc, sc in each ch across: 31 sc.

Row 2 (Right side)**:** Ch 1, turn; sc in first 7 sc, skip next sc, decrease working **behind** ch-10 loops, skip next sc, sc in next 9 sts, skip next sc, decrease working **behind** ch-10 loops, skip next sc, sc in each sc across: 25 sc.

Row 3: Ch 1, turn; sc in each sc across.

Row 4: Ch 1, turn; sc in first 4 sc, † holding next loop in front of next sc, sc in both loop **and** in next sc, sc in next 5 sc, skip next loop, holding next loop in front of next sc, sc in both loop **and** in next sc †, sc in next 3 sc, repeat from † to † once, sc in each sc across: 25 sc.

Row 5: Ch 1, turn; sc in each sc across.

Row 6: Ch 1, turn; sc in first 7 sc, holding center loop in front of next sc, 6 dc in both loop **and** in next sc, sc in next 9 sc, holding center loop in front of next sc, 6 dc in both loop **and** in next sc, sc in each sc across.

Row 7: Ch 1, turn; sc in first 7 sc, ch 1, skip next 6 dc, pushing dc to right side, sc in next 5 sc, (ch 10, sc) 3 times in same st as last sc, sc in next 4 sc, ch 1, skip next 6 dc, pushing dc to right side, sc in each sc across: 28 sts.

Row 8: Ch 1, turn; sc in first 12 sts, skip next sc, decrease working **behind** ch-10 loops, skip next sc, sc in each st across: 25 sc.

Row 9: Ch 1, turn; sc in each sc across.

Row 10: Ch 1, turn; sc in first 9 sc, holding next loop in front of next sc, sc in both loop **and** in next sc, sc in next 5 sc, skip next loop, holding next loop in front of next sc, sc in both loop **and** in next sc, sc in each sc across.

Row 11: Ch 1, turn; sc in each sc across.

Row 12: Ch 1, turn; sc in first 12 sc, holding center loop in front of next sc, 6 dc in both loop **and** in next sc, sc in each sc across.

Row 13: Ch 1, turn; sc in first 8 sc, (ch 10, sc) 3 times in same st as last sc, sc in next 4 sc, ch 1, skip next 6 dc, pushing dc to right side, sc in next 5 sc, (ch 10, sc) 3 times in same st as last sc, sc in each sc across.

Rows 14-24: Repeat Rows 2-12 once.

Row 25: Ch 1, turn; sc in first 12 sc, ch 1, skip next 6 dc, pushing dc to right side, sc in each sc across.

Row 26: Ch 1, turn; sc in each sc across; do **not** finish off.

Edging: Work same as Square B.

SQUARE D (Make 15)

With Color D, ch 24 **loosely**.

Row 1 (Right side)**:** Sc in second ch from hook and in each ch across: 23 sc.

Note: Loop a short piece of yarn around any stitch to mark last row as **right** side.

Row 2: Ch 1, turn; sc in first sc, tr in next sc, sc in next sc pushing tr to right side, tr in next sc, (sc in next 4 sc, tr in next sc, sc in next sc, tr in next sc) twice, sc in last 5 sc.

Row 3 AND ALL RIGHT SIDE ROWS: Ch 1, turn; sc in each st across.

Row 4: Ch 1, turn; sc in first 2 sc, (tr in next sc, sc in next sc, tr in next sc, sc in next 4 sc) 3 times.

Row 6: Ch 1, turn; sc in first 3 sc, tr in next sc, sc in next sc, tr in next sc, (sc in next 4 sc, tr in next sc, sc in next sc, tr in next sc) twice, sc in last 3 sc.

Row 8: Ch 1, turn; sc in first 4 sc, tr in next sc, sc in next sc, tr in next sc, (sc in next 4 sc, tr in next sc, sc in next sc, tr in next sc) twice, sc in last 2 sc.

Row 10: Ch 1, turn; sc in first 5 sc, tr in next sc, sc in next sc, tr in next sc, (sc in next 4 sc, tr in next sc, sc in next sc, tr in next sc) twice, sc in last sc.

Row 12: Ch 1, turn; sc in first sc, tr in next sc, sc in next 4 sc, tr in next sc, (sc in next sc, tr in next sc, sc in next 4 sc, tr in next sc) twice, sc in last 2 sc.

Row 14: Ch 1, turn; sc in first 2 sc, (tr in next sc, sc in next 4 sc, tr in next sc, sc in next sc) 3 times.

Rows 16-24: Repeat Rows 2-10 once; do **not** finish off.

Edging: Work same as Square B.

FINISHING

ASSEMBLY

Following Placement Diagram and using matching colors as desired, whipstitch Squares together forming 7 vertical strips of 9 Squares each *(Fig. 28a, page 140)*; then whipstitch strips together.

BORDER

Rnd 1: With **right** side facing, join Color E with slip st in any corner sc; ch 1, sc in each sc around to last sc working 3 sc in each corner sc, skip last sc; join with slip st to first sc: 771 sc.

Rnd 2: Ch 1, sc in same st and in next 2 sc, ch 3, slip st in last sc worked, ★ sc in next 3 sc, ch 3, slip st in last sc worked; repeat from ★ around; join with slip st to first sc, finish off.

LEAVES AND VINES

Using Placement Diagram as a guide and Color E, embroider Leaves and Vines over seams, using Lazy Daisy St *(Fig. 38, page 142)* and Outline St *(Figs. 32a & b, page 141)*.

PLACEMENT DIAGRAM

BUILDING BLOCKS QUILT

Diamonds in three shades of blue create the illusion of building blocks on this quilt-inspired afghan. Triangles fill in along the sides. The toasty wrap is easy to stitch in single crochet, and a color diagram makes assembly a breeze!

Finished Size: Approximately 47" x 71"

MATERIALS
Worsted Weight Yarn, approximately:
Color A (Light Blue) - 16 ounces,
(450 grams, 1,190 yards)
Color B (Blue) - 16 ounces, (450 grams, 1,190 yards)
Color C (Dark Blue) - 18 ounces,
(510 grams, 1,335 yards)
Crochet hook, size H (5.00 mm) **or** size needed for gauge
Yarn needle

GAUGE: 7 sc and 8 rows = 2"
One Diamond = 4¹/₂" wide and 7¹/₂" tall

PATTERN STITCH
DECREASE
Pull up a loop in next 2 sts, YO and draw through all 3 loops on hook **(counts as one sc).**

DIAMOND A (Make 55)
Row 1 (Right side)**:** With Color A, ch 2; 2 sc in second ch from hook.
Note: Loop a short piece of yarn around any stitch to mark last row as **right** side and bottom.
Row 2: Ch 1, turn; sc in first sc, 2 sc in next sc: 3 sc.
Row 3: Ch 1, turn; sc in first 2 sc, 2 sc in last sc: 4 sc.
Rows 4-15: Ch 1, turn; sc in each sc across to last sc, 2 sc in last sc: 16 sc.
Rows 16-29: Ch 1, turn; skip first sc, sc in next sc and in each sc across: 2 sc.
Row 30: Ch 1, turn; skip first sc, sc in next sc; finish off.

DIAMOND B (Make 60)
With Color B, work same as Diamond A.

DIAMOND C (Make 60)
With Color C, work same as Diamond A.

TRIANGLE (Make 10)
Rows 1-15: Work same as Diamond A.
Finish off.

ASSEMBLY
Following Placement Diagram, using matching colors as desired and working in end of rows, whipstitch Diamonds together placing bottom of each Diamond A towards the right edge of afghan and bottom of each Diamond B & C towards bottom edge of afghan *(Fig. 28a, page 140)*.
Whipstitch Triangles to each long side, with Row 15 along outer edge.

PLACEMENT DIAGRAM

EDGING
Rnd 1: With **right** side facing, join Color C with slip st in any st; ch 1, sc evenly around working 3 sc in each outer corner and decreasing at each inner corner; join with slip st to first sc.
Rnds 2 and 3: Ch 1, turn; sc in each sc around working 3 sc in each outer corner and decreasing at each inner corner; join with slip st to first sc.
Rnd 4: Ch 1, do **not** turn; working from **left** to **right**, work reverse sc in each sc around *(Figs. 19a-d, page 136)*; join with slip st to first st, finish off.

SNUGGLY WRAPS

Worked in strips that are joined as you go, these two snuggly afghans use front post cross stitches to create their textured ridges. Each afghan, whether fashioned in a single color or stripes, is enhanced with a lovely scalloped effect.

Finished Size: Approximately 47" x 60"

MATERIALS

Worsted Weight Yarn, approximately:

Solid

37 ounces, (1,050 grams, 2,430 yards)

Striped

Color A (Blue) - 18 ounces, (510 grams, 1,185 yards)

Color B (Ecru) - 10 ounces, (280 grams, 655 yards)

Color C (Yellow) - 9 ounces, (260 grams, 590 yards)

Crochet hook, size I (5.50 mm) **or** size needed for gauge

GAUGE: (2 dc, ch 1) 5 times = 4¼"

One Strip = 4¼" wide

PATTERN STITCHES

FRONT POST DOUBLE CROCHET *(abbreviated FPdc)*
YO, insert hook from **front** to **back** around post of dc indicated *(Fig. 13, page 135)*, YO and pull up a loop **even** with loop on hook, (YO and draw through 2 loops on hook) twice.

FRONT POST CROSS STITCH *(abbreviated FP Cross St)*
Skip next dc, work FPdc around next dc, working in **front** of FPdc just worked, work FPdc around skipped dc *(Fig. 1)*.

Fig. 1

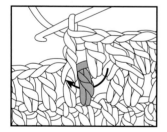

BACK POST DOUBLE CROCHET *(abbreviated BPdc)*
YO, insert hook from **back** to **front** around post of dc indicated, YO and pull up a loop **even** with loop on hook, (YO and draw through 2 loops on hook) twice.

DECREASE (uses next 2 sts)
★ YO, insert hook in Back Loop Only of **next** FPdc *(Fig. 22, page 138)*, YO and pull up a loop, YO and draw through 2 loops on hook; repeat from ★ once **more**, YO and draw through all 3 loops on hook.

FIRST STRIP

Note: For Striped Afghan, work in the following Color Sequence: 1 Rnd each Color C *(Fig. 24b, page 138)*, Color A, Color B, Color A.

Ch 198 **loosely**.

Rnd 1 (Right side): (Dc, ch 1, 2 dc) in fourth ch from hook **(3 skipped chs count as first dc)**, ch 1, (skip next ch, dc in next 2 chs, ch 1) across to last 2 chs, skip next ch, (2 dc, ch 1) 3 times in last ch; working in free loops of beginning ch *(Fig. 23b, page 138)*, (skip next ch, dc in next 2 chs, ch 1) 64 times, skip next ch, 2 dc in same ch as first dc, ch 1; join with slip st to first dc: 134 ch-1 sps.

Note: Loop a short piece of yarn around any stitch to mark last round as **right** side.

Rnd 2: Slip st in next dc and in first ch-1 sp, ch 3, 2 dc in same sp, work FP Cross St, (dc in next ch-1 sp, work FP Cross St) 65 times, (3 dc in next ch-1 sp, work FP Cross St) twice, (dc in next ch-1 sp, work FP Cross St) 65 times, 3 dc in next ch-1 sp, work FP Cross St; join with slip st to top of beginning ch-3: 134 FP Cross Sts.

Rnd 3: Ch 4, † work BPdc around next 2 dc, ch 1, decrease, ch 1, (work BPdc around next dc, ch 1, decrease, ch 1) 65 times, work BPdc around next 2 dc, ch 1 †, (dc in Back Loop Only of next st, ch 1) 4 times, repeat from † to † once, (dc in Back Loop Only of next st, ch 1) 3 times; join with slip st to third ch of beginning ch-4: 274 ch-1 sps.

Rnd 4: Slip st in first ch-1 sp, ch 3, (slip st in next ch-1 sp, ch 1, slip st in next ch-1 sp, ch 3) 67 times, (slip st, ch 1, slip st) in next ch-1 sp, ch 3, (slip st in next ch-1 sp, ch 1, slip st in next ch-1 sp, ch 3) 68 times, (slip st, ch 1, slip st) in next ch-1 sp, ch 3, slip st in next ch-1 sp, ch 1; join with slip st to first slip st, finish off.

REMAINING 10 STRIPS

Work same as First Strip through Rnd 3.

Rnd 4: Slip st in first ch-1 sp, ch 3, (slip st in next ch-1 sp, ch 1, slip st in next ch-1 sp, ch 3) 67 times, (slip st, ch 1, slip st) in next ch-1 sp, (ch 3, slip st in next ch-1 sp, ch 1, slip st in next ch-1 sp) twice; holding Strips with **wrong** sides together, ★ ch 1, slip st in corresponding ch-3 sp on **previous Strip**, (ch 1, slip st in next ch-1 sp on **new Strip**) twice; repeat from ★ 64 times **more**, ch 3, slip st in next ch-1 sp, ch 1, slip st in next ch-1 sp, ch 3, (slip st, ch 1, slip st) in next ch-1 sp, ch 3, slip st in next ch-1 sp, ch 1; join with slip st to first slip st, finish off.

Quick LACY HEXAGONS

Because it's worked with two strands of worsted weight yarn, this airy wrap is less fragile than it looks! The hexagon motifs are worked separately and then whipstitched together. The afghan is edged with reverse half double crochets.

Finished Size: Approximately 56" x 64"

MATERIALS
Worsted Weight Yarn, approximately:
57 ounces, (1,620 grams, 3,745 yards)
Crochet hook, size N (9.00 mm) **or** size needed for gauge
Yarn needle

Note: Entire Afghan is worked holding 2 strands of yarn together.

GAUGE: One Motif = 9" (from straight edge to straight edge)

MOTIF (Make 45)
Ch 5; join with slip st to form a ring.
Rnd 1 (Right side)**:** Ch 3 **(counts as first dc, now and throughout)**, 11 dc in ring; join with slip st to first dc: 12 dc.
Note: Loop a short piece of yarn around any stitch to mark last round as **right** side.
Rnd 2: Ch 3, dc in same st, 2 dc in next dc, ch 1, (2 dc in each of next 2 dc, ch 1) around; join with slip st to first dc: 24 dc.
Rnd 3: Ch 3, dc in same st and in next 2 dc, 2 dc in next dc, ch 2, ★ 2 dc in next dc, dc in next 2 dc, 2 dc in next dc, ch 2; repeat from ★ around; join with slip st to first dc: 36 dc.
Rnd 4: Ch 3, dc in same st and in next 4 dc, 2 dc in next dc, ch 3, ★ 2 dc in next dc, dc in next 4 dc, 2 dc in next dc, ch 3; repeat from ★ around; join with slip st to first dc: 48 dc.
Rnd 5: Ch 3, dc in same st and in next 6 dc, 2 dc in next dc, ch 4, ★ 2 dc in next dc, dc in next 6 dc, 2 dc in next dc, ch 4; repeat from ★ around; join with slip st to first dc, finish off: 60 dc.

ASSEMBLY
Following Placement Diagram and leaving corner ch-4 sps free, whipstitch Motifs together forming strips *(Fig. 28b, page 140)*; then whipstitch strips together.

PLACEMENT DIAGRAM

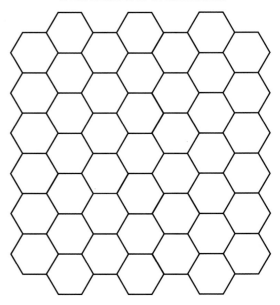

EDGING
Rnd 1: With **right** side facing, join yarn with slip st in any dc; ch 1, sc in each dc around working 4 sc in each corner ch-4 sp and 2 sc in each sp at joinings; join with slip st to first sc.
Rnd 2: Ch 1, hdc in same st, ch 1, working from **left** to **right**, ★ skip next sc, work reverse hdc in next sc *(Figs. 20a-d, page 136)*, ch 1; repeat from ★ around; join with slip st to first hdc, finish off.

BOLD APPEAL

Irresistibly soft, this luxurious fringed afghan is fashioned with cuddly brushed mohair blend and durable worsted weight yarns. The textured teal and purple panels are worked in bold graduated stripes and accented with vertical rows of navy slip stitches.

Finished Size: Approximately 49" x 65"

MATERIALS

Worsted Weight Brushed Mohair Blend, approximately:
   Color A (Purple) - 14 ounces, (400 grams, 940 yards)
Worsted Weight Yarn, approximately:
   Color B (Teal) - 32 ounces, (910 grams, 2,835 yards)
   Color C (Navy) - 4 ounces, (110 grams, 270 yards)
Crochet hooks, sizes J (6.00 mm) **and** N (9.00 mm) **or** sizes needed for gauge

GAUGE: With smaller size hook and Color B,
   13 dc and 7 rows = 4"
   With larger size hook and Color A, 13 hdc = 4"

Note: Each row is worked across length of afghan.

PATTERN STITCH
SLANT ST
Skip next 3 sts, tr in next st, working **behind** tr just made, dc in 3 skipped sts.

BODY

With larger size hook and Color A, ch 213 **loosely**.
Row 1: Hdc in third ch from hook **(2 skipped chs count as first hdc)** and in each ch across: 212 hdc.
Row 2 (Right side): Ch 3 **(counts as first dc, now and throughout)**, turn; working in Back Loops Only *(Fig. 22, page 138)*, dc in next st, work Slant Sts across to last 2 sts, dc in last 2 sts: 52 Slant Sts.
Note: Loop a short piece of yarn around last dc to mark last row as **right** side and bottom.
Row 3: Ch 2 **(counts as first hdc, now and throughout)**, turn; hdc in Front Loop Only of next st and in each st across: 212 hdc.
Rows 4-16: Repeat Rows 2 and 3, 6 times, then repeat Row 2 once **more** changing to Color B at end of Row 16 *(Fig. 24a, page 138)*.
Row 17: Using smaller size hook, ch 3, turn; dc in Front Loop Only of next st and in each st across.

Row 18: Ch 3, turn; dc in Back Loop Only of next st and in each st across.
Row 19: Ch 3, turn; dc in both loops of next dc and in each dc across.
Rows 20-24: Repeat Rows 18 and 19 twice, then repeat Row 18 once **more** changing to Color A at end of Row 24.
Row 25: Using larger size hook, ch 2, turn; hdc in both loops of next dc and in each dc across.
Rows 26-33: Repeat Rows 2 and 3, 4 times changing to Color B at end of Row 33.
Rows 34-39: Using smaller size hook, repeat Rows 18 and 19, 3 times changing to Color A at end of Row 39.
Rows 40-43: With larger size hook, repeat Rows 2 and 3, twice changing to Color B at end of Row 43.
Rows 44-48: With smaller size hook, repeat Rows 18 and 19 twice, then repeat Row 18 once **more** changing to Color A at end of Row 48.
Row 49: Repeat Row 25.
Rows 50 and 51: Repeat Rows 2 and 3 changing to Color B at end of Row 51.
Rows 52-54: Using smaller size hook, repeat Rows 18 and 19 once, then repeat Row 18 once **more** changing to Color A at end of Row 54.
Rows 55-60: Repeat Rows 49-54.
Row 61: Repeat Row 25.
Row 62: Repeat Row 2 changing to Color B in last dc.
Rows 63 and 64: Repeat Rows 17 and 18; at end of Row 64 finish off.
Row 65: With **right** side facing, larger size hook, and working in both loops, join Color A with slip st in first dc; ch 3, dc in next dc, work Slant Sts across to last 2 dc, dc in last 2 dc changing to Color B in last dc.
Row 66: Repeat Row 17; finish off.
Row 67: With **wrong** side facing, larger size hook, and working in both loops, join Color A with slip st in first dc; ch 2, hdc in next dc and in each dc across changing to Color B in last hdc.
Rows 68-94: Using smaller size hook, repeat Rows 18 and 19, 13 times, then repeat Row 18 once **more**.
Finish off.

STRIPES

With **right** side facing, larger size hook, and working from bottom to top on Row 17, hold Color C at back, insert hook from **front** to **back** in sp **between** first and second dc, YO and pull up a loop, ★ skip next sp, insert hook in next sp, YO and **loosely** draw through loop on hook; repeat from ★ across to last dc, slip st around post of last dc, ch 1, **turn**; slip st **loosely**

in each slip st across inserting hook from top to bottom; finish off.

Repeat Stripe on Rows 34, 44, 52, 58, 63, 66, and 68.

Add fringe using 6 strands each of Color A and Color B, and 3 strands of Color C, each 19" long *(Figs. 30a & b, page 140)*; attach matching color evenly spaced across end of rows on both ends of afghan.

Quick FILET RIPPLES

Using two strands of yarn and a jumbo hook makes it quick — and easy — to finish this pretty filet afghan. Worked in double crochets, a traditional ripple pattern gives the throw its lacy appeal. A simple scalloped edging borders the cozy coverlet.

Finished Size: Approximately 48" x 62"

MATERIALS
Worsted Weight Yarn, approximately:
    MC (Off-White) - 36 ounces, (1,020 grams, 2,100 yards)
    Color A (Green) - 12 ounces, (340 grams, 700 yards)
    Color B (Rose) - 10 ounces, (280 grams, 585 yards)
    Crochet hook, size P (10.00 mm) **or** size needed for gauge

Note: Entire Afghan is worked holding 2 strands of yarn together.

GAUGE: 7 dc = 3"
        In pattern, 1 repeat = 6" and 6 rows = 7"

Gauge Swatch (12" x 7")
Ch 37 **loosely.**
Rows 1-6: Work same as Body.
Finish off.

PATTERN STITCHES
BEGINNING DECREASE
Ch 2, turn; skip next st, dc in next dc **(counts as one dc).**
DECREASE
† YO, insert hook in **next** st, YO and pull up a loop, YO and draw through 2 loops on hook †, skip next 3 sts, repeat from † to † once, YO and draw through all 3 loops on hook **(counts as one dc).**
ENDING DECREASE
† YO, insert hook in **next** st, YO and pull up a loop, YO and draw through 2 loops on hook †, skip next st, repeat from † to † once, YO and draw through all 3 loops on hook **(counts as one dc).**

BODY

COLOR SEQUENCE
4 Rows MC *(Fig. 24a, page 138)*, ★ 1 row Color A, 1 row Color B, 4 rows MC; repeat from ★ throughout.

With MC, ch 157 **loosely.**
Row 1: Dc in fifth ch from hook **(4 skipped chs count as first dc plus ch 1)**, ch 1, (skip next ch, dc in next ch, ch 1) twice, skip next ch, (dc, ch 3, dc) in next ch, ★ ch 1, (skip next ch, dc in next ch, ch 1) 3 times, skip next ch, decrease,

ch 1, (skip next ch, dc in next ch, ch 1) 3 times, skip next ch, (dc, ch 3, dc) in next ch; repeat from ★ across to last 6 chs, ch 1, (skip next ch, dc in next ch, ch 1) twice, skip next ch, (dc, ch 1, dc) in last ch: 73 dc.
Row 2 (Right side): Work beginning decrease, (dc in next ch-1 sp, dc in next dc) 3 times, (2 dc, ch 3, 2 dc) in next ch-3 sp, (dc in next dc, dc in next ch-1 sp) 3 times, ★ decrease, (dc in next ch-1 sp, dc in next dc) 3 times, (2 dc, ch 3, 2 dc) in next ch-3 sp, (dc in next dc, dc in next ch-1 sp) 3 times; repeat from ★ across to last 2 dc, work ending decrease: 137 dc.
Note: Loop a short piece of yarn around any stitch to mark last row as **right** side.
Row 3: Work beginning decrease, ch 1, (skip next dc, dc in next dc, ch 1) 3 times, (dc, ch 3, dc) in next ch-3 sp, ch 1, (dc in next dc, ch 1, skip next dc) 3 times, ★ decrease, ch 1, (skip next dc, dc in next dc, ch 1) 3 times, (dc, ch 3, dc) in next ch-3 sp, ch 1, (dc in next dc, ch 1, skip next dc) 3 times; repeat from ★ across to last 3 dc, work ending decrease: 73 dc.
Rows 4-52: Repeat Rows 2 and 3, 24 times, then repeat Row 2 once **more.**
Finish off.

EDGING

With **right** side facing, join Color A with slip st in first dc; ch 1, sc in same st, skip next 2 dc, 5 dc in next dc, skip next 2 dc, sc in next dc, skip next 2 dc, 7 dc in next ch-3 sp, skip next 2 dc, sc in next dc, † (skip next 2 dc, 5 dc in next dc, skip next 2 dc, sc in next dc) twice, skip next 2 dc, 7 dc in next ch-3 sp, skip next 2 dc, sc in next dc †, repeat from † to † across to last 6 dc, skip next 2 dc, 5 dc in next dc, skip next 2 dc, sc in last dc; working in end of rows, (5 dc, sc) in first row, (5 dc in next row, sc in next row) across to last row, 7 dc in last row; working in unworked chs and in free loops of beginning ch *(Fig. 23b, page 138)* and in ch-3 sps, sc in first ch, (skip next 2 chs, 5 dc in next ch, skip next 2 chs, sc in next ch) twice, ★ skip next 2 chs, 7 dc in next ch-3 sp, skip next 2 chs, sc in next ch, (skip next 2 chs, 5 dc in next ch, skip next 2 chs, sc in next ch) twice; repeat from ★ 6 times **more**; working in end of rows, 7 dc in first row, (sc in next row, 5 dc in next row) across to last row, (sc, 5 dc) in last row; join with slip st to first sc, finish off.

18

BROWN-EYED SUSANS

Blooming against a field of green, rows of brown-eyed Susans pay tribute to a favorite wildflower. Our lacy throw is worked in squares that are joined as you stitch, and it's finished with a simple ruffled border.

Finished Size: Approximately 49" x 63"

MATERIALS
Worsted Weight Yarn, approximately:
    MC (Green) - 16 ounces, (450 grams, 1,100 yards)
    Color A (Brown) - 4 ounces, (110 grams, 275 yards)
    Color B (Gold) - 21 ounces, (600 grams, 1,440 yards)
    Crochet hook, size H (5.00 mm) **or** size needed for gauge

GAUGE: One Square = 4¹/2"

PATTERN STITCHES
TR CLUSTER
★ YO twice, insert hook in same sp, YO and pull up a loop, (YO and draw through 2 loops on hook) twice; repeat from ★ once **more**, YO and draw through all 3 loops on hook *(Figs. 10a & b, page 134)*.
DC CLUSTER
★ YO, insert hook in st indicated, YO and pull up a loop, YO and draw through 2 loops on hook; repeat from ★ 2 times **more**, YO and draw through all 4 loops on hook.

FIRST SQUARE
With Color A, ch 3; join with slip st to form a ring.
Rnd 1 (Right side): Ch 1, 6 sc in ring; join with slip st to Front Loop Only of first sc *(Fig. 22, page 138)*.
Note: Loop a short piece of yarn around any stitch to mark last round as **right** side.
Rnd 2: Working in Front Loops Only, (dc, slip st) in same st, (slip st, dc, slip st) in next sc and in each sc around pushing dc to **wrong** side; join with slip st to first slip st, finish off.
Rnd 3: With **right** side facing and working in free loops on Rnd 1 *(Fig. 23a, page 138)*, join Color B with slip st in any sc; ch 1, 2 sc in each sc around; join with slip st to first sc: 12 sc.
Rnd 4: Ch 1, sc in same st, ch 3, (sc in next sc, ch 3) around; join with slip st to first sc: 12 ch-3 sps.
Rnd 5: Slip st in first ch-3 sp, ch 1, work (sc, ch 3, tr Cluster, ch 3, sc) in same sp and in each ch-3 sp around; join with slip st to first sc, finish off: 12 Petals.
Rnd 6: With **right** side facing, join MC with slip st in top of any Petal; ch 1, sc in same st, ch 5, sc in top of next Petal, ch 5,

(work dc Cluster, ch 5) twice in top of next Petal, ★ (sc in top of next Petal, ch 5) twice, (work dc Cluster, ch 5) twice in top of next Petal; repeat from ★ around; join with slip st to first sc, finish off.

ADDITIONAL SQUARES (Make 129)
Work same as First Square through Rnd 5.
Work One-Sided or Two-Sided Joining to form 10 vertical strips of 13 Squares each.

ONE-SIDED JOINING
Rnd 6: With **right** side facing, join MC with slip st in top of any Petal; ch 1, sc in same st, ch 5, sc in top of next Petal, ch 5, † (work dc Cluster, ch 5) twice in top of next Petal, (sc in top of next Petal, ch 5) twice †, repeat from † to † once **more**, work dc Cluster in top of next Petal, ch 2, with **right** side facing, slip st in any corner loop on **previous Square**, ch 2, work dc Cluster in same st on **new Square**, ch 2, slip st in next loop on **previous Square**, ch 2, (sc in top of next Petal on **new Square**, ch 2, slip st in next loop on **previous Square**, ch 2) twice, work dc Cluster in top of next Petal on **new Square**, ch 2, slip st in next corner loop on **previous Square**, ch 2, work dc Cluster in same st on **new Square**, ch 5; join with slip st to first sc, finish off.

TWO-SIDED JOINING
Rnd 6: With **right** side facing, join MC with slip st in top of any Petal; ch 1, sc in same st, ch 5, sc in top of next Petal, ch 5, (work dc Cluster, ch 5) twice in top of next Petal, (sc in top of next Petal, ch 5) twice, ★ † work dc Cluster in top of next Petal, ch 2, with **right** side facing, slip st in corner loop on **previous Square**, ch 2, work dc Cluster in same st on **new Square** †, ch 2, slip st in next loop on **previous Square**, ch 2, (sc in top of next Petal on **new Square**, ch 2, slip st in next loop on **previous Square**, ch 2) twice; repeat from ★ once **more**, then repeat from † to † once, ch 5; join with slip st to first sc, finish off.

BORDER
Rnd 1: With **right** side facing, join MC with slip st in any corner ch-5 loop; ch 1, ★ (sc, ch 3) twice in corner loop, (sc in next loop, ch 3) across to next corner loop; repeat from ★ around; join with slip st to first sc.

Rnd 2: Ch 1, sc in same st, 3 sc in next ch-3 sp, (sc in next sc, 3 sc in next ch-3 sp) around; join with slip st to first sc, finish off.

Rnd 3: With **wrong** side facing, join Color B with slip st in same st as joining; ch 1, sc in same st, tr in next sc, (sc in next sc pushing tr to **right** side, tr in next sc) around; join with slip st to first sc, finish off.

Rnd 4: With **right** side facing, join MC with slip st in second sc to **left** of joining; ch 1, sc in same st, ch 1, skip next tr,

★ (sc in next sc, ch 1, skip next tr) across to next corner sc, (sc, ch 1) twice in corner sc, skip next tr; repeat from ★ around; join with slip st to first sc: 928 sts.

Rnd 5: Ch 1, sc in same st, (ch 5, skip next 3 sts, sc in next st) around to last 3 sts, ch 2, skip last 3 sts, dc in first sc to form last loop.

Rnd 6: Ch 1, (sc, ch 5, sc) in same loop and in each loop around; join with slip st to first sc, finish off.

HANDSOME STRIPES

Warm, rustic colors give this textured throw a strong masculine appeal. Worked in a single piece, it features stripes of ecru openwork and a blue chain that's woven through the black double crochet stripes. The coordinating border is finished with an ample fringe.

Finished Size: Approximately 48" x 63"

MATERIALS
Worsted Weight Yarn, approximately:
   MC (Beige) - 26 ounces, (740 grams, 1,635 yards)
   Color A (Rust) - 18 ounces, (510 grams, 1,130 yards)
   Color B (Black) - 10 ounces, (280 grams, 630 yards)
   Color C (Blue) - 3 ounces, (90 grams, 190 yards)
Crochet hook, size I (5.50 mm) **or** size needed for gauge
Yarn needle

GAUGE: In pattern, 16 dc = 4" and Rows 1-9 = 3"

Note: Each row is worked across length of afghan.

PATTERN STITCH
CROSS ST
Skip next 2 sc, dc in next sc, ch 1, working in **front** of last dc made, dc in first skipped sc *(Fig. 1)*.

Fig. 1

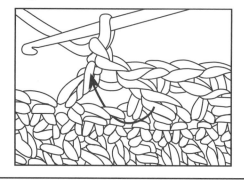

BODY

With Color A, ch 234 **loosely**.

Row 1 (Right side)**:** Sc in second ch from hook and in each ch across: 233 sc.

Note: Loop a short piece of yarn around any stitch to mark last row as **right** side.

Row 2: Ch 1, turn; sc in first sc, (tr in next sc, sc in next sc pushing tr to **right** side) across changing to Color B in last sc *(Fig. 24a, page 138)*.

Row 3: Ch 1, turn; sc in each st across.

Row 4: Ch 3 **(counts as first dc, now and throughout)**, turn; dc in next sc and in each sc across changing to Color A in last sc.

Row 5: Ch 1, turn; sc in each dc across.

Row 6: Ch 1, turn; sc in first sc, (tr in next sc, sc in next sc) across changing to MC in last sc.

Row 7: Ch 1, turn; sc in each st across.

Row 8: Ch 3, turn; work Cross St across to last sc, dc in last sc: 77 Cross Sts.

Row 9: Ch 1, turn; sc in each dc and in each ch-1 sp across; finish off: 233 sc.

Row 10: With **right** side facing, join Color A with slip st in first sc; ch 1, sc in same st and in each sc across.

Rows 11-16: Repeat Rows 2-7.

Row 17: Ch 3, turn; dc in next sc and in each sc across.

Row 18: Ch 8 **(counts as first dc plus ch 5, now and throughout)**, turn; (skip next 3 dc, dc in next 3 dc, ch 5) across to last 4 dc, skip next 3 dc, dc in last dc: 39 loops.

Rows 19 and 20: Ch 8, turn; (dc in next 3 dc, ch 5) across to last dc, dc in last dc.

Row 21: Ch 6 **(counts as first dc plus ch 3, now and throughout)**, turn; sc **around** ch-5 loops of previous 3 rows, ch 3, ★ dc in next 3 dc, ch 3, sc **around** ch-5 loops of previous 3 rows, ch 3; repeat from ★ across to last dc, dc in last dc.

Row 22: Ch 6, turn; (dc in next 3 dc, ch 3) across to last dc, dc in last dc.

Row 23: Ch 3, turn; dc in next ch and in each ch and dc across changing to Color A in last dc: 233 dc.

Row 24: Ch 1, turn; sc in each dc across.

Rows 25-125: Repeat Rows 2-24, 4 times, then repeat Rows 2-10 once **more**.

Rows 126-129: Repeat Rows 2-5.

Row 130: Ch 1, turn; sc in first sc, (tr in next sc, sc in next sc) across; finish off.

BORDER

Row 1: With **right** side facing and working in end of rows, join Color A with slip st in first row; ch 1, work 187 sc evenly spaced across.

Rows 2-7: Repeat Rows 2-7 of Body.

Row 8: Ch 1, turn; sc in first sc, (ch 3, skip next 2 sc, sc in next sc) across; finish off: 62 ch-3 sps.

Repeat on other end.

TRIM

With Color C, chain a length long enough to weave through dc of Color B stripe. With **right** side facing, weave end of chain through stripe, adjusting chs as necessary; finish off. Secure ends on wrong side.

Repeat Trim for each Color B stripe across Body and Borders.

Add fringe using 6 strands of MC, each 17" long *(Figs. 30a & b, page 140)*; attach in each ch-3 sp across both ends of afghan.

PRETTY IN PEACH

*P*retty as a peach, this cozy afghan uses double crochets and simple shell stitches to
create a pattern of alternating columns and vertical arches. The throw is finished with
a lattice edging of single crochets and chains and enhanced with a tasseled fringe.

Finished Size: Approximately 48" x 64"

MATERIALS

Worsted Weight Yarn, approximately:
    44 ounces, (1,250 grams, 2,565 yards)
    Crochet hook, size K (6.50 mm) **or** size needed for gauge

GAUGE: 12 dc and 7 rows = 4"

BODY

Ch 146 **loosely**.

Row 1: Dc in fourth ch from hook and in next 3 chs, (ch 2,
skip next 2 chs, dc in next 10 chs) across to last 7 chs, ch 2,
skip next 2 chs, dc in last 5 chs: 12 ch-2 sps.

Row 2 (Right side): Ch 3 **(counts as first dc, now and
throughout)**, turn; dc in next 2 dc, skip next 2 dc, (tr, 4 dc, tr)
in next ch-2 sp, ★ skip next 2 dc, dc in next 6 dc, skip next
2 dc, (tr, 4 dc, tr) in next ch-2 sp; repeat from ★ across to last
5 sts, skip next 2 dc, dc in last 3 sts.

Note: Loop a short piece of yarn around any stitch to mark last
row as **right** side.

Row 3: Ch 3, turn; dc in next dc, skip next dc, 2 dc in sp
before next tr, skip next 2 sts, dc in next dc, ch 2, dc in next
dc, skip next 2 sts, 2 dc in sp **before** next dc, ★ skip next dc,
dc in next 4 dc, skip next dc, 2 dc in sp **before** next tr, skip
next 2 sts, dc in next dc, ch 2, dc in next dc, skip next 2 sts,
2 dc in sp **before** next dc; repeat from ★ across to last 3 dc,
skip next dc, dc in last 2 dc.

Repeat Rows 2 and 3 until Afghan measures approximately
61½", ending by working Row 2.

Last Row: Ch 3, turn; dc in next 2 dc, hdc in next tr, sc in next
4 dc, hdc in next tr, ★ dc in next 6 dc, hdc in next tr, sc in next
4 dc, hdc in next tr; repeat from ★ across to last 3 dc, dc in
last 3 dc; do **not** finish off: 144 sts.

EDGING

TOP

Row 1: Ch 5, turn; skip next dc, sc in next dc, (ch 5, skip next
2 sts, sc in next st) across to last 3 sts, ch 2, skip next 2 sts,
dc in last dc to form last loop: 48 loops.

Row 2: Ch 1, turn; sc in same loop, (ch 5, sc in next loop)
across; finish off.

BOTTOM

Row 1: With **right** side facing and working in free loops of
beginning ch *(Fig. 23b, page 138)*, join yarn with slip st in
first ch; ch 5, skip next ch, sc in next ch, (ch 5, skip next 2 chs,
sc in next ch) across to last 3 chs, ch 2, skip next 2 chs, dc in
last ch to form last loop: 48 loops.

Row 2: Ch 1, turn; sc in same loop, (ch 5, sc in next loop)
across; finish off.

Add fringe using 6 strands, each 11" long *(Figs. 30a & b,
page 140)*; attach in each loop across both ends of afghan.

all through the house

Displayed throughout your home, handmade accents are more than just decorative pieces, they're expressions of your individual style. The unique designs we've included here are sure to inspire lots of new ideas for adding warm personal touches all through the house — from a flower-strewn boudoir to a beachside bath. So go ahead, brighten your decor with crochet!

THE LIVING ROOM

*A*dd old-fashioned elegance to the living room with these lacy accessories. (Below) A cozy chair is especially inviting when cushioned with plump pillows. These pretty throw pillows are crocheted with two strands of bedspread weight cotton thread. Coordinating coasters are quick-to-stitch projects that help unify your decor. (Opposite) Draped over a round accent table, our beautiful topper features the ever-popular pineapple pattern.

PINEAPPLE TABLE TOPPER

Finished Size: Approximately 36" in diameter

MATERIALS

Bedspread Weight Cotton Thread (size 10),
   approximately 540 yards
Steel crochet hook, size 6 (1.80 mm) **or** size needed
   for gauge

GAUGE: Rnds 1-4 = 2½"

PATTERN STITCHES

BEGINNING SHELL
Ch 3 **(counts as first dc, now and throughout)**,
(dc, ch 2, 2 dc) in same sp.

SHELL
(2 Dc, ch 2, 2 dc) in sp indicated.

DECREASE (uses next 2 dc)
★ YO, insert hook in **next** dc, YO and pull up a loop, YO
and draw through 2 loops on hook; repeat from ★ once
more, YO and draw through all 3 loops on hook **(counts
as one dc)**.

BEGINNING TR CLUSTER (uses first 4 dc)
Ch 3, ★ YO twice, insert hook in **next** dc, YO and pull up a
loop, (YO and draw through 2 loops on hook) twice; repeat
from ★ 2 times **more**, YO and draw through all 4 loops on
hook **(Figs. 11a & b, page 134)**.

TR CLUSTER (uses next 4 dc)
★ YO twice, insert hook in **next** dc, YO and pull up a loop,
(YO and draw through 2 loops on hook) twice; repeat from
★ 3 times **more**, YO and draw through all 5 loops on hook.

DC CLUSTER (uses next 4 dc)
★ YO, insert hook in **next** dc, YO and pull up a loop, YO
and draw through 2 loops on hook; repeat from ★ 3 times
more, YO and draw through all 5 loops on hook.

BODY

Ch 3; join with slip st to form a ring.

Rnd 1 (Right side)**:** Ch 1, 10 sc in ring; join with slip st to
first sc.

Rnd 2: Ch 1, sc in same st, (ch 3, sc in next sc) around, ch 1,
hdc in first sc to form last sp: 10 sps.

Rnd 3: Ch 1, sc in same sp, ch 3, (sc in next ch-3 sp, ch 3)
around; join with slip st to first sc.

Rnd 4: Slip st in first ch-3 sp, work beginning Shell, ch 3, sc in
next ch-3 sp, ch 3, (work Shell in next ch-3 sp, ch 3, sc in next
ch-3 sp, ch 3) around; join with slip st to first dc: 5 Shells.

Rnd 5: Slip st in next dc and in next ch-2 sp, work beginning
Shell, ch 3, (sc in next ch-3 sp, ch 3) twice, ★ work Shell in
next Shell (ch-2 sp), ch 3, (sc in next ch-3 sp, ch 3) twice;
repeat from ★ around; join with slip st to first dc.

Rnd 6: Slip st in next dc and in next ch-2 sp, work beginning
Shell, ch 3, (sc in next ch-3 sp, ch 3) 3 times, ★ work Shell in
next Shell, ch 3, (sc in next ch-3 sp, ch 3) 3 times; repeat from
★ around; join with slip st to first dc.

Rnd 7: Ch 3, dc in same st, 2 dc in next dc, ch 3, (dc, ch 3)
twice in next ch-2 sp, 2 dc in each of next 2 dc, ch 3, skip next
ch-3 sp, (sc in next ch-3 sp, ch 3) twice, ★ 2 dc in each of
next 2 dc, ch 3, (dc, ch 3) twice in next ch-2 sp, 2 dc in each
of next 2 dc, ch 3, skip next ch-3 sp, (sc in next ch-3 sp, ch 3)
twice; repeat from ★ around; join with slip st to first dc.

Rnd 8: Ch 3, dc in next 3 dc, ★ † ch 3, skip next ch-3 sp, dc
in next ch-3 sp, (ch 1, dc) 9 times in same sp, ch 3, skip next
ch-3 sp, dc in next 4 dc, ch 3, skip next ch-3 sp, sc in next
ch-3 sp, ch 3 †, dc in next 4 dc; repeat from ★ 3 times **more**,
then repeat from † to † once; join with slip st to first dc.

Rnd 9: Ch 3, 2 dc in each of next 2 dc, dc in next dc, ch 3,
(sc in next ch-1 sp, ch 3) 9 times, skip next ch-3 sp, dc in next
dc, 2 dc in each of next 2 dc, ★ dc in next 2 dc, 2 dc in each of
next 2 dc, dc in next dc, ch 3, (sc in next ch-1 sp, ch 3) 9
times, skip next ch-3 sp, dc in next dc, 2 dc in each of next
2 dc; repeat from ★ around to last dc, dc in last dc; join with
slip st to first dc.

Rnd 10: Ch 3, dc in next 5 dc, ch 3, skip next ch-3 sp, (sc in
next ch-3 sp, ch 3) 8 times, ★ (dc in next 6 dc, ch 3) twice,
skip next ch-3 sp, (sc in next ch-3 sp, ch 3) 8 times; repeat
from ★ around to last 6 dc, dc in last 6 dc, ch 3; join with
slip st to first dc.

Rnd 11: Ch 3, dc in next 5 dc, ch 3, skip next ch-3 sp, (sc in
next ch-3 sp, ch 3) 7 times, dc in next 6 dc, ch 3, sc in next
ch-3 sp, ch 3, ★ dc in next 6 dc, ch 3, skip next ch-3 sp, (sc in
next ch-3 sp, ch 3) 7 times, dc in next 6 dc, ch 3, sc in next
ch-3 sp, ch 3; repeat from ★ around; join with slip st to first dc.

Rnd 12: Ch 3, dc in next 5 dc, ch 3, skip next ch-3 sp, (sc in
next ch-3 sp, ch 3) 6 times, dc in next 6 dc, ch 3, (sc in next
ch-3 sp, ch 3) twice, ★ dc in next 6 dc, ch 3, skip next ch-3 sp,
(sc in next ch-3 sp, ch 3) 6 times, dc in next 6 dc, ch 3, (sc in
next ch-3 sp, ch 3) twice; repeat from ★ around; join with
slip st to first dc.

Rnd 13: Ch 3, dc in next 5 dc, ch 3, skip next ch-3 sp, (sc in
next ch-3 sp, ch 3) 5 times, dc in next 6 dc, ch 3, (sc in next
ch-3 sp, ch 3) 3 times, ★ dc in next 6 dc, ch 3, skip next
ch-3 sp, (sc in next ch-3 sp, ch 3) 5 times, dc in next 6 dc,
ch 3, (sc in next ch-3 sp, ch 3) 3 times; repeat from ★ around;
join with slip st to first dc.

Rnd 14: Ch 3, ★ † decrease twice, dc in next dc, ch 3, skip
next ch-3 sp, (sc in next ch-3 sp, ch 3) 4 times, dc in next dc,

decrease twice, dc in next dc, ch 3, (sc in next ch-3 sp, ch 3) 4 times †, dc in next dc; repeat from ★ 3 times **more**, then repeat from † to † once; join with slip st to first dc.

Rnd 15: Ch 3, dc in next 3 dc, ★ † ch 3, skip next ch-3 sp, (sc in next ch-3 sp, ch 3) 3 times, dc in next 4 dc, ch 3, (sc in next ch-3 sp, ch 3) twice, work Shell in next ch-3 sp, ch 3, (sc in next ch-3 sp, ch 3) twice †, dc in next 4 dc; repeat from ★ 3 times **more**, then repeat from † to † once; join with slip st to first dc.

Rnd 16: Ch 3, dc in next 3 dc, ★ † ch 3, skip next ch-3 sp, (sc in next ch-3 sp, ch 3) twice, dc in next 4 dc, ch 3, (sc in next ch-3 sp, ch 3) twice, skip next ch-3 sp, dc in next 2 dc, ch 3, (dc, ch 3) twice in next ch-2 sp, dc in next 2 dc, ch 3, skip next ch-3 sp, (sc in next ch-3 sp, ch 3) twice †, dc in next 4 dc; repeat from ★ 3 times **more**, then repeat from † to † once; join with slip st to first dc.

Rnd 17: Ch 2, dc in next dc, decrease, ★ † ch 3, skip next ch-3 sp, sc in next ch-3 sp, ch 3, decrease twice, ch 3, (sc in next ch-3 sp, ch 3) twice, dc in next 2 dc, ch 3, skip next ch-3 sp, dc in next ch-3 sp, (ch 1, dc) 4 times in same sp, ch 3, skip next ch-3 sp, dc in next 2 dc, ch 3, skip next ch-3 sp, (sc in next ch-3 sp, ch 3) twice †, decrease twice; repeat from ★ 3 times **more**, then repeat from † to † once; skip beginning ch-2 and join with slip st to first dc.

Rnd 18: Work beginning tr Cluster, ★ † ch 5, (sc in next ch-3 sp, ch 5) twice, dc in next 2 dc, ch 3, (sc in next ch-1 sp, ch 3) 4 times, skip next ch-3 sp, dc in next 2 dc, ch 5, skip next ch-3 sp †, (sc in next ch-3 sp, ch 5) twice, work tr Cluster; repeat from ★ 3 times **more**, then repeat from † to † once, sc in next ch-3 sp, ch 5, sc in next ch-3 sp, ch 2, dc in top of beginning tr Cluster to form last loop.

Rnd 19: Ch 1, sc in same loop, ch 10, (sc in next loop, ch 10) twice, dc in next 2 dc, ch 3, skip next ch-3 sp, (sc in next ch-3 sp, ch 3) 3 times, dc in next 2 dc, ch 10, ★ skip next loop, (sc in next loop, ch 10) 4 times, dc in next 2 dc, ch 3, skip next ch-3 sp, (sc in next ch-3 sp, ch 3) 3 times, dc in next 2 dc, ch 10; repeat from ★ around to last 2 loops, skip next loop, sc in last loop, ch 5, dtr in first sc to form last loop.

Rnd 20: Ch 1, sc in same loop, ch 10, (sc in next loop, ch 10) 3 times, dc in next 2 dc, ch 3, skip next ch-3 sp, (sc in next ch-3 sp, ch 3) twice, dc in next 2 dc, ch 10, ★ (sc in next loop, ch 10) 5 times, dc in next 2 dc, ch 3, skip next ch-3 sp, (sc in next ch-3 sp, ch 3) twice, dc in next 2 dc, ch 10; repeat from ★ around to last loop, sc in last loop, ch 5, dtr in first sc to form last loop.

Rnd 21: Ch 1, sc in same loop, ch 10, (sc in next loop, ch 10) 4 times, dc in next 2 dc, ch 3, skip next ch-3 sp, sc in next ch-3 sp, ch 3, dc in next 2 dc, ch 10, ★ (sc in next loop, ch 10) 6 times, dc in next 2 dc, ch 3, skip next ch-3 sp, sc in next ch-3 sp, ch 3, dc in next 2 dc, ch 10; repeat from ★ around to last loop, sc in last loop, ch 5, dtr in first sc to form last loop.

Rnd 22: Ch 1, sc in same loop, ch 10, (sc in next loop, ch 10) 5 times, work dc Cluster, ch 10, ★ (sc in next loop, ch 10) 7 times, work dc Cluster, ch 10; repeat from ★ around to last loop, sc in last loop, ch 5, dtr in first sc to form last loop: 40 loops.

Rnd 23: Ch 1, sc in same loop, (ch 10, sc in next loop) around, ch 8, hdc in first sc to form last loop.

Rnd 24: Ch 1, sc in same loop and in next loop, ★ (ch 3, sc) 5 times in same loop, sc in next loop; repeat from ★ around, (ch 3, sc) 4 times in same loop, ch 1, hdc in first sc to form last sp: 200 sps.

Rnd 25: Ch 1, sc in same sp, ch 3, (sc in next ch-3 sp, ch 3) around; join with slip st to first sc.

Rnds 26-30: Slip st in first ch-3 sp, ch 1, sc in same sp, ch 3, (sc in next ch-3 sp, ch 3) around; join with slip st to first sc.

Rnd 31: Slip st in first ch-3 sp, work beginning Shell, ch 3, (sc in next ch-3 sp, ch 3) 9 times, ★ work Shell in next ch-3 sp, ch 3, (sc in next ch-3 sp, ch 3) 9 times; repeat from ★ around; join with slip st to first dc: 20 Shells.

Rnd 32: Slip st in next dc and in next ch-2 sp, work beginning Shell, ch 3, (sc in next ch-3 sp, ch 3) 10 times, ★ work Shell in next Shell, ch 3, (sc in next ch-3 sp, ch 3) 10 times; repeat from ★ around; join with slip st to first dc.

Rnd 33: Ch 3, dc in same st, 2 dc in next dc, ★ † ch 3, (dc, ch 3) twice in next ch-2 sp, 2 dc in each of next 2 dc, ch 3, skip next ch-3 sp, (sc in next ch-3 sp, ch 3) 9 times †, 2 dc in each of next 2 dc; repeat from ★ 18 times **more**, then repeat from † to † once; join with slip st to first dc.

Rnd 34: Ch 3, dc in next 3 dc, ★ † ch 3, skip next ch-3 sp, dc in next ch-3 sp, (ch 1, dc) 9 times in same sp, ch 3, skip next ch-3 sp, dc in next 4 dc, ch 3, skip next ch-3 sp, (sc in next ch-3 sp, ch 3) 8 times †, dc in next 4 dc; repeat from ★ 18 times **more**, then repeat from † to † once; join with slip st to first dc.

Rnd 35: Ch 3, ★ † 2 dc in each of next 2 dc, dc in next dc, ch 3, (sc in next ch-1 sp, ch 3) 9 times, skip next ch-3 sp, dc in next dc, 2 dc in each of next 2 dc, dc in next dc, ch 3, skip next ch-3 sp, (sc in next ch-3 sp, ch 3) 7 times †, dc in next dc; repeat from ★ 18 times **more**, then repeat from † to † once; join with slip st to first dc.

Rnd 36: Ch 3, dc in next 5 dc, ★ † ch 3, skip next ch-3 sp, (sc in next ch-3 sp, ch 3) 8 times, dc in next 6 dc, ch 3, skip next ch-3 sp, (sc in next ch-3 sp, ch 3) 6 times †, dc in next 6 dc; repeat from ★ 18 times **more**, then repeat from † to † once; join with slip st to first dc.

Rnd 37: Ch 3, dc in next 5 dc, ★ † ch 3, skip next ch-3 sp, (sc in next ch-3 sp, ch 3) 7 times, dc in next 6 dc, ch 3, skip next ch-3 sp, (sc in next ch-3 sp, ch 3) 5 times †, dc in next 6 dc; repeat from ★ 18 times **more**, then repeat from † to † once; join with slip st to first dc.

Continued on page 44.

FOR THE BATH

Create a relaxing haven from the cares of the day by decorating your bathroom in seaside splendor. (Below) Comb every beach, and you still won't find a treasure as lovely as our shell-shaped rug! This fast-to-finish floor covering is stitched with three strands of long-wearing worsted weight yarn. (Opposite) Crocheted using fabric strips, a scallop-edged basket is perfect for holding bath-time essentials. Satin ribbons woven through the eyelet rounds are sweet finishing touches for our jar toppers. The delicate covers are worked using bedspread weight cotton thread. A coordinating edging turns a plain linen hand towel into a pretty accessory.

Quick SHELL JAR TOPPER

MATERIALS

Bedspread Weight Cotton Thread (size 10),
   approximately 65 yards **each**
Steel crochet hook, size 6 (1.80 mm) **or** size needed for gauge
3½" Jar lid ring
¾ yard of ¼" ribbon for **each**

GAUGE: Rnds 1-4 = 1¾"

Ch 5; join with slip st to form a ring.

Rnd 1 (Right side): Ch 1, 6 sc in ring; join with slip st to first sc.

Rnd 2: Ch 4, dc in same st, ch 1, (dc, ch 1) twice in next sc and in each sc around; join with slip st to third ch of beginning ch-4: 12 ch-1 sps.

Rnd 3: Ch 1, sc in same st, ch 3, (sc in next dc, ch 3) around; join with slip st to first sc: 12 ch-3 sps.

Rnd 4: Slip st in first ch-3 sp, ch 3 **(counts as first dc, now and throughout)**, 4 dc in same sp, ch 2, sc in next ch-3 sp, ch 2, ★ 5 dc in next ch-3 sp, ch 2, sc in next ch-3 sp, ch 2; repeat from ★ around; join with slip st to first dc: 30 dc.

Rnd 5: Ch 3, 2 dc in each of next 4 dc, ch 1, (dc in next dc, 2 dc in each of next 4 dc, ch 1) around; join with slip st to first dc: 54 dc.

Rnd 6: Ch 3, dc in same st and in next 7 dc, 2 dc in next dc, ch 1, (2 dc in next dc, dc in next 7 dc, 2 dc in next dc, ch 1) around; join with slip st to first dc: 66 dc.

Rnd 7: Ch 1, sc in same st, ch 3, (skip next dc, sc in next dc, ch 3) 4 times, ★ skip next dc, sc in next 2 dc, ch 3, (skip next dc, sc in next dc, ch 3) 4 times; repeat from ★ around to last 2 dc, skip next dc, sc in last dc; join with slip st to first sc: 30 ch-3 sps.

Rnd 8: Slip st in first ch-3 sp, ch 1, sc in same sp, ch 3, (sc in next ch-3 sp, ch 3) around; join with slip st to first sc.

Rnd 9: Slip st in first ch-3 sp, ch 3, 2 dc in same sp, 3 dc in next ch-3 sp and in each ch-3 sp around; join with slip st to first dc: 90 dc.

Rnds 10 and 11: Ch 3, dc in next dc and in each dc around; join with slip st to first dc.

Rnd 12 (Eyelet rnd): Ch 5 **(counts as first dc plus ch 2, now and throughout)**, skip next 2 dc, (dc in next dc, ch 2, skip next 2 dc) around; join with slip st to first dc: 30 dc.

Rnd 13: Ch 5, dc in next dc, ch 2, (dc, ch 2) twice in next dc, ★ (dc in next dc, ch 2) twice, (dc, ch 2) twice in next dc; repeat from ★ around; join with slip st to first dc: 40 dc.

Rnd 14: Ch 3, 4 dc in same st, ch 3, skip next dc, (sc in next dc, ch 3) 5 times, skip next dc, ★ 5 dc in next dc, ch 3, skip next dc, (sc in next dc, ch 3) 5 times, skip next dc; repeat from ★ around; join with slip st to first dc: 5 5-dc groups.

Rnd 15: Ch 3, dc in same st, 2 dc in each of next 4 dc, ch 3, skip next ch-3 sp, (sc in next ch-3 sp, ch 3) 4 times, ★ 2 dc in each of next 5 dc, ch 3, skip next ch-3 sp, (sc in next ch-3 sp, ch 3) 4 times; repeat from ★ around; join with slip st to first dc: 50 dc.

Rnd 16: Ch 3, 2 dc in next dc, (dc in next dc, 2 dc in next dc) 4 times, ch 3, skip next ch-3 sp, (sc in next ch-3 sp, ch 3) 3 times, ★ (dc in next dc, 2 dc in next dc) 5 times, ch 3, skip next ch-3 sp, (sc in next ch-3 sp, ch 3) 3 times; repeat from ★ around; join with slip st to first dc: 75 dc.

Rnd 17: Ch 3, dc in same st and in next 3 dc, 2 dc in next dc, (dc in next 4 dc, 2 dc in next dc) twice, ch 1, skip next ch-3 sp, sc in next ch-3 sp, ch 3, sc in next ch-3 sp, ch 1, ★ 2 dc in next dc, dc in next 3 dc, 2 dc in next dc, (dc in next 4 dc, 2 dc in next dc) twice, ch 1, skip next ch-3 sp, sc in next ch-3 sp, ch 3, sc in next ch-3 sp, ch 1; repeat from ★ around; join with slip st to first dc: 95 dc.

Rnd 18: Ch 1, sc in same st, (ch 3, skip next dc, sc in next dc) 9 times, ch 1, (sc, ch 3, sc) in next ch-3 sp, ch 1, ★ sc in next dc, (ch 3, skip next dc, sc in next dc) 9 times, ch 1, (sc, ch 3, sc) in next ch-3 sp, ch 1; repeat from ★ around; join with slip st to first sc, finish off.

See Washing and Blocking, page 140.

Weave ribbon through Eyelet rnd; place Topper over jar lid ring and tie ends in a bow to secure.

Quick SHELL BASKET

Finished Size: Approximately 10" long x 5" wide x 4" high

MATERIALS

100% Cotton Fabric, 44/45" wide, approximately 3 yards
Crochet hook, size N (9.00 mm) **or** size needed for gauge

Prepare fabric and tear into 1½" strips **(see Preparing Fabric Strips and Joining Fabric Strips, page 139)**.

GAUGE: 6 dc = 3"

Ch 13 **loosely**.

Rnd 1 (Right side): 6 Dc in fourth ch from hook, dc in next 8 chs, 7 dc in last ch; working in free loops of beginning ch **(Fig. 23b, page 138)**, dc in next 8 chs; join with slip st to top of beginning ch: 30 sts.

Rnd 2: Ch 3 **(counts as first dc, now and throughout)**, dc in same st, 2 dc in each of next 7 dc, dc in next 6 dc, 2 dc in each of next 9 dc, dc in next 6 dc, 2 dc in last dc; join with slip st to first dc: 48 dc.

Rnd 3: Ch 1, sc in Back Loop Only of each dc around **(Fig. 22, page 138)**; join with slip st to first sc.

Rnd 4: Ch 3, dc in both loops of next sc and in each sc around; join with slip st to first dc.

Rnd 5: Ch 1, sc in each dc around; join with slip st to first sc.

Rnd 6: Ch 3, 4 dc in same st, ch 1, skip next 2 sc, slip st in next sc, ch 1, skip next 2 sc, ★ 5 dc in next sc, ch 1, skip next 2 sc, slip st in next sc, ch 1, skip next 2 sc; repeat from ★ around; join with slip st to first dc, finish off.

Lower Edging: With **right** side facing, top of Basket toward you, and working in free loops on Rnd 2 *(Fig. 23a, page 138)*, join fabric with slip st in any st; slip st in each st around; join with slip st to first slip st, finish off.

Quick SHELL TOWEL EDGING

Finished Size: Approximately 1¾" wide

MATERIALS

Bedspread Weight Cotton Thread (size 10), approximately 40 yards
Steel crochet hook, size 6 (1.80 mm) **or** size needed for gauge
Linen - 14" x 18½"
Straight pins
Sewing needle and thread

GAUGE: Dc, (ch 1, dc) 12 times = 4"

Ch 149 **loosely**.

Row 1 (Right side): Dc in eighth ch from hook **(7 skipped chs count as first dc plus ch 2)**, (ch 2, skip next 2 chs, dc in next ch) across: 48 sps.

Row 2: Ch 1, turn; sc in first dc, ch 3, (sc in next dc, ch 3) twice, skip next dc, 5 dc in next dc, ch 3, ★ skip next dc, (sc in next dc, ch 3) 5 times, skip next dc, 5 dc in next dc, ch 3; repeat from ★ across to last 4 dc, skip next dc, sc in next dc, (ch 3, sc in next dc) twice: 6 5-dc groups.

Row 3: Ch 6, turn; skip first ch-3 sp, sc in next ch-3 sp, ch 3, 2 dc in each of next 5 dc, ch 3, ★ skip next ch-3 sp, (sc in next ch-3 sp, ch 3) 4 times, 2 dc in each of next 5 dc, ch 3; repeat from ★ across to last 3 ch-3 sps, skip next ch-3 sp, sc in next ch-3 sp, ch 3, dc in last sc.

Row 4: Ch 1, turn; sc in first dc, ch 3, (dc in next dc, 2 dc in next dc) 5 times, ch 3, ★ skip next ch-3 sp, (sc in next ch-3 sp, ch 3) 3 times, (dc in next dc, 2 dc in next dc) 5 times, ch 3; repeat from ★ across to last 2 sps, skip next sp, sc in third ch of beginning ch-6.

Row 5: Ch 1, turn; sc in first sc, ch 3, 2 dc in next dc, dc in next 3 dc, 2 dc in next dc, (dc in next 4 dc, 2 dc in next dc) twice, ch 3, ★ skip next ch-3 sp, sc in next ch-3 sp, ch 1, sc in next ch-3 sp, ch 3, 2 dc in next dc, dc in next 3 dc, 2 dc in next dc, (dc in next 4 dc, 2 dc in next dc) twice, ch 3; repeat from ★ across to last ch-3 sp, skip last ch-3 sp, sc in last sc.

Row 6: Ch 1, turn; sc in first sc, ch 1, sc in next dc, (ch 3, skip next dc, sc in next dc) 9 times, ch 1, ★ sc in next ch-1 sp, ch 1, sc in next dc, (ch 3, skip next dc, sc in next dc) 9 times, ch 1; repeat from ★ across to last ch-3 sp, skip last ch-3 sp, sc in last sc; finish off.

Lower Edging: With **right** side facing and working over beginning ch, join thread with slip st in first ch-2 sp; ch 1, (sc, ch 3, sc) in same sp and in each ch-2 sp across; finish off.

FINISHING

See Washing and Blocking, page 140.

Make a ¼" hem on each side of linen.

Using photo as a guide for placement, pin Edging along hem line on right side of linen and sew in place.

Quick SHELL RUG

Finished Size: Approximately 22" x 27"

MATERIALS

Worsted Weight Yarn, approximately:
  MC (Clay) - 9 ounces, (260 grams, 615 yards)
  CC (Ecru) - 5 ounces, (140 grams, 345 yards)
Crochet hook, size N (9.00 mm) **or** size needed for gauge

Note: Rug is worked holding 2 strands of MC and 1 strand of CC together.

GAUGE: In pattern, 7 sts and 6 rows = 4"

PATTERN STITCHES

FRONT POST TREBLE CROCHET (abbreviated FPtr)
YO twice, insert hook from **front** to **back** around post of st indicated, YO and pull up a loop **even** with last st worked, (YO and draw through 2 loops on hook) 3 times *(Fig. 13, page 135)*. Skip st behind FPtr.

FRONT POST SINGLE CROCHET (abbreviated FPsc)
Insert hook from **front** to **back** around post of st indicated, YO and pull up a loop **even** with last st worked, YO and draw through both loops on hook. Skip st behind FPsc.

Ch 13 **loosely**.

Row 1 (Right side): 2 Dc in fourth ch from hook and in each of next 3 chs, dc in next 2 chs, 2 dc in each of last 4 chs: 19 sts.

Note: Loop a short piece of yarn around any stitch to mark last row as **right** side.

Continued on page 43.

FOR THE BEDROOM

A garden retreat awaits with these pretty pansy accents for the bedroom. (Below) Our floral fantasy afghan is enhanced with three-dimensional flowers. Stitched with worsted weight yarn, the snuggly throw is worked in motifs and then crocheted together. (Opposite) Featuring the charm of a woven basket, our boutique tissue box cover is abloom with pansies. The dainty sachet, worked in bedspread weight cotton thread, offers a lovely way to sweeten the air.

PANSY GARDEN AFGHAN

Finished Size: Approximately 48" x 74"

MATERIALS

Worsted Weight Yarn, approximately:
- MC (White) - 45 ounces, (1,280 grams, 2,545 yards)
- Color A (Lilac) - 22 ounces, (620 grams, 1,245 yards)
- Color B (Green) - 1¾ ounces, (50 grams, 100 yards)
- Color C (Black) - 1 ounce, (30 grams, 55 yards)
- Color D (Yellow) - 15 yards

Crochet hook, size G (4.00 mm) **or** size needed for gauge

GAUGE: One Motif = 7" (from straight edge to straight edge)

PATTERN STITCHES

BEGINNING CLUSTER

Ch 2, ★ YO, insert hook in st or sp indicated, YO and pull up a loop, YO and draw through 2 loops on hook; repeat from ★ once **more**, YO and draw through all 3 loops on hook *(Figs. 10a & b, page 134)*.

CLUSTER

★ YO, insert hook in st or sp indicated, YO and pull up a loop, YO and draw through 2 loops on hook; repeat from ★ 2 times **more**, YO and draw through all 4 loops on hook.

PICOT

Ch 4, sc in fourth ch from hook.

MOTIF A (Make 25)

With Color C, ch 4; join with slip st to form a ring.

Rnd 1 (Right side): Ch 3 **(counts as first dc, now and throughout)**, 2 dc in ring, (ch 3, 3 dc in ring) 3 times changing to Color D in last dc worked *(Fig. 24a, page 138)*, ch 5, sc **around** ring in sp **between** second and third dc groups *(Fig. 1)*, ch 5; join with slip st to first dc, finish off.

Fig. 1

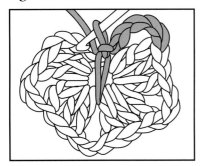

Note: Loop a short piece of yarn around any stitch to mark last round as **right** side.

Rnd 2: With **right** side facing, join Color A with slip st in first ch-5 loop; ch 1, in same loop work [sc, ch 4, dc, ch 1, (tr, ch 1) 7 times, dc, ch 4, sc], sc in next sc, in next loop work [sc, ch 4, dc, ch 1, (tr, ch 1) 7 times, dc, ch 4, sc], skip next dc, sc in next dc, skip next dc, ★ (5 dc, ch 1, 5 dc) in next ch-3 sp, skip next dc, sc in next dc, skip next dc; repeat from ★ 2 times **more**; join with slip st to first sc: 5 Petals.

Rnd 3: Ch 3, (sc in next sp, ch 3) 10 times, skip next sc, sc in next sc, ch 3, (sc in next sp, ch 3) 10 times, slip st in next sc, sc in next sc, ch 4, keeping Petals to front, (sc in next sc, ch 4) 3 times, working in sts of Rnd 2, (slip st in center tr of next Petal, ch 4) twice; join with slip st to sc between Petals, finish off: 6 ch-4 sps.

Rnd 4: With **right** side facing, join Color B with slip st in same st as joining; [ch 8 **loosely**, sc in third ch from hook, dc in next ch, tr in last 4 chs **(Leaf made)**], slip st in next ch-4 sp, ch 3, slip st in next ch-4 sp, (work Leaf, slip st in next ch-4 sp) twice; finish off: 3 Leaves.

Rnd 5: With **right** side facing and keeping Leaves to front, join MC with slip st in same ch-4 sp as last slip st; ch 1, 8 sc in same sp and in next 3 ch-4 sps, (working in next ch-4 sp, 4 sc on each side of slip st) twice **(Fig. 2)**; join with slip st to first sc: 48 sc.

Fig. 2

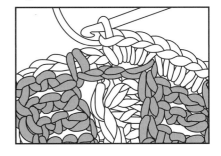

Rnd 6: Ch 5 **(counts as first dc plus ch 2, now and throughout)**, dc in same st, ch 1, (skip next sc, dc in next sc, ch 1) 3 times, skip next sc, ★ (dc, ch 2, dc) in next sc, ch 1, skip next sc, (dc in next sc, ch 1, skip next sc) 3 times; repeat from ★ around; join with slip st to first dc: 30 dc.

Rnd 7: Slip st in first ch-2 sp, ch 5, dc in same sp and in next dc, (dc in next ch-1 sp and in next dc) 4 times, ★ (dc, ch 2, dc) in next ch-2 sp, dc in next dc, (dc in next ch-1 sp and in next dc) 4 times; repeat from ★ around; join with slip st to first dc: 66 dc.

Rnd 8: Slip st in first ch-2 sp, work (beginning Cluster, ch 2, Cluster) in same sp, ch 2, (skip next 2 dc, work Cluster in next dc, ch 2) 3 times, skip next 2 dc, ★ (work Cluster, ch 2) twice in next ch-2 sp, (skip next 2 dc, work Cluster in next dc, ch 2) 3 times, skip next 2 dc; repeat from ★ around; join with slip st to top of beginning Cluster, finish off: 30 Clusters.

Rnd 9: With **right** side facing, join Color A with slip st in first ch-2 sp; ch 1, 3 sc in same sp, sc in next Cluster, (2 sc in next ch-2 sp, sc in next Cluster) 4 times, ★ 3 sc in next ch-2 sp, sc in next Cluster, (2 sc in next ch-2 sp, sc in next Cluster) 4 times; repeat from ★ around; join with slip st to first sc, finish off: 96 sc.

MOTIF B (Make 42)

With MC, ch 5; join with slip st to form a ring.

Rnd 1 (Right side)**:** Ch 3, 17 dc in ring; join with slip st to first dc: 18 dc.

Note: Mark last round as **right** side.

Rnd 2: Work (beginning Cluster, ch 2, Cluster) in same st, ch 2, skip next 2 dc, ★ (work Cluster, ch 2) twice in next dc, skip next 2 dc; repeat from ★ around; join with slip st to top of beginning Cluster: 12 Clusters.

Rnd 3: Slip st in first ch-2 sp, ch 1, 3 sc in same sp, sc in next Cluster, (3 sc in next ch-2 sp, sc in next Cluster) around; join with slip st to first sc: 48 sc.

Rnd 4: Slip st in next sc, ch 5, dc in same st, ch 1, (skip next sc, dc in next sc, ch 1) 3 times, skip next sc, ★ (dc, ch 2, dc) in next sc, ch 1, (skip next sc, dc in next sc, ch 1) 3 times, skip next sc; repeat from ★ around; join with slip st to first dc: 30 dc.

Rnds 5-7: Work same as Motif A, Rnds 7-9.

ASSEMBLY

Following Placement Diagram and placing each Motif A with Pansies facing the same direction, join Motifs together forming strips as follows:

With **right** sides together, matching sts and working through outside loops of **both** thicknesses, join Color A with slip st in any corner sc; ch 1, sc in same st and in each st across to next corner sc; finish off.

Join strips in same manner.

EDGING

Rnd 1: With **right** side facing and working in Back Loops Only, join Color A with slip st in any corner sc; ch 1, 3 sc in same st, sc in each sc around working 3 sc in each corner sc; join with slip st to first sc, finish off.

Rnd 2: With **right** side facing, join MC with slip st in any corner sc; ch 7, sc in fourth ch from hook, (dc, work Picot, dc) in same st, skip next 2 sc, [(dc, work Picot, dc) in next sc, skip next 2 sc] across to next corner sc, ★ dc in corner sc, (work Picot, dc) twice in same st, skip next 2 sc, [(dc, work Picot, dc) in next sc, skip next 2 sc] across next corner sc; repeat from ★ around; join with slip st to third ch of beginning ch-7, finish off.

PLACEMENT DIAGRAM

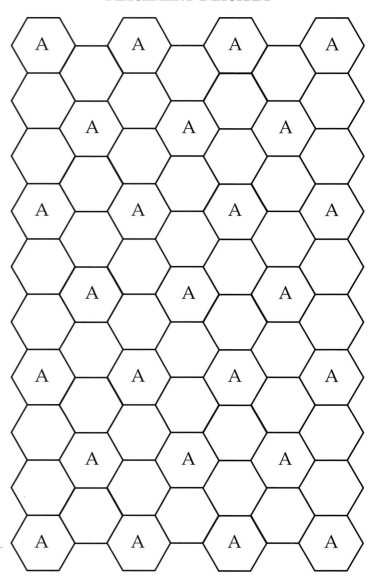

PANSY BASKET TISSUE COVER

MATERIALS

Worsted Weight Yarn, approximately:
    MC (Brown) - 1½ ounces, (40 grams, 85 yards)
    CC (Green) - 1 ounce, (30 grams, 55 yards)
Sport Weight Yarn, approximately:
    Color A (Lilac) - ¾ ounce, (20 grams, 75 yards)
    Color B (Green) - 16 yards
    Color C (Black) - 7 yards
    Color D (Yellow) - 2 yards
Crochet hooks, size C (2.75 mm) **and** size G (4.00 mm)
    or sizes needed for gauge
Ribbon bow
Yarn needle
2 - 16" lengths of 22 gauge wire

GAUGE: With larger size hook, 8 sc and 8 rows = 2"
           Pansy = 2½"

COVER

Using larger size hook and CC, ch 20 **loosely**; being careful not to twist ch, join with slip st to form a ring.

Rnd 1 (Right side): Ch 1, sc in first 4 chs, 3 sc in next ch, (sc in next 4 chs, 3 sc in next ch) around; do **not** join, place marker *(see Markers, page 138)*: 28 sc.

Note: Loop a short piece of yarn around any stitch to mark last round as **right** side.

Rnd 2: Sc in next 5 sc, 3 sc in next sc, (sc in next 6 sc, 3 sc in next sc) 3 times, sc in next sc: 36 sc.

Rnd 3: Sc in next 7 sc, 3 sc in next sc, (sc in next 8 sc, 3 sc in next sc) 3 times, sc in next sc: 44 sc.

Rnd 4: Sc in next 9 sc, 3 sc in next sc, (sc in next 10 sc, 3 sc in next sc) 3 times, sc in next sc: 52 sc.

Rnd 5: Sc in next 11 sc, 3 sc in next sc, (sc in next 12 sc, 3 sc in next sc) 3 times, sc in next sc: 60 sc.

Rnd 6: Sc in next 13 sc, 3 sc in next sc, (sc in next 14 sc, 3 sc in next sc) 3 times, sc in next sc: 68 sc.

Rnd 7: Sc in next 15 sc, 2 sc in next sc, (sc in next 16 sc, 2 sc in next sc) 3 times, sc in next sc: 72 sc.

Rnds 8-15: Sc in each sc around; at end of Rnd 15, change to MC in last sc *(Fig. 24a, page 138)*.

Rnd 16: Sc in each sc around; remove marker, slip st in next sc.

Rnd 17 (Edging): Ch 2 **(counts as first hdc, now and throughout)**, turn; working in Back Loops Only *(Fig. 22, page 138)*, hdc in next sc and in each sc around; join with slip st to first hdc.

Rnd 18: Ch 1, working from **left** to **right**, work reverse sc in each st around *(Figs. 19a-d, page 136)*; join with slip st to first st, finish off.

Rnd 19: Fold Edging toward work. With **right** side facing and working in free loops on Rnd 16 *(Fig. 23a, page 138)*, join MC with slip st in any sc; ch 2, hdc in next sc and in each sc around; join with slip st to first hdc.

Rnds 20 and 21: Ch 1, work FPhdc around first 4 sts *(Fig. 14, page 135)*, work BPhdc around next 4 sts *(Fig. 15, page 135)*, ★ work FPhdc around next 4 sts, work BPhdc around next 4 sts; repeat from ★ around; join with slip st to first FPhdc.

Rnds 22 and 23: Ch 1, work BPhdc around first 4 sts, work FPhdc around next 4 sts, ★ work BPhdc around next 4 sts, work FPhdc around next 4 sts; repeat from ★ around; join with slip st to first BPhdc.

Repeat Rnds 20-23 once or until sides measure approximately 5¼" from Rnd 7.

Last Rnd: Slip st in each st around; join with slip st to first st, finish off.

HANDLE

Using larger size hook and MC, ch 58 **loosely**.

Row 1 (Right side): Hdc in third ch from hook and in each ch across: 57 sts.

Note: Mark last row as **right** side.

Row 2: Ch 1, do **not** turn; working from **left** to **right** and working over wire *(Fig. 25, page 138)*, work reverse sc in each hdc across; finish off leaving a long end for sewing.

Row 3: With **right** side facing, working in free loops of beginning ch *(Fig. 23b, page 138)* and working over second wire, join MC with slip st in first ch on left; ch 1, work reverse sc in same st and in each st across; finish off leaving a long end for sewing.

Bend wires on each end to wrong side.

PANSY (Make 5)

With Color C and using smaller size hook, ch 4; join with slip st to form a ring.

Rnd 1 (Right side): Ch 2, 2 hdc in ring, (ch 3, 3 hdc in ring) 3 times changing to Color D in last hdc worked, ch 5, sc **around** ring in sp **between** second and third hdc groups *(Fig. 1, page 16)*, ch 5; join with slip st to first hdc, finish off.

Note: Mark last round as **right** side.

Rnd 2: With **right** side facing, join Color A with slip st in first ch-5 loop; ch 1, [sc, ch 3, hdc, ch 1, (dc, ch 1) 6 times, hdc, ch 3, sc] in same loop and in next loop, skip next hdc, sc in next hdc, ★ (4 hdc, ch 1, 4 hdc) in next ch-3 sp, skip next hdc, sc in next hdc, skip next hdc; repeat from ★ around; join with slip st to first sc.

Edging: Ch 3, (sc in next sp, ch 3) 9 times, skip next sc, sc in next sc, (ch 3, sc in next sp) 9 times, slip st in next sc; finish off.

LEAF (Make 15)

With Color B and using smaller size hook, ch 8 **loosely**; sc in third ch from hook, hdc in next ch, dc in last 4 chs; finish off leaving a long end for sewing.

FINISHING

Using photo as a guide for placement, sew Handle to sides of Cover sliding ends of wire through sides of Cover.
Sew Pansies and Leaves to Cover as desired.
Add bow to Handle.

Quick PANSY SACHET

Finished Size: Approximately 5" in diameter

MATERIALS

Bedspread Weight Cotton Thread (size 10), approximately:
  MC (White) - 45 yards
  Color A (Lilac) - 22 yards
  Color B (Green) - 2 yards
  Color C (Black) - 1 yard
  Color D (Yellow) - ½ yard
Steel crochet hook, size 6 (1.80 mm) **or** size needed
  for gauge
¾ yard of ⅛" ribbon
Cotton balls or polyester fiberfill
Tapestry needle
Scented oil

GAUGE: Front or Back, Rnds 1-3 = 1½"

PATTERN STITCHES

BEGINNING CLUSTER

Ch 2, ★ YO, insert hook in st or sp indicated, YO and pull up a loop, YO and draw through 2 loops on hook; repeat from ★ once **more**, YO and draw through all 3 loops on hook *(Figs. 10a & b, page 134)*.

CLUSTER

★ YO, insert hook in st or sp indicated, YO and pull up a loop, YO and draw through 2 loops on hook; repeat from ★ 2 times **more**, YO and draw through all 4 loops on hook.

FRONT

Work same as Pansy Afghan Motif A, page 36, through Rnd 9; at end of Rnd 9, do **not** finish off.

Rnd 10 (Eyelet rnd)**:** Slip st in next sc, ch 5, dc in same st, ch 1, skip next sc, (dc in next sc, ch 1, skip next sc) 7 times, ★ (dc, ch 2, dc) in next sc, ch 1, skip next sc, (dc in next sc, ch 1, skip next sc) 7 times; repeat from ★ around; join with slip st to first dc: 54 sps.

Rnd 11: Slip st in next ch-2 sp, ch 1, 3 sc in same sp, sc in next dc, (sc in next ch-1 sp and in next dc) across to next ch-2 sp, ★ 3 sc in next ch-2 sp, sc in next dc, (sc in next ch-1 sp and in next dc) across to next ch-2 sp; repeat from ★ around; join with slip st to first sc, finish off: 120 sc.

Rnd 12: With **right** side facing, join MC with slip st in any corner sc; ch 1, (sc, ch 3) twice in same st, (skip next sc, sc in next sc, ch 3) 9 times, skip next sc, ★ (sc, ch 3) twice in next sc, (skip next sc, sc in next sc, ch 3) 9 times, skip next sc; repeat from ★ around; join with slip st to first sc: 66 ch-3 sps.

Rnd 13: Slip st in next ch-3 sp, ch 1, sc in same sp, ch 2, work (Cluster, ch 4, sc in fourth ch from hook, Cluster) in next ch-3 sp, ch 2, ★ sc in next ch-3 sp, ch 2, work (Cluster, ch 4, sc in fourth ch from hook, Cluster) in next ch-3 sp, ch 2; repeat from ★ around; join with slip st to first sc, finish off.

BACK

Work same as Pansy Afghan Motif B, through Rnd 7; at end of Rnd 7, do **not** finish off.

Rnd 8 (Eyelet rnd)**:** Work same as Front, Rnd 10; finish off.

FINISHING

See Washing and Blocking, page 140.
Sprinkle scented oil on the fiberfill.

JOINING

With **wrong** sides together and matching spaces, weave ribbon through Eyelet rnd, stuffing before closing. Tie ribbon in a bow to secure.

THE DINING ROOM

*Set the scene for intimate dining with these handcrafted table dressings. (Below and opposite top)
Perfect for those special dinners, our handy casserole cozy holds a standard-size baking dish,
and the matching cutlery caddy keeps utensils neatly separated and close at hand. These fast-to-
stitch projects are crafted using fabric strips and a large hook. (Opposite bottom) It's fun — and
easy — to fashion our lovely table setting by adding a lacy edging to a purchased place mat.
The same frilly edging is worked around a plastic ring to gather a coordinating napkin.*

41

FRILLY NAPKIN RING AND PLACE MAT EDGING

Finished Size: Napkin Ring - 4" in diameter
Place Mat Edging - 1¼" wide

MATERIALS
Bedspread Weight Cotton Thread (size 10), approximately:
Napkin Ring - 30 yards **each**
Place Mat Edging - 135 yards **each** (for an Edging 50" long)
Steel crochet hooks, sizes 7 (1.65 mm) **and** 10 (1.30 mm)
or sizes needed for gauge
2" Plastic ring
Purchased place mat (ours measures 12½" x 17")
Straight pins
Sewing needle and thread

GAUGE: With smaller size hook, 15 sc = 1"
With larger size hook, 9 dc = 1"

NAPKIN RING
Rnd 1 (Right side)**:** With smaller size hook, join thread with slip st around ring; ch 1, 95 sc in ring; join with slip st to first sc.
Note: Loop a short piece of thread around any stitch to mark last round as **right** side.
Rnd 2: With larger size hook, ch 3, skip next sc, dc in next sc, ch 4, skip next 2 sc, ★ dc in next sc, skip next sc, dc in next sc, ch 4, skip next 2 sc; repeat from ★ around; join with slip st to top of beginning ch-3: 19 ch-4 sps.
Rnd 3: Slip st in next dc and in next ch-4 sp, ch 1, [sc, ch 2, dc, ch 2, (tr, ch 2) twice, dc, ch 2, sc] in same sp and in each ch-4 sp around; join with slip st to first sc: 38 tr.
Rnd 4: ★ Ch 3, skip next ch-2 sp, sc in next ch-2 sp, ch 5, in next ch-2 sp work (sc, ch 3, slip st in last sc worked, sc, ch 5, slip st in last sc worked, sc, ch 3, slip st in last sc worked, sc), ch 5, sc in next ch-2 sp, ch 3, sc in sp **between** next 2 sc; repeat from ★ around; join with slip st to base of beginning ch-3, finish off.

PLACE MAT EDGING
BEGINNING CHAIN
With larger size hook, make a chain to fit around the place mat. The number of chains must be divisible by 5. For example, as in ours, 450 (5 goes into 450, 90 times evenly). Count the chains and adjust as needed. Being careful not to twist ch, join with slip st to form a ring.

Rnd 1 (Right side)**:** Ch 1, sc in each ch around; join with slip st to first sc.
Note: Loop a short piece of thread around any stitch to mark last round as **right** side.
Rnds 2-4: With smaller size hook, work same as Napkin Ring.

FINISHING
See Washing and Blocking, page 140.
Using photo as a guide, pin Edging along hem line on right side of place mat and sew in place.

Quick CASEROLE COZY

Quick **CASSEROLE COZY**

Finished Size: To fit a 9" x 13" casserole dish

MATERIALS
100% Cotton Fabric, 44/45" wide, approximately:
4½ yards
Crochet hook, size P (10.00 mm) **or** size needed for gauge
2 yards of 1½" grosgrain ribbon

Prepare fabric and tear into 2" strips *(see Preparing Fabric Strips and Joining Fabric Strips, page 139)*.

GAUGE: 6 sc and 6 rows = 4"

Ch 7 **loosely.**
Rnd 1 (Right side)**:** Sc in second ch from hook, (ch 2, sc) twice in same st, sc in last 5 chs, (ch 2, sc) twice in same st; working in free loops of beginning ch *(Fig. 23b, page 138)*, sc in next 4 chs; do **not** join, place fabric marker *(see Markers, page 138)*: 14 sc.
Note #1: Loop a short piece of fabric around any stitch to mark last round as **right** side.
Note #2: Work in Back Loops Only throughout *(Fig. 22, page 138)*.
Rnds 2-5: Sc in each sc around working (sc, ch 2, sc) in each corner ch-2 sp: 46 sc.
Rnd 6: Sc in each sc around working 2 sc in each corner ch-2 sp; remove marker, slip st in next sc: 54 sc.
Rnds 7-9: Ch 1, sc in each sc around; join with slip st to first sc.
Rnd 10: Ch 3, skip next sc, (slip st in next sc, ch 3, skip next sc) around; join with slip st to base of beginning ch-3, finish off.

Beginning in center of one long side, weave ribbon between sc on Rnd 9. Pull ends of ribbon tight around casserole dish and tie in a bow to secure. Trim ends.

Quick

CUTLERY CADDY

Finished Size: Approximately 5" high x 3¹/₂" in diameter **each**

MATERIALS
100% Cotton Fabric, 44/45" wide, approximately: 3¹/₂ yards
Crochet hook, size P (10.00 mm) **or** size needed for gauge
1¹/₂ yards of 1¹/₂" grosgrain ribbon

Prepare fabric and tear into 2" strips *(see Preparing Fabric Strips and Joining Fabric Strips, page 139)*.

GAUGE: Rnds 1 and 2 = 3¹/₂"

HOLDER (Make 3)
Rnd 1 (Right side)**:** Ch 2, 7 sc in second ch from hook; do **not** join, place fabric marker *(see Markers, page 138)*. *Note:* Loop a short piece of fabric around any stitch to mark last round as **right** side.
Rnd 2: 2 Sc in each sc around: 14 sc.
Rnd 3: Sc in Back Loop Only of each sc around *(Fig. 22, page 138)*.
Rnds 4-7: Sc in both loops of each sc around; at end of Rnd 7, remove marker, slip st in next sc.
Rnd 8: Ch 3, skip next sc, (slip st in next sc, ch 3, skip next sc) around; join with slip st to base of beginning ch-3, finish off.

Beginning with any Holder and working between sc on Rnd 6, weave ribbon between 7 sc, continue to weave through 7 sc on Rnd 6 on each Holder in same manner to form a group; tie ribbon in a bow to secure. Trim ends.

SHELL RUG
Continued from page 33.

Row 2 AND ALL WRONG SIDE ROWS THROUGH ROW 28: Ch 1, turn; sc in each st across.
Row 3: Ch 3 **(counts as first dc, now and throughout)**, turn; (work FPtr around dc in row **below** next sc, 2 dc in next sc) 4 times, dc in next 2 sc, work FPtr around dc in row **below** next sc, (2 dc in next sc, work FPtr around dc in row **below** next sc) 3 times, dc in last sc: 26 sts.
Row 5: Ch 3, turn; work FPtr around next FPtr, (dc in next sc, 2 dc in next sc, work FPtr around next FPtr) 3 times, 2 dc in next sc, dc in next 2 sc, 2 dc in next sc, work FPtr around next FPtr, (dc in next sc, 2 dc in next sc, work FPtr around next FPtr) 3 times, dc in last sc: 34 sts.
Row 7: Ch 3, turn; work FPtr around next FPtr, ★ dc in each sc across to next FPtr, work FPtr around next FPtr; repeat from ★ across to last sc, dc in last sc.

Row 9: Ch 3, turn; work FPtr around next FPtr, (dc in next 2 sc, 2 dc in next sc, work FPtr around next FPtr) 3 times, 2 dc in next sc, dc in next 4 sc, 2 dc in next sc, work FPtr around next FPtr, (dc in next 2 sc, 2 dc in next sc, work FPtr around next FPtr) 3 times, dc in last sc: 42 sts.
Rows 11 and 13: Repeat Row 7.
Row 15: Ch 3, turn; work FPtr around next FPtr, (dc in next 3 sc, 2 dc in next sc, work FPtr around next FPtr) 3 times, 2 dc in next sc, dc in next 6 sc, 2 dc in next sc, work FPtr around next FPtr, (dc in next 3 sc, 2 dc in next sc, work FPtr around next FPtr) 3 times, dc in last sc: 50 sts.
Rows 17, 19, and 21: Repeat Row 7.
Row 23: Ch 3, turn; work FPtr around next FPtr, (dc in next 5 sc, work FPtr around next FPtr) 3 times, 2 dc in next sc, dc in next 8 sc, 2 dc in next sc, work FPtr around next FPtr, (dc in next 5 sc, work FPtr around next FPtr) 3 times, dc in last sc: 52 sts.
Rows 25 and 27: Repeat Row 7.
Row 29: Ch 1, turn; sc in first sc, work FPsc around next FPtr, (sc in next sc, 2 dc in each of next 3 sc, sc in next sc, work FPsc around next FPtr) twice, sc in next sc, dc in next 4 sc, work FPtr around next FPtr, dc in next 12 sc, work FPtr around next FPtr, dc in next 4 sc, sc in next sc, work FPsc around next FPtr, leave remaining 13 sts unworked.
Row 30: Turn; slip st in first st, sc in next 24 sts, slip st in next st, leave remaining sts unworked.
Row 31: Ch 1, turn; work FPsc around first FPsc, sc in next sc, 2 dc in each of next 3 sc, sc in next sc, work FPsc around next FPtr, sc in next 12 sc, work FPsc around next FPtr, leave remaining sts unworked.
Row 32: Turn; slip st in first st, sc in next 12 sc, slip st in next st, leave remaining sts unworked.
Row 33: Ch 1, turn; work FPsc around first FPsc, sc in next sc, 2 hdc in each of next 2 sc, 2 dc in each of next 2 sc, dc in next 2 sc, 2 dc in each of next 2 sc, 2 hdc in each of next 2 sc, sc in next sc, work FPsc around next FPsc, sc in next sc, 2 dc in each of next 3 sc, sc in next sc, work FPsc around next FPsc, sc in next sc, (2 dc in each of next 3 sc, sc in next sc, work FPsc around next FPtr, sc in next sc) twice; finish off.
Lower Edge: With **right** side facing, having beginning ch toward the left, and working in end of rows, join yarn with slip st in end of Row 6; sc in same row, 2 hdc in next row, dc in next row, 2 dc in next row, tr in next row, 5 tr in last row; working in free loops of beginning ch *(Fig. 23b, page 138)*, tr in next 10 chs; working in end of rows, 5 tr in first row, tr in next row, 2 dc in next row, dc in next row, 2 hdc in next row, (sc, slip st) in next row; finish off.

43

PINEAPPLE TABLE TOPPER

Continued from page 29.

Rnd 38: Ch 3, dc in next 5 dc, ★ † ch 3, skip next ch-3 sp, (sc in next ch-3 sp, ch 3) 6 times, dc in next 6 dc, ch 3, skip next ch-3 sp, (sc in next ch-3 sp, ch 3) 4 times †, dc in next 6 dc; repeat from ★ 18 times **more**, then repeat from † to † once; join with slip st to first dc.

Rnd 39: Ch 3, dc in next 5 dc, ★ † ch 3, skip next ch-3 sp, (sc in next ch-3 sp, ch 3) 5 times, dc in next 6 dc, ch 5, skip next ch-3 sp, (sc in next ch-3 sp, ch 5) 3 times †, dc in next 6 dc; repeat from ★ 18 times **more**, then repeat from † to † once; join with slip st to first dc.

Rnd 40: Ch 3, ★ † decrease twice, dc in next dc, ch 3, skip next ch-3 sp, (sc in next ch-3 sp, ch 3) 4 times, dc in next dc, decrease twice, dc in next dc, ch 7, skip next loop, (sc in next loop, ch 7) twice †, dc in next dc; repeat from ★ 18 times **more**, then repeat from † to † once; join with slip st to first dc.

Rnd 41: Ch 3, dc in next 3 dc, ★ † ch 3, skip next ch-3 sp, (sc in next ch-3 sp, ch 3) 3 times, dc in next 4 dc, ch 10, skip next loop, sc in next loop, ch 10 †, dc in next 4 dc; repeat from ★ 18 times **more**, then repeat from † to † once; join with slip st to first dc.

Rnd 42: Ch 3, dc in next 3 dc, ★ † ch 3, skip next ch-3 sp, (sc in next ch-3 sp, ch 3) twice, dc in next 4 dc, ch 10, (sc in next loop, ch 10) twice †, dc in next 4 dc; repeat from ★ 18 times **more**, then repeat from † to † once; join with slip st to first dc.

Rnd 43: Ch 2, dc in next dc, decrease, ★ † ch 3, skip next ch-3 sp, sc in next ch-3 sp, ch 3, decrease twice, ch 10, (sc in next loop, ch 10) 3 times †, decrease twice; repeat from ★ 18 times **more**, then repeat from † to † once; skip beginning ch-2 and join with slip st to first dc.

Rnd 44: Work beginning tr Cluster, (ch 10, sc in next loop) 4 times, ★ ch 10, work tr Cluster, (ch 10, sc in next loop) 4 times; repeat from ★ around, ch 5, dtr in top of beginning tr Cluster to form last loop: 100 loops.

Rnd 45: Ch 1, sc in same loop, ch 10, (sc in next loop, ch 10) around; join with slip st to first sc.

Rnd 46: Slip st in first 3 chs, ch 3, (dc, ch 4, slip st in third ch from hook, ch 1, 2 dc) in same loop, ch 5, ★ (2 dc, ch 4, slip st in third ch from hook, ch 1, 2 dc) in next loop, ch 5; repeat from ★ around; join with slip st to first dc, finish off.

See Washing and Blocking, page 140.

PRETTY PILLOWS

Finished Size: Pillow #1 - approximately 14" in diameter
Pillow #2 - approximately 15" in diameter

MATERIALS

Bedspread Weight Cotton Thread (size 10), approximately:
Pillow #1 - 430 yards
Pillow #2 - 650 yards
Crochet hook, size E (3.50 mm) **or** size needed for gauge
Pillow #1 - 14" round pillow or $1/2$ yard 44/45" wide fabric and polyester fiberfill
Pillow #2 - $5/8$ yard 44/45" wide fabric and polyester fiberfill

---

PATTERN STITCHES

DECREASE

★ YO, insert hook in **next** dc, YO and pull up a loop, YO and draw through 2 loops on hook; repeat from ★ once **more**, YO and draw through all 3 loops on hook (**counts as one dc**).

BEGINNING CLUSTER (uses first 4 dc)

Ch 3, ★ YO twice, insert hook in **next** dc, YO and pull up a loop, (YO and draw through 2 loops on hook) twice; repeat from ★ 2 times **more**, YO and draw through all 4 loops on hook (*Figs. 11a & b, page 134*).

CLUSTER (uses next 4 dc)

★ YO twice, insert hook in **next** dc, YO and pull up a loop, (YO and draw through 2 loops on hook) twice; repeat from ★ 3 times **more**, YO and draw through all 5 loops on hook.

2-DC CLUSTER

★ YO, insert hook in sp indicated, YO and pull up a loop, YO and draw through 2 loops on hook; repeat from ★ once **more**, YO and draw through all 3 loops on hook (*Figs. 10a & b, page 134*).

PILLOW #1

GAUGE: Rnds 1-4 = $3^1/2$"

Note: Pillow is worked holding 2 strands of thread together.

BACK

Ch 5; join with slip st to form a ring.

Rnd 1 (Right side)**:** Ch 1, 10 sc in ring; join with slip st to first sc.

Note: Loop a short piece of thread around any stitch to mark last round as **right** side.

Rnd 2: Ch 1, sc in same st, (ch 5, sc in next sc) around, ch 2, dc in first sc to form last loop: 10 loops.

Rnd 3: Ch 1, sc in same loop, (ch 5, sc in next loop) around, ch 2, dc in first sc to form last loop.

Rnd 4: Ch 3 **(counts as first dc, now and throughout)**, (dc, ch 2, 2 dc) in same loop, ch 5, sc in next loop, ★ ch 5, (2 dc, ch 2, 2 dc) in next loop, ch 5, sc in next loop; repeat from ★ around, ch 2, dc in first dc to form last loop: 10 loops.

Rnd 5: Ch 1, sc in same loop, ch 5, (2 dc, ch 2, 2 dc) in next ch-2 sp, ch 5, ★ (sc in next loop, ch 5) twice, (2 dc, ch 2, 2 dc) in next ch-2 sp, ch 5; repeat from ★ around to last loop, sc in last loop, ch 2, dc in first sc to form last loop: 15 loops.

Rnd 6: Ch 1, sc in same loop, ch 5, sc in next loop, ch 3, (dc in next 2 dc, ch 3) twice, sc in next loop, ★ (ch 5, sc in next loop) twice, ch 3, (dc in next 2 dc, ch 3) twice, sc in next loop; repeat from ★ around, ch 2, dc in first sc to form last loop.

Rnd 7: Ch 1, sc in same loop, ch 5, sc in next loop, ch 3, skip next ch-3 sp, 2 dc in each of next 2 dc, ch 3, (tr, ch 3) twice in next ch-3 sp, 2 dc in each of next 2 dc, ch 3, skip next ch-3 sp, ★ sc in next loop, ch 5, sc in next loop, ch 3, skip next ch-3 sp, 2 dc in each of next 2 dc, ch 3, (tr, ch 3) twice in next ch-3 sp, 2 dc in each of next 2 dc, ch 3, skip next ch-3 sp; repeat from ★ around; join with slip st to first sc.

Rnd 8: Slip st in first loop, ch 1, sc in same loop, ch 3, skip next ch-3 sp, 2 dc in next dc, dc in next 3 dc, ch 3, skip next ch-3 sp, dc in next ch-3 sp, (ch 1, dc) 7 times in same sp, ch 3, skip next ch-3 sp, dc in next 3 dc, 2 dc in next dc, ch 3, skip next ch-3 sp, ★ sc in next loop, ch 3, skip next ch-3 sp, 2 dc in next dc, dc in next 3 dc, ch 3, skip next ch-3 sp, dc in next ch-3 sp, (ch 1, dc) 7 times in same sp, ch 3, skip next ch-3 sp, dc in next 3 dc, 2 dc in next dc, ch 3, skip next ch-3 sp; repeat from ★ around; join with slip st to first sc.

Rnd 9: Slip st in next 3 chs and in next dc, ch 3, dc in same st and in next 4 dc, ch 3, (sc in next ch-1 sp, ch 3) 7 times, skip next ch-3 sp, dc in next 4 dc, 2 dc in next dc, ch 1, ★ 2 dc in next dc, dc in next 4 dc, ch 3, (sc in next ch-1 sp, ch 3) 7 times, skip next ch-3 sp, dc in next 4 dc, 2 dc in next dc, ch 1; repeat from ★ around; join with slip st to first dc.

Rnd 10: Ch 3, dc in next 5 dc, ch 3, skip next ch-3 sp, (sc in next ch-3 sp, ch 3) 6 times, ★ (dc in next 6 dc, ch 3) twice, skip next ch-3 sp, (sc in next ch-3 sp, ch 3) 6 times; repeat from ★ around to last 6 dc, dc in last 6 dc, ch 3; join with slip st to first dc.

Rnd 11: Ch 3, dc in next 5 dc, ch 3, skip next ch-3 sp, (sc in next ch-3 sp, ch 3) 5 times, dc in next 6 dc, ch 3, sc in next ch-3 sp, ch 3, ★ dc in next 6 dc, ch 3, skip next ch-3 sp, (sc in next ch-3 sp, ch 3) 5 times, dc in next 6 dc, ch 3, sc in next ch-3 sp, ch 3; repeat from ★ around; join with slip st to first dc.

Rnd 12: Ch 3, dc in next 5 dc, ch 3, skip next ch-3 sp, (sc in next ch-3 sp, ch 3) 4 times, dc in next 6 dc, ch 3, (sc in next ch-3 sp, ch 3) twice, ★ dc in next 6 dc, ch 3, skip next ch-3 sp, (sc in next ch-3 sp, ch 3) 4 times, dc in next 6 dc, ch 3, (sc in next ch-3 sp, ch 3) twice; repeat from ★ around; join with slip st to first dc.

Rnd 13: Ch 2, dc in next 5 dc, ch 3, skip next ch-3 sp, (sc in next ch-3 sp, ch 3) 3 times, dc in next 4 dc, decrease, ch 3, (sc in next ch-3 sp, ch 3) 3 times, ★ decrease, dc in next 4 dc, ch 3, skip next ch-3 sp, (sc in next ch-3 sp, ch 3) 3 times, dc in next 4 dc, decrease, ch 3, (sc in next ch-3 sp, ch 3) 3 times; repeat from ★ around; skip beginning ch-2 and join with slip st to first dc.

Rnd 14: Ch 2, dc in next 4 dc, ch 3, skip next ch-3 sp, (sc in next ch-3 sp, ch 3) twice, dc in next 3 dc, decrease, ch 3, (sc in next ch-3 sp, ch 3) 4 times, ★ decrease, dc in next 3 dc, ch 3, skip next ch-3 sp, (sc in next ch-3 sp, ch 3) twice, dc in next 3 dc, decrease, ch 3, (sc in next ch-3 sp, ch 3) 4 times; repeat from ★ around; skip beginning ch-2 and join with slip st to first dc.

Rnd 15: Ch 3, dc in next 3 dc, ch 5, skip next ch-3 sp, sc in next ch-3 sp, ch 5, dc in next 4 dc, ch 3, (sc in next ch-3 sp, ch 3) 5 times, ★ dc in next 4 dc, ch 5, skip next ch-3 sp, sc in next ch-3 sp, ch 5, dc in next 4 dc, ch 3, (sc in next ch-3 sp, ch 3) 5 times; repeat from ★ around; join with slip st to first dc.

Rnd 16: Ch 3, dc in next 3 dc, ch 3, sc in next sc, ch 3, dc in next 4 dc, ch 3, (sc in next ch-3 sp, ch 3) 6 times, ★ dc in next 4 dc, ch 3, sc in next sc, ch 3, dc in next 4 dc, ch 3, (sc in next ch-3 sp, ch 3) 6 times; repeat from ★ around; join with slip st to first dc.

Rnd 17: Work beginning Cluster, ch 1, work Cluster, ch 7, sc in next ch-3 sp, (ch 4, sc in next ch-3 sp) 6 times, ch 7, ★ work Cluster, ch 1, work Cluster, ch 7, sc in next ch-3 sp, (ch 4, sc in next ch-3 sp) 6 times, ch 7; repeat from ★ around; join with slip st to top of beginning Cluster.

Rnd 18: Slip st in first ch-1 sp, ch 1, sc in same sp, (ch 5, sc in next ch-sp) around, ch 2, dc in first sc to form last loop.

Rnd 19: Ch 1, sc in same loop, ch 5, (sc in next loop, ch 5) around; join with slip st to first sc, finish off.

FRONT
Work same as Back; at end of Rnd 19, do **not** finish off.

FINISHING
Make pillow form if desired, page 140.

JOINING
Ch 1, hold Front and Back with **wrong** sides together and Front facing; matching pattern and working through **both** pieces, (3 sc, ch 3, slip st in sc just made, 2 sc) in first loop and in each loop around inserting pillow form before closing; join with slip st to first sc, finish off.

PILLOW #2

GAUGE: Rnds 1-3 = 4"

Note: Pillow is worked holding 2 strands of thread together.

BACK

Ch 8; join with slip st to form a ring.

Rnd 1 (Right side)**:** Ch 3 **(counts as first dc, now and throughout)**, 15 dc in ring; join with slip st to first dc: 16 dc.
Note: Loop a short piece of thread around any stitch to mark last round as **right** side.

Rnd 2: Ch 12, (dc in next 2 dc, ch 9) around to last dc, dc in last dc; join with slip st to third ch of beginning ch-12: 8 loops.

Rnd 3: Slip st in first 2 chs, ch 3, dc in next 2 chs, ch 3, skip next ch, dc in next 3 chs, skip next 2 dc and next ch, ★ dc in next 3 chs, ch 3, skip next ch, dc in next 3 chs, skip next 2 dc and next ch; repeat from ★ around; join with slip st to first dc: 48 dc.

Rnd 4: Slip st in next dc, ch 3, dc in next dc, (2 dc, ch 3, 2 dc) in next ch-3 sp, dc in next 2 dc, skip next 2 dc, ★ dc in next 2 dc, (2 dc, ch 3, 2 dc) in next ch-3 sp, dc in next 2 dc, skip next 2 dc; repeat from ★ around; join with slip st to first dc: 64 dc.

Rnd 5: Slip st in next dc, ch 3, dc in next 2 dc, (2 dc, ch 3, 2 dc) in next ch-3 sp, dc in next 3 dc, skip next 2 dc, ★ dc in next 3 dc, (2 dc, ch 3, 2 dc) in next ch-3 sp, dc in next 3 dc, skip next 2 dc; repeat from ★ around; join with slip st to first dc: 80 dc.

Rnd 6: Slip st in next dc, ch 3, dc in next 3 dc, (2 dc, ch 3, 2 dc) in next ch-3 sp, dc in next 4 dc, skip next 2 dc, ★ dc in next 4 dc, (2 dc, ch 3, 2 dc) in next ch-3 sp, dc in next 4 dc, skip next 2 dc; repeat from ★ around; join with slip st to first dc: 96 dc.

Rnd 7: Slip st in next dc, ch 3, dc in next 4 dc, (2 dc, ch 3, 2 dc) in next ch-3 sp, dc in next 5 dc, skip next 2 dc, ★ dc in next 5 dc, (2 dc, ch 3, 2 dc) in next ch-3 sp, dc in next 5 dc, skip next 2 dc; repeat from ★ around; join with slip st to first dc: 112 dc.

Rnd 8: Slip st in next dc, ch 3, dc in next 5 dc, (2 dc, ch 3, 2 dc) in next ch-3 sp, dc in next 6 dc, skip next 2 dc, ★ dc in next 6 dc, (2 dc, ch 3, 2 dc) in next ch-3 sp, dc in next 6 dc, skip next 2 dc; repeat from ★ around; join with slip st to first dc: 128 dc.

Rnd 9: Slip st in next 2 dc, ch 3, dc in next 5 dc, (2 dc, ch 3, 2 dc) in next ch-3 sp, dc in next 6 dc, ch 3, skip next 4 dc, ★ dc in next 6 dc, (2 dc, ch 3, 2 dc) in next ch-3 sp, dc in next 6 dc, ch 3, skip next 4 dc; repeat from ★ around; join with slip st to first dc: 128 dc.

Rnd 10: Slip st in next 3 dc, ch 3, dc in next 4 dc, (2 dc, ch 3, 2 dc) in next ch-3 sp, dc in next 5 dc, ch 3, (dc, ch 5, dc) in next ch-3 sp, ch 3, skip next 3 dc, ★ dc in next 5 dc, (2 dc, ch 3, 2 dc) in next ch-3 sp, dc in next 5 dc, ch 3, (dc, ch 5, dc) in next ch-3 sp, ch 3, skip next 3 dc; repeat from ★ around; join with slip st to first dc.

Rnd 11: Slip st in next 3 dc, ch 3, dc in next 3 dc, (2 dc, ch 3, 2 dc) in next ch-3 sp, dc in next 4 dc, ch 3, skip next ch-3 sp, 7 dc in next loop, ch 3, skip next ch-3 sp and next 3 dc, ★ dc in next 4 dc, (2 dc, ch 3, 2 dc) in next ch-3 sp, dc in next 4 dc, ch 3, skip next ch-3 sp, 7 dc in next loop, ch 3, skip next ch-3 sp and next 3 dc; repeat from ★ around; join with slip st to first dc: 152 dc.

Rnd 12: Slip st in next 3 dc, ch 3, dc in next 2 dc, (2 dc, ch 3, 2 dc) in next ch-3 sp, dc in next 3 dc, ch 3, skip next 3 dc, dc in next dc, (ch 1, dc in next dc) 6 times, ch 3, skip next 3 dc, ★ dc in next 3 dc, (2 dc, ch 3, 2 dc) in next ch-3 sp, dc in next 3 dc, ch 3, skip next 3 dc, dc in next dc, (ch 1, dc in next dc) 6 times, ch 3, skip next 3 dc; repeat from ★ around; join with slip st to first dc: 136 dc.

Rnd 13: Slip st in next 3 dc, ch 3, dc in next dc, (2 dc, ch 3, 2 dc) in next ch-3 sp, dc in next 2 dc, ch 5, work 2-dc Cluster in next ch-1 sp, (ch 2, work 2-dc Cluster in next ch-1 sp) 5 times, ch 5, skip next ch-3 sp and next 3 dc, ★ dc in next 2 dc, (2 dc, ch 3, 2 dc) in next ch-3 sp, dc in next 2 dc, ch 5, work 2-dc Cluster in next ch-1 sp, (ch 2, work 2-dc Cluster in next ch-1 sp) 5 times, ch 5, skip next ch-3 sp and next 3 dc; repeat from ★ around; join with slip st to first dc: 48 2-dc Clusters.

Rnd 14: Slip st in next 3 dc, ch 3, (2 dc, ch 3, 2 dc) in next ch-3 sp, dc in next dc, ch 5, work 2-dc Cluster in next ch-2 sp, (ch 2, work 2-dc Cluster in next ch-2 sp) 4 times, ch 5, skip next 3 dc, ★ dc in next dc, (2 dc, ch 3, 2 dc) in next ch-3 sp, dc in next dc, ch 5, work 2-dc Cluster in next ch-2 sp, (ch 2, work 2-dc Cluster in next ch-2 sp) 4 times, ch 5, skip next 3 dc; repeat from ★ around; join with slip st to first dc, finish off.

FRONT

Work same as Back; at end of Rnd 14, do **not** finish off.

FINISHING

Make pillow form if desired, page 140.

JOINING

Rnd 1: Slip st in next 2 dc and in next ch-3 sp, ch 1, hold Front and Back with **wrong** sides together and Front facing; matching pattern and working through **both** pieces, sc in same sp, ch 5, sc in next loop, ch 5, sc in next ch-2 sp, (ch 3, sc in next ch-2 sp) 3 times, ★ (ch 5, sc in next ch-sp) 4 times, (ch 3, sc in next ch-2 sp) 3 times; repeat from ★ around to last loop inserting pillow form before closing, ch 5, sc in last loop, ch 5; join with slip st to first sc: 56 ch-sps.

Rnd 2: Slip st in first loop, ch 1, 5 sc in same loop and in next loop, (2 sc, ch 3, slip st in sc just made, sc) in each of next 3 ch-3 sps, ★ 5 sc in each of next 4 loops, (2 sc, ch 3, slip st in sc just made, sc) in each of next 3 ch-3 sps; repeat from ★ around to last 2 loops, 5 sc in each of last 2 loops; join with slip st to first sc, finish off.

Quick LACY COASTER

Finished Size: Approximately 5¼" in diameter

MATERIALS
Bedspread Weight Cotton Thread (size 10), approximately
    45 yards **each**
Steel crochet hook, size 6 (1.80 mm) **or** size needed for gauge

GAUGE: Rnds 1-5 = 2"

PATTERN STITCHES
DECREASE

★ YO, insert hook in **next** dc, YO and pull up a loop, YO and draw through 2 loops on hook; repeat from ★ once **more**, YO and draw through all 3 loops on hook **(counts as one dc)**.

BEGINNING CLUSTER (uses first 4 dc)

Ch 3, ★ YO twice, insert hook in **next** dc, YO and pull up a loop, (YO and draw through 2 loops on hook) twice; repeat from ★ 2 times **more**, YO and draw through all 4 loops on hook *(Figs. 11a & b, page 134)*.

CLUSTER (uses next 4 dc)

★ YO twice, insert hook in **next** dc, YO and pull up a loop, (YO and draw through 2 loops on hook) twice; repeat from ★ 3 times **more**, YO and draw through all 5 loops on hook.

Ch 5; join with slip st to form a ring.

Rnd 1 (Right side)**:** Ch 1, 10 sc in ring; join with slip st to first sc.

Note: Loop a short piece of thread around any stitch to mark last round as **right** side.

Rnd 2: Ch 1, sc in same st, (ch 5, sc in next sc) around, ch 2, dc in first sc to form last loop: 10 loops.

Rnd 3: Ch 1, sc in same loop, (ch 5, sc in next loop) around, ch 2, dc in first sc to form last loop.

Rnd 4: Ch 3 **(counts as first dc, now and throughout)**, (dc, ch 2, 2 dc) in same loop, ch 5, sc in next loop, ★ ch 5, (2 dc, ch 2, 2 dc) in next loop, ch 5, sc in next loop; repeat from ★ around, ch 2, dc in first dc to form last loop: 10 loops.

Rnd 5: Ch 1, sc in same loop, ch 5, (2 dc, ch 2, 2 dc) in next ch-2 sp, ch 5, ★ (sc in next loop, ch 5) twice, (2 dc, ch 2, 2 dc) in next ch-2 sp, ch 5; repeat from ★ around to last loop, sc in last loop, ch 2, dc in first sc to form last loop: 15 loops.

Rnd 6: Ch 1, sc in same loop, ch 5, sc in next loop, ch 3, (dc in next 2 dc, ch 3) twice, sc in next loop, ★ (ch 5, sc in next loop) twice, ch 3, (dc in next 2 dc, ch 3) twice, sc in next loop; repeat from ★ around, ch 2, dc in first sc to form last loop.

Rnd 7: Ch 1, sc in same loop, ch 5, sc in next loop, ch 3, skip next ch-3 sp, 2 dc in each of next 2 dc, ch 3, (tr, ch 3) twice in next ch-3 sp, 2 dc in each of next 2 dc, ch 3, skip next ch-3 sp,

★ sc in next loop, ch 5, sc in next loop, ch 3, skip next ch-3 sp, 2 dc in each of next 2 dc, ch 3, (tr, ch 3) twice in next ch-3 sp, 2 dc in each of next 2 dc, ch 3, skip next ch-3 sp; repeat from ★ around; join with slip st to first sc.

Rnd 8: Slip st in first loop, ch 1, sc in same loop, ch 3, skip next ch-3 sp, 2 dc in next dc, dc in next 3 dc, ch 3, skip next ch-3 sp, dc in next ch-3 sp, (ch 1, dc) 4 times in same sp, ch 3, dc in next 3 dc, 2 dc in next dc, ch 3, skip next ch-3 sp, ★ sc in next loop, ch 3, skip next ch-3 sp, 2 dc in next dc, dc in next 3 dc, ch 3, skip next ch-3 sp, dc in next ch-3 sp, (ch 1, dc) 4 times in same sp, ch 3, dc in next 3 dc, 2 dc in next dc, ch 3, skip next ch-3 sp; repeat from ★ around; join with slip st to first sc.

Rnd 9: Slip st in first 3 chs and in next dc, ch 3, dc in next 4 dc, ch 3, (sc in next ch-1 sp, ch 3) 4 times, skip next ch-3 sp, dc in next 5 dc, ch 1, ★ dc in next 5 dc, ch 3, (sc in next ch-1 sp, ch 3) 4 times, skip next ch-3 sp, dc in next 5 dc, ch 1; repeat from ★ around; join with slip st to first dc.

Rnd 10: Ch 2, dc in next 4 dc, ch 4, skip next ch-3 sp, sc in next ch-3 sp, (ch 3, sc in next ch-3 sp) twice, ch 4, dc in next 3 dc, decrease, ch 3, sc in next ch-1 sp, ch 3, ★ decrease, dc in next 3 dc, ch 4, skip next ch-3 sp, sc in next ch-3 sp, (ch 3, sc in next ch-3 sp) twice, ch 4, dc in next 3 dc, decrease, ch 3, sc in next ch-1 sp, ch 3; repeat from ★ around; skip beginning ch-2 and join with slip st to first dc.

Rnd 11: Ch 3, dc in next 3 dc, ch 4, skip next ch-4 sp, sc in next ch-3 sp, ch 3, sc in next ch-3 sp, ch 4, dc in next 4 dc, ch 3, (sc in next ch-3 sp, ch 3) twice, ★ dc in next 4 dc, ch 4, skip next ch-4 sp, sc in next ch-3 sp, ch 3, sc in next ch-3 sp, ch 4, dc in next 4 dc, ch 3, (sc in next ch-3 sp, ch 3) twice; repeat from ★ around; join with slip st to first dc.

Rnd 12: Ch 3, dc in next 3 dc, ch 5, skip next ch-4 sp, sc in next ch-3 sp, ch 5, dc in next 4 dc, ch 3, sc in next ch-3 sp, (ch 5, sc in next ch-3 sp) twice, ch 3, ★ dc in next 4 dc, ch 5, skip next ch-4 sp, sc in next ch-3 sp, ch 5, dc in next 4 dc, ch 3, sc in next ch-3 sp, (ch 5, sc in next ch-3 sp) twice, ch 3; repeat from ★ around; join with slip st to first dc.

Rnd 13: Ch 3, dc in next 3 dc, ch 3, sc in next sc, ch 3, dc in next 4 dc, ch 5, (sc in next ch-sp, ch 5) 4 times, ★ dc in next 4 dc, ch 3, sc in next sc, ch 3, dc in next 4 dc, ch 5, (sc in next ch-sp, ch 5) 4 times; repeat from ★ around; join with slip st to first dc.

Rnd 14: Work beginning Cluster, ch 1, work Cluster, ch 7, sc in next loop, (ch 5, slip st in third ch from hook, ch 3, sc in next loop) 4 times, ch 7, ★ work Cluster, ch 1, work Cluster, ch 7, sc in next loop, (ch 5, slip st in third ch from hook, ch 3, sc in next loop) 4 times, ch 7; repeat from ★ around; join with slip st to top of beginning Cluster, finish off.

See Washing and Blocking, page 140.

FLOWERPOT LACE

Shell and cluster stitches form a flower-like motif on this sunny flowerpot cover. Fashioned in bedspread weight cotton thread, the pretty cover is finished with ribbons laced through the eyelet rounds. Presented with a blooming plant, it's a lovely gift for a secret pal.

Finished Size: Approximately 3¹/₂" high (Body)

MATERIALS
    Bedspread Weight Cotton Thread (size 10),
        approximately 180 yards
    Steel crochet hook, size 5 (1.90 mm) **or** size needed
        for gauge
    1¹/₂ yards of ¹/₈" ribbon
    Flower pot - 4" top diameter x 3" to 3¹/₂" high

GAUGE: 14 dc and 7 rows = 2"

PATTERN STITCHES

CLUSTER
★ YO, insert hook in st indicated, YO and pull up a loop, YO and draw through 2 loops on hook; repeat from ★ 5 times **more**, YO and draw through all 7 loops on hook *(Figs. 10a & b, page 134)*.

SHELL
(2 Dc, ch 2, 2 dc) in st or sp indicated.

DOUBLE SHELL
2 Dc in sp indicated, (ch 2, 2 dc) twice in **same** sp.

V-ST
(Dc, ch 2, dc) in sp indicated.

DECREASE (uses next 3 sps)
★ YO twice, insert hook in **next** ch-3 sp, YO and pull up a loop, (YO and draw through 2 loops on hook) twice; repeat from ★ 2 times **more**, YO and draw through all 4 loops on hook.

BODY

Ch 84 **loosely**; being careful not to twist ch, join with slip st to form a ring.

Rnd 1 (Right side): Ch 3 **(counts as first dc, now and throughout)**, dc in next ch and in each ch around; join with slip st to first dc: 84 dc.

Note: Loop a short piece of thread around any stitch to mark last round as **right** side.

Rnd 2 (Eyelet rnd): Ch 4 **(counts as first dc plus ch 1, now and throughout)**, skip next dc, (dc in next dc, ch 1, skip next dc) around; join with slip st to first dc: 42 ch-1 sps.

Rnd 3: Ch 3, dc in next ch and in each st around; join with slip st to first dc: 84 dc.

Rnd 4: Ch 3, dc in next dc, work Cluster in next dc, ★ dc in next 11 dc, work Cluster in next dc; repeat from ★ 5 times **more**, dc in last 9 dc; join with slip st to first dc: 7 Clusters.

Rnd 5: Ch 3, work Cluster in next dc, dc in next Cluster, work Cluster in next dc, ★ dc in next 9 dc, work Cluster in next dc, dc in next Cluster, work Cluster in next dc; repeat from ★ 5 times **more**, dc in last 8 dc; join with slip st to first dc: 14 Clusters.

Rnd 6: Ch 3, dc in next Cluster, work Cluster in next dc, ★ dc in next 11 sts, work Cluster in next dc; repeat from ★ 5 times **more**, dc in last 9 sts; join with slip st to first dc: 7 Clusters.

Rnd 7: Ch 3, dc in next dc and in each st around; join with slip st to first dc: 84 dc.

Rnds 8 and 9: Repeat Rnds 2 and 3.

Rnd 10: Slip st in next 2 dc, ch 3, (dc, ch 2, 2 dc) in same st, skip next 2 dc, (work Shell in next dc, skip next 2 dc) around; join with slip st to first dc: 28 Shells.

Rnd 11: Slip st in next dc and in next ch-2 sp, ch 4, dc in same sp, (ch 1, dc in same sp) 6 times, sc in next Shell (ch-2 sp), ★ dc in next Shell, (ch 1, dc in same sp) 7 times, sc in next Shell; repeat from ★ around; join with slip st to first dc: 14 sc.

Rnd 12: Ch 1, sc in same st, (sc in next ch-1 sp, sc in next dc) 7 times, skip next sc, ★ sc in next dc, (sc in next ch-1 sp, sc in next dc) 7 times, skip next sc; repeat from ★ around; join with slip st to first sc, finish off.

RUFFLE

Rnd 1: With **right** side facing and working in free loops of beginning ch *(Fig. 23b, page 138)*, join thread with slip st in second ch; ch 3, (dc, ch 2, 2 dc) in same st, skip next 2 chs, (work Shell in next ch, skip next 2 chs) around; join with slip st to first dc: 28 Shells.

Rnd 2: Slip st in next dc and in next ch-2 sp, ch 5 **(counts as first dc plus ch 2, now and throughout)**, dc in same sp, work Shell in next Shell, ★ work V-St in next 3 Shells, work Shell in next Shell; repeat from ★ 5 times **more**, work V-St in last 2 Shells; join with slip st to first dc: 7 Shells and 21 V-Sts.

Rnd 3: Slip st in first ch-2 sp, ch 5, dc in same sp, ★ † work Shell in next Shell, work V-St in next V-St (ch-2 sp), 7 dc in next V-St †, work V-St in next V-St; repeat from ★ 5 times **more**, then repeat from † to † once; join with slip st to first dc: 7 7-dc groups.

Rnd 4: Slip st in first ch-2 sp, ch 5, dc in same sp, ★ † ch 1, work Double Shell in next Shell, ch 1, work V-St in next V-St, ch 1, (dc in next dc, ch 1) 7 times †, work V-St in next V-St; repeat from ★ 5 times **more**, then repeat from † to † once; join with slip st to first dc.

Rnd 5: Slip st in first ch-2 sp, ch 5, dc in same sp, ★ † ch 1, work Shell in next 2 ch-2 sps, ch 1, work V-St in next V-St, ch 1, skip next ch-1 sp, sc in next ch-1 sp, (ch 3, sc in next ch-1 sp) 5 times, ch 1 †, work V-St in next V-St; repeat from ★ 5 times **more**, then repeat from † to † once; join with slip st to first dc.

Rnd 6: Slip st in first ch-2 sp, ch 5, dc in same sp, ★ † ch 3, work Shell in next 2 Shells, ch 3, work V-St in next V-St, ch 3, skip next ch-1 sp, (sc in next ch-3 sp, ch 3) 5 times †, work V-St in next V-St; repeat from ★ 5 times **more**, then repeat from † to † once; join with slip st to first dc.

Rnd 7: Slip st in first ch-2 sp, ch 5, dc in same sp, ★ † ch 3, work Double Shell in next 2 Shells, ch 3, work V-St in next V-St, ch 3, skip next ch-3 sp, (sc in next ch-3 sp, ch 3) 4 times †, work V-St in next V-St; repeat from ★ 5 times **more**, then repeat from † to † once; join with slip st to first dc.

Rnd 8: Slip st in first ch-2 sp, ch 5, dc in same sp, ★ † ch 3, work Shell in next 4 ch-2 sps, ch 3, work V-St in next V-St, skip next ch-3 sp, decrease †, work V-St in next V-St; repeat from ★ 5 times **more**, then repeat from † to † once; join with slip st to first dc, finish off.

FINISHING

See Washing and Blocking, page 140.
Weave ribbon through both Eyelet rnds on Body.
Insert pot in Cover and pull ribbons to gather Cover around pot.
Tie each ribbon in a bow to secure Cover to pot.

$\mathcal{C}$uick HAPPY HOUSEWARMING!

$\mathcal{C}$*rocheted in worsted weight yarn, this handy set makes a thoughtful housewarming gift. The round hot pad is crocheted using front post double crochet stitches. A coordinating pot holder has the same pretty pattern and is finished with a loop for hanging.*

Finished Size: Hot Pad - 9" in diameter
Pot Holder - 8" in diameter

MATERIALS

Worsted Weight Yarn, approximately:
MC (White) - 3½ ounces, (100 grams, 230 yards)
CC (Blue) - 1 ounce, (30 grams, 65 yards)
Crochet hook, size G (4.00 mm) **or** size needed for gauge

GAUGE: Rnds 1 and 2 of Front = 2¼"

PATTERN STITCH

FRONT POST DOUBLE CROCHET *(abbreviated FPdc)*
YO, insert hook from **front** to **back** around post of st indicated *(Fig. 13, page 135)*, YO and pull up a loop **even** with loop on hook, (YO and draw through 2 loops on hook) twice.

HOT PAD

FRONT

Rnd 1 (Right side)**:** With CC, ch 4, 11 dc in fourth ch from hook; join with slip st to top of beginning ch: 12 sts.

Note: Loop a short piece of yarn around any stitch to mark last round as **right** side.

Rnd 2: Ch 3 **(counts as first dc, now and throughout)**, dc in same st, 2 dc in next dc and in each dc around; join with slip st to first dc, finish off: 24 dc.

Rnd 3: With **right** side facing, join MC with slip st in any dc; ch 3, work FPdc around same st, (dc in next dc, work FPdc around same st) around; join with slip st to first dc: 48 sts.

Rnd 4: Ch 3, dc in same st, work FPdc around next FPdc, (2 dc in next dc, work FPdc around next FPdc) around; join with slip st to first dc, finish off: 72 sts.

Rnd 5: With **right** side facing and working in Back Loops Only *(Fig. 22, page 138)*, join CC with slip st in first dc; ch 3, dc in next 10 sts, 2 dc in next st, (dc in next 11 sts, 2 dc in next st) around; join with slip st to first dc, finish off: 78 dc.

Rnd 6: With **right** side facing, join MC with slip st in first dc; ch 3, dc in next dc, work FPdc around next dc, (dc in next 2 dc, work FPdc around next dc) around; join with slip st to first dc: 26 FPdc.

Rnd 7: Ch 3, 2 dc in next dc, work FPdc around next FPdc, (dc in next dc, 2 dc in next dc, work FPdc around next FPdc) around; join with slip st to first dc: 104 sts.

Rnd 8: Ch 3, dc in next 2 dc, work FPdc around next FPdc, (dc in next 3 dc, work FPdc around next FPdc) around; join with slip st to first dc, finish off.

BACK

Rnd 1 (Right side)**:** With MC, ch 4, 11 dc in fourth ch from hook; join with slip st to top of beginning ch: 12 sts.
Note: Mark last round as **right** side.

Rnds 2 and 3: Ch 3, dc in same st, 2 dc in next dc and in each dc around; join with slip st to first dc: 48 dc.

Rnd 4: Ch 1, sc in first 7 dc, 2 sc in next dc, (sc in next 7 dc, 2 sc in next dc) around; do **not** join, place marker *(see Markers, page 138)*: 54 sc.

Rnd 5: (Sc in next 8 sc, 2 sc in next sc) around: 60 sc.

Rnd 6: (Sc in next 9 sc, 2 sc in next sc) around: 66 sc.

Rnd 7: (Sc in next 10 sc, 2 sc in next sc) around: 72 sc.

Rnd 8: (Sc in next 11 sc, 2 sc in next sc) around: 78 sc.

Rnd 9: (Sc in next 12 sc, 2 sc in next sc) around: 84 sc.

Rnd 10: (Sc in next 13 sc, 2 sc in next sc) around: 90 sc.

Rnd 11: (Sc in next 14 sc, 2 sc in next sc) around: 96 sc.

Rnd 12: (Sc in next 15 sc, 2 sc in next sc) around: 102 sc.

Rnd 13: (Sc in next 50 sc, 2 sc in next sc) twice: 104 sc.

Rnd 14: Sc in each sc around; slip st in next sc, finish off.

JOINING

Rnd 1: With **wrong** sides together, Front facing and working through inside loops only of **both** pieces, join CC with slip st in any st; ch 1, sc in each st around; join with slip st to Back Loop Only of first sc.

Rnd 2: Ch 1, sc in Back Loop Only of each sc around; join with slip st to both loops of first sc, finish off.

POT HOLDER

FRONT

Rnds 1-7: Work same as Hot Pad: 104 sts.
Finish off.

BACK

Rnds 1-5: Work same as Hot Pad: 60 sc.

Rnd 6: (Sc in next 4 sc, 2 sc in next sc) around: 72 sc.

Rnd 7: (Sc in next 5 sc, 2 sc in next sc) around: 84 sc.

Rnd 8: (Sc in next 6 sc, 2 sc in next sc) around: 96 sc.

Rnd 9: (Sc in next 11 sc, 2 sc in next sc) around: 104 sc.

Rnd 10: Sc in each sc around; slip st in next sc, finish off.

JOINING

Rnd 1: Work same as Hot Pad.

Rnd 2: Ch 1, sc in Back Loop Only of each sc around; join with slip st to both loops of first sc, ch 9, skip next 2 sc, slip st in both loops of next sc; finish off.

Quick PETITE TISSUE COVER

A lovely accessory for a lady's dressing table, this lacy tissue cover is created using bedspread weight cotton thread. Purse-size tissues fit nicely inside the petite holder, which is worked in shell stitches and accented with satin bows.

Finished Size: Approximately 2½" x 5¼"

MATERIALS

Bedspread Weight Cotton Thread (size 10), approximately 50 yards
Crochet hook, size 5 (1.90 mm) **or** size needed for gauge
1 yard of ⅛" ribbon
Purse-size tissues

GAUGE: In pattern, (V-St, Shell) twice and 7 rows = 2"

PATTERN STITCHES
V-ST
(Dc, ch 2, dc) in st or sp indicated.
SHELL
5 Dc in sp indicated.

BODY

Ch 46 **loosely**.

Row 1 (Right side): Dc in sixth ch from hook, (ch 1, skip next ch, dc in next ch) across: 21 sps.

Note: Loop a short piece of thread around any stitch to mark last row as **right** side.

Row 2: Ch 4 **(counts as first dc plus ch 1, now and throughout)**, dc in next dc, skip next ch-1 sp, work V-St in next ch-1 sp, ★ skip next ch-1 sp, work Shell in next ch-1 sp, skip next ch-1 sp, work V-St in next ch-1 sp; repeat from ★ 3 times **more**, skip next ch-1 sp, dc in next dc, ch 1, skip next ch, dc in next ch: 4 Shells.

Row 3: Ch 4, turn; dc in next dc, work Shell in next V-St (ch-2 sp), ★ work V-St in center dc of next Shell, work Shell in next V-St; repeat from ★ across, dc in next dc, ch 1, dc in last dc.

Row 4: Ch 4, turn; dc in next dc, work V-St in center dc of next Shell, ★ work Shell in next V-St, work V-St in center dc of next Shell; repeat from ★ across, dc in next dc, ch 1, dc in last dc.

Rows 5-20: Repeat Rows 3 and 4, 8 times.

Row 21: Ch 4, turn; dc in next dc, ch 1, (dc, ch 1) twice in next V-St, ★ working across next Shell, (skip next dc, dc in next dc, ch 1) twice, (dc, ch 1) twice in next V-St; repeat from ★ across, dc in next dc, ch 1, dc in last dc; finish off: 21 ch-1 sps.

EDGING

With **wrong** side facing, fold ends of Body up, placing beginning ch and Row 21 on each side of center row. Working through **both** thicknesses and matching sps on end of rows carefully (5 sps **each** side of center), join thread with slip st in first sp; ch 2, 2 dc in same sp, (slip st, ch 2, 2 dc) in next sp and in each sp across to last sp, slip st in last sp; finish off. Repeat for other end.

FINISHING

Insert tissues (without packaging) into Cover.

Cut ribbon in half.

Begin with center of each ribbon in sps at opposite ends. Lace ribbon through every other sp on Rows 1 and 21, criss-crossing as if lacing a shoe, and leaving 7 center sps on each row free; tie each ribbon in a bow.

BABY BROTHER

With his rosy cheeks and big smile, this soft crocheted doll makes a great buddy for a child who's adjusting to the arrival of a new sibling. Dressed in a newborn-size sleeper, he'll help teach big brother or sister how to handle the new baby safely.

Finished Size: Approximately 23" tall

MATERIALS

Worsted Weight Yarn, approximately:
   MC (Peach) - 5 ounces, (140 grams, 330 yards)
   CC (Brown) - 12 yards
Crochet hook, size I (5.50 mm) **or** size needed for gauge
Embroidery floss - blue and pink
Pink felt
Yarn and tapestry needles
Brown sewing thread
Polyester fiberfill
Cardboard - 1³/₄" x 5"
Sleeper (size 0-3 months)

GAUGE: 14 sc and 13 rows = 4"

PATTERN STITCHES

CLUSTER

★ YO, insert hook in st indicated, YO and pull up a loop, YO and draw through 2 loops on hook; repeat from ★ 2 times **more**, YO and draw through all 4 loops on hook *(Figs. 10a & b, page 134)*.

Note: Always push Cluster to **right** side unless otherwise specified.

SC DECREASE

Pull up a loop in next 2 sts, YO and draw through all 3 loops on hook **(counts as one sc)**.

DC DECREASE (uses next 2 sts)

★ YO, insert hook in **next** st, YO and pull up a loop, YO and draw through 2 loops on hook; repeat from ★ once **more**, YO and draw through all 3 loops on hook **(counts as one dc)**.

LEFT LEG

With MC, ch 6 **loosely**.

Rnd 1 (Right side): Sc in second ch from hook and in next 2 chs, 2 sc in next ch, 5 sc in next ch; working in free loops of beginning ch *(Fig. 23b, page 138)*, 2 sc in next ch, sc in next 2 chs, 2 sc in next ch; do **not** join, place marker *(see Markers, page 138)*: 16 sc.

Rnd 2: 2 Sc in next sc, sc in next 4 sc, 2 sc in next sc, (sc in next sc, 2 sc in next sc) twice, sc in next 5 sc, 2 sc in next sc: 21 sc.

Rnd 3: 2 Sc in next sc, sc in next 6 sc, (hdc, dc) in next sc, hdc in next sc, 2 sc in each of next 3 sc, hdc in next sc, (dc, hdc) in next sc, sc in next 6 sc, 2 sc in next sc: 28 sts.

Rnd 4: 2 Sc in next sc, sc in next 8 sts, (sc, tr, sc) in next dc, (work Cluster in next st, sc in next st) twice, 3 dc in next sc, drop loop from hook, insert hook in first dc of 3-dc group, hook dropped loop and draw through, sc in next sc, 5 dc in next sc, drop loop from hook, insert hook in first dc of 5-dc group, hook dropped loop and draw through, sc in next 11 sts: 31 sts.

Rnd 5: Sc in next 9 sc, sc decrease, skip next tr, YO, insert hook in next sc, YO and pull up a loop, YO and draw through 2 loops on hook, skip next st, YO, insert hook in next sc, YO and pull up a loop, YO and draw through 2 loops on hook, YO and draw through all 3 loops on hook, dc decrease twice, sc decrease twice, sc in next 8 sc: 23 sts.

Rnd 6: Sc decrease, sc in next 7 sc, sc decrease, (sc in next st, sc decrease) twice, sc in next 6 sc: 19 sts.

Rnd 7: Sc decrease, (sc in next 6 sc, sc decrease) twice, sc in next sc: 16 sc.

Rnds 8 and 9: Sc in each sc around.

Rnd 10: (Sc in next 3 sc, 2 sc in next sc) around: 20 sc.

Rnds 11-16: Sc in each sc around.

Rnd 17: (Sc in next 3 sc, sc decrease) around: 16 sc.

Rnd 18: Sc in next 15 sc, slip st in next sc, remove marker.

Note: Begin working in rows for knee.

Row 1: Turn; skip first slip st, sc in next 8 sc, slip st in next sc, leave remaining 6 sc unworked.

Rows 2 and 3: Turn; skip first slip st, sc in next 8 sc, slip st in same sc as previous slip st.

Note: Begin working in rounds.

Rnd 1: Turn; skip first slip st, sc in next 8 sc, sc in same sc as previous slip st, sc in next 6 sc on Rnd 18, sc in same sc as slip st on Row 1; do **not** join, place marker: 16 sc.

Rnd 2: (Sc in next 3 sc, 2 sc in next sc) around: 20 sc.

Rnd 3: (Sc in next 4 sc, 2 sc in next sc) around: 24 sc.

Rnds 4-10: Sc in each sc around.

Rnd 11: Sc in next 14 sc, slip st in next sc, leave remaining 9 sts unworked; finish off.

RIGHT LEG

Work same as Left Leg through Rnd 3: 28 sts.

Rnd 4: Sc in next 11 sts, 5 dc in next sc, drop loop from hook, insert hook in first dc of 5-dc group, hook dropped loop and draw through, sc in next sc, 3 dc in next sc, drop loop from hook, insert hook in first dc of 3-dc group, hook dropped loop and draw through, (sc in next st, work Cluster in next st) twice, (sc, tr, sc) in next dc, sc in next 8 sts, 2 sc in next st: 31 sts.

Rnd 5: Sc in next 8 sc, sc decrease twice, dc decrease twice, YO, insert hook in next sc, YO and pull up a loop, YO and draw through 2 loops on hook, skip next st, YO, insert hook in next sc, YO and pull up a loop, YO and draw through 2 loops on hook, YO and draw through all 3 loops on hook, skip next tr, sc decrease, sc in next 9 sc: 23 sts.

Rnd 6: Sc in next 6 sc, sc decrease, (sc in next st, sc decrease) twice, sc in next 7 sc, sc decrease: 19 sts.
Complete same as Left Leg; do **not** finish off.
Stuff Legs.

BODY

Joining Row: Ch 1, fold Rnd 11 of Leg in half with ch 1 at fold; matching sts and working through **both** thicknesses, sc in each sc across Right Leg; fold Rnd 11 of Left Leg in half with toes pointing away from you; matching sts and working through **both** thicknesses, sc in each sc across Left Leg: 24 sc.

Rnd 1 (Right side): Ch 1, turn; sc in Front Loop Only of each sc across *(Fig. 22, page 138)*, turn; working in free loops *(Fig. 23a, page 138)*, 2 sc in each sc across; do **not** join, place marker: 72 sc.

Rnds 2-12: Sc in each sc around.

Rnd 13: Sc in next 14 sc, work Cluster in next sc, push Cluster to **wrong** side (belly button), sc in each sc around.

Rnds 14-16: Sc in each st around.

Rnd 17: (Sc in next 10 sc, sc decrease) around: 66 sc.

Rnd 18: Sc in each sc around.

Rnd 19: (Sc in next 9 sc, sc decrease) around: 60 sc.

Rnd 20: Sc in each st around.

Rnd 21: (Sc in next 8 sc, sc decrease) around: 54 sc.

Rnd 22: Sc in each sc around.

Rnd 23: (Sc in next 7 sc, sc decrease) around: 48 sc.

Rnd 24: Sc in each sc around.

Rnd 25: (Sc in next 6 sc, sc decrease) around: 42 sc.

Rnd 26: Sc in each sc around.

Rnd 27: (Sc in next 5 sc, sc decrease) around: 36 sc.

Rnd 28: Sc in each sc around.

Rnd 29: (Sc in next 4 sc, sc decrease) around: 30 sc.

Rnds 30-32: Sc in each sc around; do **not** finish off.
Stuff Body.

HEAD

Rnd 1: 2 Sc in each sc around: 60 sc.

Rnds 2-7: Sc in each sc around.

Rnd 8: Sc in first 23 sc, work Cluster in next sc (nose), sc in each sc around.

Rnds 9-19: Repeat Rnds 20-30 of Body: 30 sc.

Rnd 20: (Sc in next sc, sc decrease) around: 20 sc.
Stuff Head.

Rnd 21: Sc decrease around; slip st in next sc, finish off leaving a long end for sewing: 10 sc.

Thread yarn needle with end and weave through remaining sts; gather tightly and secure.

RIGHT ARM

With MC, ch 18 **loosely**; being careful not to twist ch, join with slip st to form a ring.

Rnd 1 (Right side): Sc in each ch around; do **not** join, place marker: 18 sc.

Rnds 2-7: Sc in each sc around.

Rnd 8: (Sc in next 7 sc, sc decrease) twice: 16 sc.

Rnd 9: Sc in each sc around.

Note: Begin working in rows for elbow.

Row 1: Sc in next 12 sc, slip st in next sc, leave remaining 3 sc unworked, remove marker.

Row 2: Turn; skip first slip st, sc in next 8 sc, slip st in next sc, leave remaining sc unworked.

Rows 3 and 4: Turn; skip first slip st, sc in next 8 sc, slip st in same sc as previous slip st.

Note: Begin working in rounds.

Rnd 1: Turn; skip first slip st, sc in next 8 sc, sc in same sc as previous slip st, sc in next 6 sc on Rnd 9, sc in same sc as slip st on Row 2; do **not** join, place marker.

Rnds 2-8: Sc in each sc around: 16 sc.

Rnds 9 and 10: (Sc in next 2 sc, sc decrease) around: 9 sc.

Rnd 11: (Sc in next 2 sc, 2 sc in next sc) around: 12 sc.

Rnds 12 and 13: Sc in each sc around.

Rnd 14: Ch 2, skip next 2 sc (for Thumb), sc in each sc around: 12 sts.
Stuff Arm.

Rnd 15: Sc in next 2 chs, (sc in next 3 sc, sc decrease) twice; do **not** finish off: 10 sts.

FINGERS

Sc in next sc, slip st in next sc, ch 5 **loosely**, sc in second ch from hook and in each ch across (finger), fold Rnd 15 in half with ch-5 at fold; ★ matching sts and working through **both** thicknesses, slip st in next sc, ch 6 **loosely**, sc in second ch from hook and in each ch across (finger); repeat from ★ once **more**, slip st in next sc, ch 4 **loosely**, sc in second ch from hook and in each ch across (finger), slip st in last sc; finish off.

Continued on page 58.

ELEGANT HANDKERCHIEF

Our elegant handkerchief is fashioned by adding a dainty edging to a square of linen.
Triple picot stitches, worked in fine cotton thread, create the feminine trim.

Finished Size: Approximately 5/8" wide

MATERIALS

Cotton Crochet Thread (size 30), approximately 55 yards
Steel crochet hook, size 13 (0.85 mm)
Handkerchief linen - 11" square

Note: Gauge is not important. Edging can be smaller or larger without changing the overall effect.

PREPARING HANDKERCHIEF

Press edges of linen 1/8" to wrong side; press 1/8" to wrong side again.

Note: When working sc on first round of Edging, insert hook through linen, 1/8" from pressed edge.

PATTERN STITCHES
BEGINNING TRIPLE PICOT

Ch 15, slip st in tenth ch from hook, (ch 10, slip st in same ch) twice.

TRIPLE PICOT

Ch 10, slip st in adjacent loop of **previous** Triple Picot, ch 5, slip st in tenth ch from hook, (ch 10, slip st in same ch) twice.

EDGING

Rnd 1 (Right side): With **right** side of linen facing, join thread with slip st in any corner; ch 1, 2 sc in same corner, work 114 sc evenly spaced across to next corner, ★ 3 sc in next corner, work 114 sc evenly spaced across to next corner; repeat from ★ 2 times **more**, sc in same corner as first sc; join with slip st to first sc: 468 sc.

Rnd 2: Ch 1, sc in same st, (ch 5, skip next 2 sc, sc in next sc) around to last 2 sc, ch 2, skip last 2 sc, dc in first sc to form last loop: 156 loops.

Rnd 3: Ch 1, sc in same loop, work beginning Triple Picot, ch 5, sc in next loop, ★ (work Triple Picot, ch 5, skip next loop, sc in next loop) across to next corner sc, work Triple Picot, ch 5, sc in next loop; repeat from ★ 2 times **more**, (work Triple Picot, ch 5, skip next loop, sc in next loop) across to last loop, ch 10, slip st in adjacent loop of **previous** Triple Picot, ch 5, slip st in tenth ch from hook, ch 10, slip st in same ch, ch 5, slip st in adjacent loop of **beginning** Triple Picot, ch 5, slip st in same ch, ch 5; join with slip st to first sc, finish off.

See Washing and Blocking, page 140.

BABY BROTHER

Continued from page 56.

THUMB

Rnd 1: Join MC with sc in first skipped sc on Rnd 13 of Arm *(see Joining With Sc, page 137)*, sc in next sc, sc in free loop of next 2 chs; do **not** join: 4 sc.

Rnd 2: Sc in next 2 sc, sc decrease; slip st in next sc, finish off.

LEFT ARM

Work same as Right Arm.

FINGERS

Sc in next 7 sc, slip st in next sc, ch 4 **loosely**, sc in second ch from hook and in each ch across (finger), fold Rnd 15 in half with ch-4 at fold; ★ matching sts and working through **both** thicknesses, slip st in next sc, ch 6 **loosely**, sc in second ch from hook and in each ch across (finger); repeat from ★ once **more**, slip st in next sc, ch 5 **loosely**, sc in second ch from hook and in each ch across (finger), slip st in last sc; finish off.

THUMB

Work same as Right Hand.

Cheek

EAR (Make 2)

Rnd 1 (Right side)**:** With MC, ch 2, 6 sc in second ch from hook; do **not** join, place marker.

Rnd 2: 2 Sc in each sc around: 12 sc.

Joining Rnd: Ch 1, fold Ear in half with ch-1 at fold; matching sts and working through **both** thicknesses, sc in each sc across; finish off leaving a long end for sewing: 6 sc.

FINISHING

Using photo as a guide for placement, sew Ears to Head. Fold beginning ch of Arm in half; sew each Arm to Body. Cut cheeks from pink felt using pattern. Sew to face using pink embroidery floss and Blanket St *(Figs. 35a & b, page 141)*. Add facial features using blue embroidery floss and Satin St for eyes *(Fig. 34, page 141)* and pink embroidery floss and Outline St for mouth *(Figs. 32a & b, page 141)*.

HAIR

Wind CC **loosely** and **evenly** around the cardboard until the card is filled, then cut across one end; repeat as needed. Thread tapestry needle with sewing thread. Holding several 3¹/₂" strands of CC at a time, stitch across center of strands working from side to side on top of Head.

Quick MALLARD JAR TOPPER

*R*emind Dad that he's special by giving him a jar of his favorite goodies topped with this handsome mallard. The miniature duck is lightly stuffed for extra appeal.

MATERIALS

Bedspread Weight Cotton Thread (size 10), approximately:
    MC (Ecru) - 15 yards
    Color A (Green) - 5 yards
    Color B (Brown) - 9 yards
    Color C (Gold) - 1 yard
Crochet hook, size 6 (1.80 mm) **or** size needed for gauge
Glue
2⁵/₈" Circle self-sticking mounting board
Ribbons - 14" each color
Polyester fiberfill
Sewing needle and thread
Black embroidery floss

GAUGE: Rnds 1 and 2 of Cover = 1"

PATTERN STITCH

DECREASE

Pull up a loop in next 2 sts, YO and draw through all 3 loops on hook **(counts as one sc)**.

COVER

Rnd 1 (Right side)**:** With MC, ch 4, 17 dc in fourth ch from hook; join with slip st to top of beginning ch: 18 sts.

Note: Loop a short piece of thread around any stitch to mark last round as **right** side.

Rnd 2: Ch 3 **(counts as first dc, now and throughout)**, dc in same st, 2 dc in next dc and in each dc around; join with slip st to first dc: 36 dc.

Rnd 3: Ch 3, dc in next 2 dc, 2 dc in next dc, (dc in next 3 dc, 2 dc in next dc) around; join with slip st to first dc: 45 dc.

Rnd 4: Ch 3, dc in next 3 dc, 2 dc in next dc, (dc in next 4 dc, 2 dc in next dc) around; join with slip st to first dc: 54 dc.

Rnd 5: Ch 3, dc in next 4 dc, 2 dc in next dc, (dc in next 5 dc, 2 dc in next dc) around; join with slip st to first dc: 63 dc.

Rnd 6: Ch 3, dc in next 5 dc, 2 dc in next dc, (dc in next 6 dc, 2 dc in next dc) around; join with slip st to first dc, finish off: 72 dc.

MALLARD

HEAD

Rnd 1 (Right side): With Color A, ch 2, 6 sc in second ch from hook; do **not** join, place marker *(see Markers, page 138)*.

Rnd 2: 2 Sc in each sc around: 12 sc.

Rnd 3: (Sc in next sc, 2 sc in next sc) around: 18 sc.

Rnds 4-7: Sc in each sc around.

Rnd 8: (Decrease, sc in next sc) around: 12 sc.

Rnd 9: Sc in each sc around; drop Color A, slip st in next sc changing to MC *(Fig. 24b, page 138)*.

Rnd 10: Ch 1, sc in each sc around; cut MC, join with slip st to first sc changing to Color A.

Rnd 11: Ch 1, sc in each sc around; join with slip st to first sc, finish off.

BODY

Row 1: With **right** side facing, join Color B with slip st in same st as joining, ch 17 **loosely**; sc in second ch from hook and in each ch across; sc in next 12 sc of Head; working in free loops of beginning ch *(Fig. 23b, page 138)*, sc in next 16 chs; do **not** join: 44 sc.

Row 2: Turn; slip st in first 3 sc, ch 1, working in Front Loops Only *(Fig. 22, page 138)*, sc in same st and in next 18 sc, 2 sc in each of next 2 sc, sc in next 19 sc, leave last 2 sc unworked: 42 sc.

Row 3: Ch 1, turn; sc in Back Loop Only of each sc across.

Row 4: Turn; slip st in first 3 sc, ch 1, sc in Front Loop Only of same st and in each sc across to last 2 sc, leave last 2 sc unworked: 38 sc.

Row 5: Ch 1, turn; sc in Back Loop Only of each sc across.

Rows 6 and 7: Repeat Rows 4 and 5: 34 sc.

Finish off.

BEAK

With Color C, ch 4, slip st in second ch from hook, sc in last 2 chs; finish off.

FINISHING

Sew Beak to Head.

With embroidery floss, add French Knot eyes *(Fig. 37, page 142)*.

Stuff Mallard lightly and sew to right side of Cover.

Attach Cover to mounting board.

Tie ribbons around jar lid.

TULIP DOILY

Featuring a charming tulip design, this hexagon-shaped doily brings Victorian elegance to any room. The old-fashioned piece is worked using bedspread weight cotton thread and finished with an edging of dainty picots.

Finished Size: Approximately 13" in diameter

MATERIALS
Bedspread Weight Cotton Thread (size 10),
   approximately 135 yards
Steel crochet hook, size 3 (2.10 mm) **or** size needed
   for gauge

GAUGE: Rnds 1-3 = 1½"

PATTERN STITCHES

DECREASE (uses next 2 dc)
★ YO, insert hook in **next** dc, YO and pull up a loop, YO and draw through 2 loops on hook; repeat from ★ once **more**, YO and draw through all 3 loops on hook **(counts as one dc)**.

DOUBLE DECREASE (uses next 3 dc)
★ YO, insert hook in **next** dc, YO and pull up a loop, YO and draw through 2 loops on hook; repeat from ★ 2 times **more**, YO and draw through all 4 loops on hook **(counts as one dc)**.

CLUSTER (uses next 6 dc)
★ YO, insert hook in **next** dc, YO and pull up a loop, YO and draw through 2 loops on hook; repeat from ★ 5 times **more**; YO and draw through all 7 loops on hook **(Figs. 11a & b, page 134)**.

Ch 6; join with slip st to form a ring.
Rnd 1 (Right side)**:** Ch 1, (sc in ring, ch 3) 6 times; join with slip st to first sc.
Rnd 2: Slip st in first ch-3 sp, ch 1, (sc, ch 3) twice in same sp and in each ch-3 sp around; join with slip st to first sc: 12 ch-3 sps.
Rnds 3 and 4: Slip st in first ch-3 sp, ch 1, sc in same sp, ch 3, (sc in next ch-3 sp, ch 3) around; join with slip st to first sc.
Rnd 5: Slip st in first ch-3 sp, ch 1, sc in same sp, (ch 6, sc in next ch-3 sp) around, ch 3, dc in first sc to form last loop.
Rnd 6: Ch 1, sc in same loop, (ch 6, sc in next loop) around, ch 3, dc in first sc to form last loop.
Rnd 7: Ch 1, sc in same loop, (ch 7, sc in next loop) around, ch 3, tr in first sc to form last loop.
Rnd 8: Ch 3 **(counts as first dc, now and throughout)**, (2 dc, ch 3, 3 dc) in same sp, ch 6, sc in next loop, ch 6,

★ (3 dc, ch 3, 3 dc) in next loop, ch 6, sc in next loop, ch 6; repeat from ★ around; join with slip st to first dc: 6 sc.
Rnd 9: Ch 3, dc in same st, 2 dc in each of next 2 dc, ch 3, sc in next ch-3 sp, ch 3, 2 dc in each of next 3 dc, ch 3, (sc in next loop, ch 3) twice, ★ 2 dc in each of next 3 dc, ch 3, sc in next ch-3 sp, ch 3, 2 dc in each of next 3 dc, ch 3, (sc in next loop, ch 3) twice; repeat from ★ around; join with slip st to first dc.
Rnd 10: Ch 3, dc in next 5 dc, ch 3, (sc in next ch-3 sp, ch 3) twice, dc in next 6 dc, ch 3, skip next ch-3 sp, sc in next ch-3 sp, ch 3, ★ dc in next 6 dc, ch 3, (sc in next ch-3 sp, ch 3) twice, dc in next 6 dc, ch 3, skip next ch-3 sp, sc in next ch-3 sp, ch 3; repeat from ★ around; join with slip st to first dc.
Rnd 11: Ch 3, dc in next 5 dc, ch 3, skip next ch-3 sp, 2 dc in next ch-3 sp, ch 3, dc in next 6 dc, ch 3, (sc in next ch-3 sp, ch 3) twice, ★ dc in next 6 dc, ch 3, skip next ch-3 sp, 2 dc in next ch-3 sp, ch 3, dc in next 6 dc, ch 3, (sc in next ch-3 sp, ch 3) twice; repeat from ★ around; join with slip st to first dc.
Rnd 12: Ch 3, dc in next 5 dc, ch 3, dc in next 2 dc, ch 3, dc in next 6 dc, ch 3, (sc in next ch-3 sp, ch 3) 3 times, ★ dc in next 6 dc, ch 3, dc in next 2 dc, ch 3, dc in next 6 dc, ch 3, (sc in next ch-3 sp, ch 3) 3 times; repeat from ★ around; join with slip st to first dc.
Rnd 13: Ch 2, dc in next dc, decrease twice, ch 4, 3 dc in next dc, ch 3, 3 dc in next dc, ch 4, decrease 3 times, ch 3, (sc in next ch-3 sp, ch 3) 4 times, ★ decrease 3 times, ch 4, 3 dc in next dc, ch 3, 3 dc in next dc, ch 4, decrease 3 times, ch 3, (sc in next ch-3 sp, ch 3) 4 times; repeat from ★ around; skip beginning ch-2 and join with slip st to first dc.
Rnd 14: Ch 2, decrease, ch 3, 2 dc in each of next 3 dc, ch 1, 3 dc in next ch-3 sp, ch 1, 2 dc in each of next 3 dc, ch 3, work double decrease, ch 3, (sc in next ch-3 sp, ch 3) 5 times, ★ work double decrease, ch 3, 2 dc in each of next 3 dc, ch 1, 3 dc in next ch-3 sp, ch 1, 2 dc in each of next 3 dc, ch 3, work double decrease, ch 3, (sc in next ch-3 sp, ch 3) 5 times; repeat from ★ around; skip beginning ch-2 and join with slip st to top of first decrease.
Rnd 15: Slip st in first ch-3 sp, ch 1, sc in same sp, ch 3, decrease 3 times, ch 3, 2 dc in each of next 3 dc, ch 3, decrease 3 times, ch 3, ★ (sc in next ch-3 sp, ch 3) 8 times, decrease 3 times, ch 3, 2 dc in each of next 3 dc, ch 3, decrease 3 times, ch 3; repeat from ★ around to last 7 ch-3 sps, (sc in next ch-3 sp, ch 3) 7 times; join with slip st to first sc.

Rnd 16: Slip st in first ch-3 sp, ch 1, sc in same sp, ch 3, work double decrease, ch 3, sc in next ch-3 sp, ch 4, work Cluster, ch 4, sc in next ch-3 sp, ch 3, work double decrease, ch 3, ★ (sc in next ch-3 sp, ch 3) 9 times, work double decrease, ch 3, sc in next ch-3 sp, ch 4, work Cluster, ch 4, sc in next ch-3 sp, ch 3, work double decrease, ch 3; repeat from ★ around to last 8 ch-3 sps, (sc in next ch-3 sp, ch 3) 8 times; join with slip st to first sc.

Rnd 17: Slip st in first ch-3 sp, ch 1, sc in same sp, ch 3, sc in next ch-3 sp, (ch 5, slip st in third ch from hook, ch 2, sc in next ch-3 sp) 3 times, ★ (ch 3, sc in next ch-3 sp) 11 times, (ch 5, slip st in third ch from hook, ch 2, sc in next ch-3 sp) 3 times; repeat from ★ around to last 9 ch-3 sps, ch 3, (sc in next ch-3 sp, ch 3) 9 times; join with slip st to first sc.

Rnd 18: Ch 9, (tr in next sc, ch 5) around; join with slip st to fourth ch of beginning ch-9: 84 loops.

Rnd 19: Ch 9, (tr in next tr, ch 5) around; join with slip st to fourth ch of beginning ch-9.

Rnd 20: Slip st in first loop, ch 1, (3 sc, ch 3, slip st in third ch from hook, 3 sc) in same loop and in each loop around; join with slip st to first sc, finish off.

See Washing and Blocking, page 140.

COUNTRY BREAD CLOTH

Cheer up a special friend with a batch of homemade muffins delivered in a basket lined with this country bread cloth. The cozy warmer is crafted by adding a colorful edging, crocheted with bedspread weight cotton thread, to a coordinating plaid fabric square.

Finished Size: Approximately 21" square

MATERIALS
Bedspread Weight Cotton Thread (size 10),
    approximately 265 yards
Steel crochet hook, size 6 (1.80 mm) **or** size needed
    for gauge
Fabric - 17" square
Washable fabric marker
Sewing needle and thread

GAUGE: 16 dc and 8 rows = 2"

PREPARING BREAD CLOTH
Press edges of fabric ¼" to wrong side; press ¼" to wrong side again. Hem with matching sewing thread.
Along **each** side of square, make a mark at every inch.
With a single strand of bedspread weight cotton thread, make 4 backstitches between each inch mark on fabric *(Figs. 36a & b, page 141)*: 64 sts **each** side.

PATTERN STITCH
CLUSTER
★ YO twice, insert hook in loop indicated, YO and pull up a loop, (YO and draw through 2 loops on hook) twice; repeat from ★ 2 times **more**, YO and draw through all 4 loops on hook *(Figs. 10a & b, page 134)*.

EDGING

Rnd 1 (Right side): With **right** side of fabric facing, join thread with slip st in first backstitch **before** any corner; ch 8 **(counts as first dc plus ch 5, now and throughout)**, ★ 2 dc in each backstitch across to within one backstitch of next corner, 3 dc in last backstitch, ch 5; repeat from ★ 2 times **more**, 2 dc in each backstitch across, 2 dc in same backstitch as beginning ch-8; join with slip st to first dc: 129 dc **each** side.

Rnd 2: Slip st in first corner ch-5 sp, ch 8, dc in same sp, ch 1, dc in next dc, ch 1, ★ (skip next dc, dc in next dc, ch 1) across to next corner ch-5 sp, (dc, ch 5, dc) in corner ch-5 sp, ch 1, dc in next dc, ch 1; repeat from ★ 2 times **more**, (skip next dc, dc in next dc, ch 1) across; join with slip st to first dc: 66 ch-1 sps **each** side.

Rnd 3: Slip st in first corner ch-5 sp, ch 8, 2 dc in same sp, dc in each dc and in each ch-1 sp across to next corner ch-5 sp, ★ (2 dc, ch 5, 2 dc) in corner ch-5 sp, dc in each dc and in each ch-1 sp across to next corner ch-5 sp; repeat from ★ around, dc in same corner as beginning ch-8; join with slip st to first dc: 137 dc **each** side.

Rnd 4: Repeat Rnd 2: 70 ch-1 sps **each** side.

Rnd 5: Ch 3 **(counts as first dc, now and throughout)**, (2 dc, ch 5, 2 dc) in first corner ch-5 sp, ★ † dc in next dc, dc in next ch-1 sp, dc in next dc, ch 5, skip next 2 ch-1 sps, sc in next ch-1 sp, (sc in next dc, sc in next ch-1 sp) 3 times, ch 5, skip next 2 dc, dc in next dc, dc in next ch-1 sp †, repeat from † to † across to within one dc of next corner ch-5 sp, dc in next dc, (2 dc, ch 5, 2 dc) in next corner ch-5 sp; repeat from ★ 2 times **more**, then repeat from † to † across; join with slip st to first dc.

Rnd 6: Slip st in next 2 dc, ch 3, (2 dc, ch 5, 2 dc) in first corner ch-5 sp, dc in next dc, ch 3, ★ † skip next 3 dc, dc in next dc, 2 dc in next ch-5 sp, ch 5, skip next sc, sc in next 5 sc, ch 5, 2 dc in next ch-5 sp, dc in next dc, ch 3 †, repeat from † to † across to within 4 dc of next corner ch-5 sp, skip next 3 dc, dc in next dc, (2 dc, ch 5, 2 dc) in next corner ch-5 sp, dc in next dc, ch 3; repeat from ★ 2 times **more**, then repeat from † to † across to last 3 dc, skip last 3 dc; join with slip st to first dc.

Rnd 7: Slip st in next 2 dc, ch 3, (2 dc, ch 5, 2 dc) in first corner ch-5 sp, dc in next dc, ch 5, sc in next ch-3 sp, ch 5, ★ † skip next 2 dc, dc in next dc, 2 dc in next ch-5 sp, ch 5, skip next sc, sc in next 3 sc, ch 5, 2 dc in next ch-5 sp, dc in next dc, ch 5, sc in next ch-3 sp, ch 5 †, repeat from † to † across to within 3 dc of next corner ch-5 sp, skip next 2 dc, dc in next dc, (2 dc, ch 5, 2 dc) in next corner ch-5 sp, dc in next dc, ch 5, sc in next ch-3 sp, ch 5; repeat from ★ 2 times **more**, then repeat from † to † across to last 2 dc, skip last 2 dc; join with slip st to first dc.

Rnd 8: Slip st in next 2 dc, ch 3, (2 dc, ch 5, 2 dc) in first corner ch-5 sp, dc in next dc, ch 5, sc in next ch-5 sp, ch 7, sc in next ch-5 sp, ch 5, ★ † skip next 2 dc, dc in next dc, 2 dc in next ch-5 sp, ch 5, skip next sc, sc in next sc, ch 5, 2 dc in next ch-5 sp, dc in next dc, ch 5, sc in next ch-5 sp, ch 7, sc in next ch-5 sp, ch 5 †, repeat from † to † across to within 3 dc of

next corner ch-5 sp, skip next 2 dc, dc in next dc, (2 dc, ch 5, 2 dc) in next corner ch-5 sp, dc in next dc, ch 5, sc in next ch-5 sp, ch 7, sc in next ch-5 sp, ch 5; repeat from ★ 2 times **more**, then repeat from † to † across to last 2 dc, skip last 2 dc; join with slip st to first dc.

Rnd 9: Slip st in next 2 dc, ch 3, (2 dc, ch 5, 2 dc) in first corner ch-5 sp, dc in next dc, ch 3, skip next ch-5 sp, (work Cluster, ch 3) 5 times in next loop, ★ † skip next 2 dc, dc in next dc, 2 dc in each of next 2 ch-5 sps, dc in next dc, ch 3,

skip next ch-5 sp, (work Cluster, ch 3) 5 times in next loop †, repeat from † to † across to within 3 dc of next corner ch-5 sp, skip next 2 dc, dc in next dc, (2 dc, ch 5, 2 dc) in next corner ch-5 sp, dc in next dc, ch 3, skip next ch-5 sp, (work Cluster, ch 3) 5 times in next loop; repeat from ★ 2 times **more**, then repeat from † to † across to last 2 dc, skip last 2 dc; join with slip st to first dc, finish off.

See Washing and Blocking, page 140.

just for fun

These innovative designs give you lots of fun ideas for accenting your life with crochet. You'll find several projects, like our seasonal magnets, that are not only quick to stitch, but they also help you use up scrap yarn. There's even a clever rug that you can craft from recycled plastic bags! This whimsical collection provides a variety of ways to enjoy your stitching time.

KID-PLEASING PLAID AFGHAN

Fashioned with fun in mind, this reversible plaid afghan is worked in kid-pleasing colors. Stripes of yellow, green, white, and blue crisscross the bright red throw, creating the look of tartan plaid. A playful accent for a child's room, the heavy, durable cover-up will be enjoyed for years.

Finished Size: Approximately 48" x 67"

MATERIALS

Worsted Weight Yarn, approximately:

MC (Red) - 29 ounces, (820 grams, 1,905 yards)

Color A (White) - 4½ ounces, (130 grams, 295 yards)

Color B (Blue) - 6 ounces, (170 grams, 395 yards)

Color C (Yellow) - 3 ounces, (90 grams, 200 yards)

Color D (Green) - 2½ ounces, (70 grams, 165 yards)

Crochet hook, size H (5.00 mm) **or** size needed for gauge

GAUGE: 15 tr and 5 rows = 4"

BODY

With MC, ch 184 **loosely**.

Row 1 (Right side)**:** Tr in fifth ch from hook (**4 skipped chs count as first tr**), tr in next 8 chs, ★ † ch 2, skip next 2 chs, tr in next 7 chs, ch 2, (skip next 2 chs, tr in next ch, ch 2) twice, skip next 2 chs †, tr in next 31 chs, ch 2, skip next 2 chs, tr in next ch, ch 2, skip next 2 chs, tr in next 19 chs; repeat from ★ once **more**, then repeat from † to † once, tr in each ch across: 149 tr.

Note: Loop a short piece of yarn around any stitch to mark last row as **right** side and bottom edge.

Row 2: Ch 4 **(counts as first tr, now and throughout)**, turn; tr in next 9 tr, ★ † ch 2, (skip next ch-2 sp, tr in next tr, ch 2) twice, skip next ch-2 sp, tr in next 7 tr, ch 2, skip next ch-2 sp †, tr in next 19 tr, ch 2, skip next ch-2 sp, tr in next tr, ch 2, skip next ch-2 sp, tr in next 31 tr; repeat from ★ once **more**, then repeat from † to † once, tr in each st across.

Row 3: Ch 4, turn; tr in next 9 tr, ★ † ch 2, skip next ch-2 sp, tr in next 7 tr, ch 2, (skip next ch-2 sp, tr in next tr, ch 2) twice, skip next ch-2 sp †, tr in next 31 tr, ch 2, skip next ch-2 sp, tr in next tr, ch 2, skip next ch-2 sp, tr in next 19 tr; repeat from ★ once **more**, then repeat from † to † once, tr in each tr across.

Row 4: Repeat Row 2.

Row 5 (Eyelet row)**:** Ch 6 **(counts as first tr plus ch 2, now and throughout)**, turn; skip next 2 tr, tr in next tr, (ch 2, skip next 2 tr, tr in next tr) twice, ★ † ch 2, skip next ch-2 sp, tr in next tr, (ch 2, skip next 2 tr, tr in next tr) twice, (ch 2, skip next ch-2 sp, tr in next tr) 3 times †, (ch 2, skip next 2 tr, tr in next tr) 10 times, (ch 2, skip next ch-2 sp, tr in next tr) twice, (ch 2, skip next 2 tr, tr in next tr) 6 times; repeat from ★ once **more**, then repeat from † to † once, (ch 2, skip next 2 tr, tr in next tr) across: 60 ch-2 sps.

Rows 6 and 7 (Eyelet rows)**:** Ch 6, turn; skip next ch-2 sp, tr in next tr, (ch 2, skip next ch-2 sp, tr in next tr) across.

Row 8: Ch 4, turn; (tr in next 2 chs, tr in next tr) 3 times, ★ † (ch 2, skip next ch-2 sp, tr in next tr) 3 times, (tr in next 2 chs, tr in next tr) twice, ch 2, skip next ch-2 sp, tr in next tr †, (tr in next 2 chs, tr in next tr) 6 times, (ch 2, skip next ch-2 sp, tr in next tr) twice, (tr in next 2 chs, tr in next tr) 10 times; repeat from ★ once **more**, then repeat from † to † once, (tr in next 2 chs, tr in next tr) across: 149 tr.

Rows 9-17: Repeat Row 3 once, then repeat Rows 2 and 3, 4 times **more**.

Row 18 (Eyelet row)**:** Ch 6, turn; skip next 2 tr, tr in next tr, (ch 2, skip next 2 tr, tr in next tr) twice, ★ † (ch 2, skip next ch-2 sp, tr in next tr) 3 times, (ch 2, skip next 2 tr, tr in next tr) twice, ch 2, skip next ch-2 sp, tr in next tr †, (ch 2, skip next 2 tr, tr in next tr) 6 times, (ch 2, skip next ch-2 sp, tr in next tr) twice, (ch 2, skip next 2 tr, tr in next tr) 10 times; repeat from ★ once **more**, then repeat from † to † once, (ch 2, skip next 2 tr, tr in next tr) across: 60 ch-2 sps.

Rows 19 and 20: Repeat Rows 7 and 8.

Rows 21-25: Repeat Row 3 once, then repeat Rows 2 and 3 twice.

Row 26: Repeat Row 18.

Row 27: Ch 4, turn; (tr in next 2 chs, tr in next tr) 3 times, ★ † ch 2, skip next ch-2 sp, tr in next tr, (tr in next 2 chs, tr in next tr) twice, (ch 2, skip next ch-2 sp, tr in next tr) 3 times †, (tr in next 2 chs, tr in next tr) 10 times, (ch 2, skip next ch-2 sp, tr in next tr) twice, (tr in next 2 chs, tr in next tr) 6 times; repeat from ★ once **more**, then repeat from † to † once, (tr in next 2 chs, tr in next tr) across.

Row 28: Repeat Row 2.

Rows 29-83: Repeat Rows 5-28 twice, then repeat Rows 5-11 once **more**.
Finish off.

STRIPES

Note: Always join yarn and finish off leaving a 4" end for fringe.

Referring to Placement Diagram for color placement, work all Vertical Lines of one color and then all Horizontal Lines of the same color. Work colors in the following sequence: White, Blue, Yellow, Green.

PLACEMENT DIAGRAM

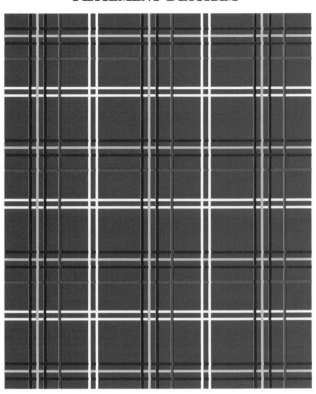

VERTICAL LINE

Front Stripe: Hold afghan with **right** side facing and top edge toward you; working upward, join yarn with slip st around first ch-2; (ch 3 **loosely**, sc around next skipped ch-2) across; finish off.

Back Stripe: Hold afghan with **wrong** side facing and bottom edge toward you; working to **left** of Front Stripe and around same skipped ch-2, join yarn with slip st around skipped ch-2 of beginning ch; working upward, (ch 3 **loosely**, sc around next skipped ch-2) across; finish off.

HORIZONTAL LINE

Front Stripe: Hold afghan with **right** side facing and bottom edge toward the left; join yarn with slip st around post of first tr of Eyelet row; working upward, (ch 3 **loosely**, sc around post of next tr) across; finish off.

Back Stripe: Hold afghan with **wrong** side facing and bottom edge toward the left; working to **right** of Front Stripe and around same tr, join yarn with slip st around post of first tr; working upward, (ch 3 **loosely**, sc around post of next tr) across; finish off.

Add additional fringe to each end of every Stripe Line around afghan using 3 strands of matching color, each 9" long **(Figs. 30a & b, page 140)**, and add fringe to both ends of afghan, evenly spacing fringe between Stripes and using 4 strands of MC, each 9" long.

SUNFLOWER BASKET

*P*ick *our pretty sunflower basket to bring nature's delights indoors! The petals of the cheery carrier are stiffened and slightly curved to form a shallow basket. It's perfect for displaying on your table.*

Finished Size: Approximately 9" in diameter after shaping and 6" tall

MATERIALS
Cotton Crochet Thread (size 3), approximately:
    MC (Gold) - 110 yards
    Color A (Brown) - 10 yards
    Color B (Green) - 22 yards
Steel crochet hook, size 0 (3.25 mm) **or** size needed for gauge
3 - 18" lengths of 22 gauge wire
Tapestry needle
Starching materials: Commercial fabric stiffener, blocking board, plastic wrap, resealable plastic bag, 9" plastic foam ring, terry towel, paper towels, and stainless steel pins

GAUGE: Rnds 1-5 = 3"

PATTERN STITCHES
CROSS ST
Skip next dc, dc in next dc, working **around** last dc, dc in skipped dc *(Fig. 1)*.

Fig. 1

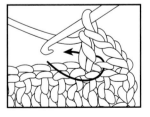

DECREASE (uses next 2 dc)
★ YO, insert hook in **next** st, YO and pull up a loop, YO and draw through 2 loops on hook; repeat from ★ once **more**, YO and draw through all 3 loops on hook.

BOTTOM

With Color A, ch 6; join with slip st to form a ring.

Rnd 1 (Right side)**:** Ch 3, (hdc, ch 1) 7 times in ring; join with slip st to second ch of beginning ch-3: 8 ch-1 sps.

Note: Loop a short piece of thread around any stitch to mark last round as **right** side.

Rnd 2: Slip st in first ch-1 sp, ch 3, hdc in same sp, (hdc, ch 1, hdc) in next ch-1 sp and in each ch-1 sp around; join with slip st to second ch of beginning ch-3: 8 ch-1 sps.

Rnd 3: Slip st in first ch-1 sp, ch 3, hdc in same sp, ch 2, ★ (hdc, ch 1, hdc) in next ch-1 sp, ch 2; repeat from ★ around; join with slip st to second ch of beginning ch-3: 16 sps.

Rnd 4: Slip st in first ch-1 sp, ch 3, hdc in same sp, ch 1, (hdc, ch 1) twice in next sp and in each sp around; join with slip st to second ch of beginning ch-3, finish off: 32 ch-1 sps.

Rnd 5: With **right** side facing and working in Back Loops Only *(Fig. 22, page 138)*, join MC with slip st in same st as joining; ch 1, sc in same st and in each ch and in each hdc around; join with slip st to first sc: 64 sc.

Rnd 6: Ch 3 **(counts as first dc, now and throughout)**, working in both loops, dc in same st and in next 6 sc, ★ 2 dc in each of next 2 sc, dc in next 6 sc; repeat from ★ around to last sc, 2 dc in last sc; join with slip st to first dc: 80 dc.

Rnd 7: Ch 3, dc in next dc, work 3 Cross Sts, dc in next 2 dc, ch 2, ★ dc in next 2 dc, work 3 Cross Sts, dc in next 2 dc, ch 2; repeat from ★ around; join with slip st to first dc: 8 ch-2 sps.

Rnd 8: Ch 5, **turn**; 2 dc in next dc, dc in next dc, work 3 Cross Sts, dc in next dc, ★ 2 dc in next dc, ch 2, 2 dc in next dc, dc in next dc, work 3 Cross Sts, dc in next dc; repeat from ★ around, dc in same st as beginning ch-5; join with slip st to third ch of beginning ch-5.

Rnd 9: Ch 3, turn; dc in same st, work 5 Cross Sts, 2 dc in next dc, ch 3, ★ 2 dc in next dc, work 5 Cross Sts, 2 dc in next dc, ch 3; repeat from ★ around; join with slip st to first dc.

Rnd 10: Ch 3, turn; working around beginning ch-3, dc in st to the **right**, ch 3, (work 7 Cross Sts, ch 3) 7 times, work 6 Cross Sts; join with slip st to first dc.

Rnd 11: Ch 3, turn; working around beginning ch-3, dc in st to the **right**, work 6 Cross Sts, ch 3, (work 7 Cross Sts, ch 3) around; join with slip st to first dc.

Rnd 12: Ch 3, turn; working around beginning ch-3, dc in st to the **right**, ch 4, (work 7 Cross Sts, ch 4) 7 times, work 6 Cross Sts; join with slip st to first dc, do **not** finish off.

FIRST PETAL

Row 1: Slip st in next dc, ch 2, turn; dc in next dc, work 5 Cross Sts, decrease, leave remaining sts unworked.

Row 2: Ch 2, turn; decrease, work 3 Cross Sts, decrease, hdc in next dc, leave turning ch unworked.

Row 3: Ch 2, turn; dc in next st, work 3 Cross Sts, decrease; finish off.

REMAINING 7 PETALS

Row 1: With **right** side facing, join MC with slip st in first unworked dc on Rnd 12; ch 2, dc in next dc, work 5 Cross Sts, decrease, leave remaining sts unworked.

Rows 2 and 3: Work same as First Petal; on last Petal, do **not** finish off.

EDGING

Ch 1, do **not** turn; working in end of rows, ★ 2 sc in each of first 3 rows, 4 sc in next ch-4 sp, 2 sc in each of next 3 rows, sc in next 8 sts; repeat from ★ around; join with slip st to first sc, finish off.

HANDLE

CENTER SECTION

Fold up 1" on each end of wire and twist to secure.
With Color B, ch 91 **loosely**.

Row 1 (Right side)**:** Working over first wire *(Fig. 25, page 138)*, sc in back ridge of second ch from hook and in each ch across *(Fig. 2a, page 133)*; finish off leaving a long end for sewing: 90 sc.

Note: Mark last row as **right** side.

FIRST SIDE

Foundation Chain: With **right** side facing, join Color B with slip st in tenth sc from **left** edge, ch 9 **loosely**; finish off.
With **right** side facing, join Color B with slip st in tenth sc from **right** edge, ch 10 **loosely**.

Row 1: Working over second wire, sc in back ridge of second ch from hook and in next 8 chs, sc in same sc as joining and in each sc across to Foundation Chain, sc in same sc as joining, sc in back ridge of last 9 chs; finish off leaving a long end for sewing: 90 sc.

SECOND SIDE

Working in both loops of beginning ch *(Fig. 23b, page 138)*, work same as First Side.

FINISHING

Using photo as a guide for placement, sew Handle to Bottom, joining Center Section to center 2 sc between Petals and joining First and Second Sides to side of Petals leaving 5 sc from Center Section free.

See Starching and Blocking, page 143.

PINCUSHION BONNET

Pretty as a spring bonnet, this dainty pincushion keeps pins and needles safely in one spot. Sewing enthusiasts will love the notion, which is worked in bedspread weight cotton thread and lightly stuffed before finishing. A delicate floral spray lends a charming touch.

Finished Size: Approximately 6" in diameter

MATERIALS
Bedspread Weight Cotton Thread (size 10),
    approximately 120 yards
Steel crochet hook, size 6 (1.80 mm) **or** size needed
    for gauge
Polyester fiberfill
Tapestry needle
Finishing materials: Ribbon, flowers

GAUGE: Rnds 1 and 2 of Cushion = 1"

PATTERN STITCH
DECREASE (uses next 2 sts)
★ YO, insert hook in **next** st, YO and pull up a loop, YO and draw through 2 loops on hook; repeat from ★ once **more**, YO and draw through all 3 loops on hook **(counts as one dc)**.

CUSHION
Rnd 1 (Right side): Ch 4, 15 dc in fourth ch from hook; join with slip st to top of beginning ch: 16 sts.

Rnd 2: Ch 3 **(counts as first dc, now and throughout)**, dc in same st, 2 dc in each dc around; join with slip st to first dc: 32 dc.

Rnd 3: Ch 3, dc in same st and in next dc, (2 dc in next dc, dc in next dc) around; join with slip st to first dc: 48 dc.

Rnd 4: Ch 3, dc in same st and in next 2 dc, (2 dc in next dc, dc in next 2 dc) around; join with slip st to first dc: 64 dc.

Rnd 5: Ch 3, dc in same st and in next 3 dc, (2 dc in next dc, dc in next 3 dc) around; join with slip st to Back Loop Only of first dc *(Fig. 22, page 138)*: 80 dc.

Rnd 6: Ch 3, dc in Back Loop Only of next dc and in each dc around; join with slip st to both loops of first dc.

Rnds 7-9: Ch 3, dc in both loops of next dc and in each dc around; join with slip st to first dc.

Rnd 10: Ch 3, dc in next dc and in each dc around; join with slip st to Back Loop Only of first dc.

Rnd 11: Ch 2, working in Back Loops Only, dc in next 4 dc, (decrease, dc in next 3 dc) around; skip beginning ch-2 and join with slip st to both loops of first dc: 64 dc.

Rnd 12: Ch 2, working in both loops, dc in next 3 dc, (decrease, dc in next 2 dc) around; skip beginning ch-2 and join with slip st to first dc: 48 dc.

Stuff Cushion **lightly** and shape.

Rnd 13: Ch 2, dc in next 2 dc, (decrease, dc in next dc) around; skip beginning ch-2 and join with slip st to first dc: 32 dc.

Rnd 14: Ch 2, dc in next dc, decrease around; skip beginning ch-2 and join with slip st to first dc: 16 dc.

Rnd 15: Ch 2, dc in next st, decrease around; skip beginning ch-2 and join with slip st to first dc, finish off leaving a long end for sewing: 8 dc.

Add additional stuffing, if necessary.

Thread needle with end and weave through remaining sts; gather tightly and secure.

TRIM

With top toward you and working in free loops on Rnd 5 *(Fig. 23a, page 138)*, join thread with slip st in any dc; ch 1, working from **left** to **right**, work reverse sc in each st around *(Figs. 19a-d, page 136)*; join with slip st to first st, finish off.

BRIM

Rnd 1: With top toward you and working in free loops on Rnd 10, join thread with slip st in any dc; ch 3, dc in next dc, ch 3, skip next 2 dc, (dc in next 2 dc, ch 3, skip next 2 dc) around; join with slip st to first dc: 20 ch-3 sps.

Rnd 2: Ch 3, dc in next dc and in next ch, ch 3, skip next ch, dc in next ch, ★ dc in next 2 dc and in next ch, ch 3, skip next ch, dc in next ch; repeat from ★ around; join with slip st to first dc: 80 dc.

Rnd 3: Ch 3, dc in next 2 dc and in next ch, ch 3, skip next ch, dc in next ch, ★ dc in next 4 dc and in next ch, ch 3, skip next ch, dc in next ch; repeat from ★ around to last dc, dc in last dc; join with slip st to first dc: 120 dc.

Rnd 4: Ch 3, dc in next 3 dc and in next ch, ch 3, skip next ch, dc in next ch, ★ dc in next 6 dc and in next ch, ch 3, skip next ch, dc in next ch; repeat from ★ around to last 2 dc, dc in last 2 dc; join with slip st to first dc: 160 dc.

Rnd 5: Ch 3, dc in next 4 dc, ch 3, skip next 2 chs, dc in next ch, ch 3, ★ skip next 2 dc, dc in next 6 dc, ch 3, skip next 2 chs, dc in next ch, ch 3; repeat from ★ around to last 3 dc, skip next 2 dc, dc in last dc; join with slip st to first dc: 140 dc.

Rnd 6: Slip st in next dc, ch 3, dc in next 3 dc, ch 3, (skip next 2 chs, dc in next ch, ch 3) twice, skip next 2 dc, ★ dc in next 4 dc, ch 3, (skip next 2 chs, dc in next ch, ch 3) twice, skip next 2 dc; repeat from ★ around; join with slip st to first dc: 120 dc.

Rnd 7: Slip st in next 2 dc, ch 3, dc in next dc, ch 3, (skip next 2 chs, dc in next ch, ch 3) 3 times, skip next 2 dc, ★ dc in next 2 dc, ch 3, (skip next 2 chs, dc in next ch, ch 3) 3 times, skip next 2 dc; repeat from ★ around; join with slip st to first dc: 80 ch-3 sps.

Rnd 8: Ch 1, sc in same st and in next dc, 3 sc in each of next 4 ch-3 sps, ★ sc in next 2 dc, 3 sc in each of next 4 ch-3 sps; repeat from ★ around; join with slip st to first sc, finish off.

FINISHING

Using photo as a guide for placement, place ribbon around Cushion and glue in place. Add flowers and bows as desired.

Quick COLORFUL BAG RUG

U nique home fashions are in the bag — or rather, made out of them — when you craft this colorful bath mat using plastic bags and a jumbo hook! Worked in rounds of double crochets, the eye-catching rug can be created from new garbage bags or recycled shopping bags.

Finished Size: 24" in diameter

MATERIALS

Plastic Garbage or Shopping Bag Strips, approximately:
  MC (Red) - 100 yards
  CC (White) - 70 yards
Crochet hook, size S
Optional: Rotary cutter and mat

PREPARING PLASTIC STRIPS

Lay each bag flat on a hard surface and cut bottom and handles (if any) off. Do **not** cut sides.

Cut across each bag forming 6" wide strips *(Fig. 1a, page 71)*, ending with a circle of plastic *(Fig. 1b, page 71)*.

Note: A rotary cutter and mat can be used to cut approximately 10 bags at the same time.

Link the strips together by pulling one strip through the loop of another strip and then back through itself *(Fig. 1c)*; pull tightly to form knot.

Fig. 1a

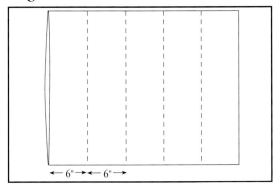

← 6" → ← 6" →

Fig. 1b

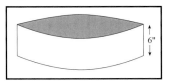

6"

Fig. 1c

GAUGE: Rnds 1 and 2 = 7¹/₂"

Rnd 1 (Right side)**:** With CC, ch 4, 9 dc in fourth ch from hook; join with slip st to top of beginning ch: 10 sts.

Rnd 2: Ch 3 **(counts as first dc, now and throughout)**, dc in same st, 2 dc in next dc and in each dc around; join with slip st to first dc changing to MC *(Fig. 24b, page 138)*: 20 dc.

Rnd 3: Ch 3, dc in same st and in next dc, (2 dc in next dc, dc in next dc) around; join with slip st to first dc: 30 dc.

Rnd 4: Ch 3, dc in same st and in next 2 dc, (2 dc in next dc, dc in next 2 dc) around; join with slip st to first dc changing to CC: 40 dc.

Rnd 5: Ch 3, dc in same st and in next 4 dc, (2 dc in next dc, dc in next 4 dc) around; join with slip st to first dc: 48 dc.

Rnd 6: Ch 3, dc in same st and in next 3 dc, (2 dc in next dc, dc in next 3 dc) around; join with slip st to first dc changing to MC: 60 dc.

Rnd 7: Ch 3, dc in next dc, 2 dc in next dc, (dc in next 2 dc, 2 dc in next dc) around; join with slip st to first dc: 80 dc.

Rnd 8: Ch 1, sc in same st and in next dc, hdc in next dc, dc in next dc, hdc in next dc, ★ sc in next 2 dc, hdc in next dc, dc in next dc, hdc in next dc; repeat from ★ around; join with slip st to first sc, finish off.

71

PLAYTIME DINOSAUR

*A*dd adventure to a child's day with this "dino-riffic" dinosaur! Sure to stimulate young imaginations, the prehistoric playmate is crocheted with fabric strips and stuffed.

Finished Size: Approximately 28" long x 10" high

MATERIALS
100% Cotton Fabric, 44/45" wide, approximately:
MC (Brown) - 7½ yards
Color A (Tan) - 4 yards
Color B (Black) - ¹⁄₁₆ yard
Crochet hook, size K (6.50 mm) **or** size needed for gauge
2 - 18 mm eyes
Polyester fiberfill
Yarn needle
Sewing needle and thread

Prepare fabric and cut into 1" strips *(see Preparing Fabric Strips and Joining Fabric Strips, page 139)*.

GAUGE: 8 sc and 8 rows = 4"

PATTERN STITCH
DECREASE
Pull up a loop in next 2 sts, YO and draw through all 3 loops on hook **(counts as one sc)**.

HEAD AND BODY

Rnd 1 (Right side)**:** With MC, ch 2, 6 sc in second ch from hook; do **not** join, place fabric marker *(see Markers, page 138)*.
Rnd 2: (Sc in next sc, 2 sc in next sc) around: 9 sc.
Rnd 3: Sc in next 2 sc, 2 sc in next sc, ★ sc in next sc changing to Color B *(Fig. 24a, page 138)*, sc in next sc changing to MC, 2 sc in next sc; repeat from ★ once **more**: 12 sc.
Rnd 4: Sc in next 6 sc, 3 sc in next sc, sc in next sc, 3 sc in next sc, sc in next 3 sc: 16 sc.
Rnd 5: (Sc in next 5 sc, decrease) twice, sc in next 2 sc: 14 sc.
Rnd 6: Sc in each sc around.
Rnd 7: (Sc in next sc, 2 sc in next sc) around: 21 sc.
Rnd 8: Sc in each sc around.
Rnd 9: Sc in next 14 sc, 4 sc in next sc, sc in next 6 sc: 24 sc.
Rnds 10-13: Sc in each sc around.
Rnd 14: (Sc in next 4 sc, decrease) around: 20 sc.
Rnd 15: Sc in each sc around.
Rnd 16: (Sc in next 3 sc, decrease) around: 16 sc.

Rnds 17 and 18: Sc in each sc around.
Rnd 19: (Sc in next 3 sc, 2 sc in next sc) around: 20 sc.
Rnd 20: Sc in next sc, 2 sc in next sc, sc in next 11 sc, 2 sc in next sc, (sc in next sc, 2 sc in next sc) 3 times: 25 sc.
Rnd 21: Sc in each sc around.
Rnd 22: 2 Sc in next sc, sc in next 16 sc, (2 sc in next sc, sc in next sc) 4 times: 30 sc.
Rnds 23 and 24: Sc in each sc around.
Rnd 25: (Sc in next sc, 2 sc in next sc) twice, sc in next 13 sc, 2 sc in next sc, (sc in next sc, 2 sc in next sc) 6 times: 39 sc.
Rnds 26-30: Sc in each sc around.
Rnd 31: Sc in next 2 sc, 2 sc in next sc, sc in next 16 sc, (2 sc in next sc, sc in next 3 sc) 5 times: 45 sc.
Rnds 32-35: Sc in each sc around; at end of Rnd 35, slip st in next sc, finish off leaving a long end for sewing.

TAIL

Rnd 1: With MC, ch 2, 6 sc in second ch from hook; do **not** join, place marker.
Rnd 2: (2 Sc in next sc, sc in next sc) around: 9 sc.
Rnds 3 and 4: Sc in each sc around.
Rnd 5: (2 Sc in next sc, sc in next 2 sc) around: 12 sc.
Rnds 6 and 7: Sc in each sc around.
Rnd 8: (2 Sc in next sc, sc in next 3 sc) around: 15 sc.
Rnds 9 and 10: Sc in each sc around.
Rnd 11: (2 Sc in next sc, sc in next 4 sc) around: 18 sc.
Rnds 12-15: Sc in each sc around.
Rnd 16: Sc in next 16 sc, leave remaining 2 sc unworked.
Note: Begin working in rows.
Row 1: Ch 1, turn; decrease, sc in next 12 sc, decrease: 14 sc.
Rows 2-5: Ch 1, turn; decrease, sc in each sc across to last 2 sc, decrease: 6 sc.
Note: Begin working in rounds.
Rnd 1: Ch 1, turn; sc in each sc across; work 6 sc evenly spaced across end of rows; sc in next 2 sc on Rnd 15; work 6 sc evenly spaced across end of rows; do **not** join, place marker: 20 sc.
Rnd 2: (Sc in next 4 sc, 2 sc in next sc) around: 24 sc.
Rnds 3 and 4: Sc in each sc around.
Note: Begin working in rows.
Row 1: Sc in next 2 sc, leave remaining 22 sc unworked.
Row 2: Ch 1, turn; decrease, sc in next 18 sc, decrease, leave remaining 2 sc unworked: 20 sc.

Rows 3-8: Ch 1, turn; decrease, sc in each sc across to last 2 sc, decrease; place marker around last st worked on Row 8: 8 sc.
Note: Begin working in rounds.
Rnd 1: Ch 1, turn; sc in each sc across; work 8 sc evenly spaced across end of rows; sc in next 2 sc on Row 1; work 7 sc evenly spaced across end of rows; do **not** join, place marker: 25 sc.
Rnd 2: (Sc in next 4 sc, 2 sc in next sc) around: 30 sc.
Rnd 3: Sc in next 3 sc, 2 sc in next sc, sc in next 13 sc, 2 sc in next sc, (sc in next 3 sc, 2 sc in next sc) 3 times: 35 sc.
Rnd 4: Sc in next 4 sc, 2 sc in next sc, sc in next 14 sc, 2 sc in next sc, (sc in next 4 sc, 2 sc in next sc) 3 times: 40 sc.
Rnd 5: Sc in next 4 sc, 2 sc in next sc, sc in next 19 sc, 2 sc in next sc, (sc in next 4 sc, 2 sc in next sc) 3 times; slip st in next sc, finish off leaving a long end for sewing: 45 sc.

RIGHT BACK LEG

Rnd 1: With Color A, ch 2, 6 sc in second ch from hook; do **not** join, place marker.
Rnd 2: 2 Sc in each sc around: 12 sc.
Rnd 3: (Sc in next 2 sc, 2 sc in next sc) around: 16 sc.

Rnd 4: (Sc in next 3 sc, 2 sc in next sc) around; slip st in next sc: 20 sc.
Rnd 5: Ch 1, **turn**; sc in FLO of first 3 sc *(Fig. 22, page 138)*, (slip st, ch 2, dc, ch 2, slip st) in BLO of next sc (toe), ★ sc in FLO of next sc, (slip st, ch 2, dc, ch 2, slip st) in BLO of next sc (toe); repeat from ★ 2 times **more**, sc in FLO of last 10 sc; join with slip st to first sc: 4 toes.
Rnd 6: Ch 1, **turn**; sc in both loops of first 10 sc, hdc in free loop of next sc on Rnd 4 (behind toe) *(Fig. 23a, page 138)*, (sc in next sc, hdc in free loop of next sc on Rnd 4) 3 times, sc in last 3 sc; join with slip st to first sc changing to MC *(Fig. 24b, page 138)*, place marker: 20 sts.
Rnds 7-10: Sc in each sc around.
Note: Begin working in rows.
Row 1: Sc in next 6 sc, remove marker, ch 1, turn; decrease, sc in next 13 sc, decrease, leave remaining 3 sc unworked: 15 sc.
Row 2: Ch 1, turn; sc in each sc across.
Row 3: Ch 1, turn; decrease, sc in each sc across to last 2 sc, decrease: 13 sc.
Rows 4-11: Repeat Rows 2 and 3, 4 times; at end of Row 11, finish off leaving a long end for sewing: 5 sc.

LEFT BACK LEG

Rnds 1-10: Work same as Right Back Leg.
Note: Begin working in rows.
Row 1: Sc in next sc, ch 1, turn; decrease, sc in next 13 sc, decrease, leave remaining 3 sc unworked: 15 sc.
Rows 2-11: Work same as Right Back Leg.

LEFT FRONT LEG

Rnd 1: With Color A, ch 2, 6 sc in second ch from hook; do **not** join, place marker.
Rnd 2: 2 Sc in each sc around: 12 sc.
Rnd 3: (Sc in next sc, 2 sc in next sc) around; slip st in next sc: 18 sc.
Rnd 4: Ch 1, turn; sc in FLO of first 2 sc, (slip st, ch 2, dc, ch 2, slip st) in BLO of next sc (toe), ★ sc in FLO of next sc, (slip st, ch 2, dc, ch 2, slip st) in BLO of next sc (toe); repeat from ★ 2 times **more**, sc in FLO of last 9 sc; join with slip st to first sc: 4 toes.
Rnd 5: Ch 1, turn; sc in both loops of first 9 sc, hdc in free loop of next sc on Rnd 3, (sc in next sc, hdc in free loop of next sc on Rnd 3) 3 times, sc in last 2 sc; join with slip st to first sc changing to MC, place marker: 18 sts.
Rnds 6-8: Sc in each sc around.
Note: Begin working in rows.
Row 1: Slip st in next sc, ch 1, turn; decrease, sc in next 10 sc, decrease, leave remaining 4 sts unworked: 12 sc.
Row 2: Ch 1, turn; sc in each sc across.
Row 3: Ch 1, turn; decrease, sc in each sc across to last 2 sc, decrease: 10 sc.
Rows 4-8: Repeat Rows 2 and 3 twice, then repeat Row 2 once **more**: 6 sc.
Row 9: Ch 1, turn; decrease across: 3 sc.
Row 10: Ch 1, turn; sc in each sc across; finish off leaving a long end for sewing.

RIGHT FRONT LEG

Rnds 1-8: Work same as Left Front Leg.
Note: Begin working in rows.
Row 1: Sc in next 5 sc, slip st in next sc, ch 1, turn; decrease, sc in next 10 sc, decrease, leave remaining 4 sc unworked: 12 sc.
Rows 2-10: Work same as Left Front Leg.

PLATES

LARGE (Make 10)
With Color A, ch 6 **loosely**.
Row 1 (Right side)**:** Sc in second ch from hook and in each ch across: 5 sc.
Note: Loop a short piece of fabric around any stitch to mark last row as **right** side.

Row 2: Ch 1, turn; sc in each sc across.
Row 3: Ch 1, turn; decrease, sc in next sc, decrease: 3 sc.
Row 4: Ch 1, turn; sc in each sc across.
Row 5: Ch 1, turn; pull up a loop in each sc across, YO and draw through all 4 loops on hook; finish off.
Edging: With **right** side facing and working in end of rows, join Color A with slip st in first row; ch 1, 2 sc in same row, sc in next 3 rows, 3 sc in next row, sc in next 3 rows, 2 sc in last row; finish off leaving a long end for sewing.

SMALL (Make 8)
With Color A, ch 4 **loosely**.
Row 1 (Right side)**:** Sc in second ch from hook and in each ch across: 3 sc.
Note: Mark last row as **right** side.
Row 2: Ch 1, turn; sc in each sc across.
Row 3: Ch 1, turn; pull up a loop in each sc across, YO and draw through all 4 loops on hook; finish off.
Edging: With **right** side facing and working in end of rows, join Color A with slip st in first row; ch 1, 2 sc in same row, sc in next row, 3 sc in next row, sc in next row, 2 sc in last row; finish off leaving a long end for sewing.

SPIKES

LARGE (Make 3)
Rnd 1: With Color A, ch 2, 6 sc in second ch from hook; do **not** join, place marker.
Rnds 2-5: Sc in each sc around.
Rnd 6: (Sc in next 2 sc, 2 sc in next sc) twice; slip st in next sc, finish off leaving a long end for sewing: 8 sc.
Stuff **lightly**.

SMALL (Make 2)
Work same as Large Spike through Rnd 4; at end of Rnd 4, slip st in next sc, finish off leaving a long end for sewing.
Stuff **lightly**.

FINISHING

Add eyes.
Stuff Head, Body, Tail, and Legs.
Using photo as a guide for placement, sew Tail to Body.
Sew Legs in place with toes facing forward.
Sew a Large Spike to tip of Tail.
Sew 2 Small Spikes on each side of Large Spike near Tail.
Sew remaining 2 Large Spikes on each side of Tail.
Starting at Tail and working toward Neck, with wrong side facing inward, sew a double row of Plates in the following sequence: 1 Small, 5 Large, 3 Small.

Quick POPPY POT HOLDER

*W*ith its familiar red and black colors, this vibrant poppy pot holder will brighten
your kitchen. The easy-to-make pad is crocheted with rug yarn for extra durability.

Finished Size: Approximately 7¹/₂" in diameter

MATERIALS

    Rug Yarn, approximately:
        MC (Red) - 40 yards
        CC (Black) - 5 yards
    Crochet hook, size H (5.00 mm) **or** size needed for gauge

GAUGE: Rnds 1 and 2 (Center) = 2¹/₂"

CENTER

Rnd 1 (Right side): With CC, ch 2, 6 sc in second ch from
hook; join with slip st to first sc.

Note: Loop a short piece of yarn around any stitch to mark last
round as **right** side.

Rnd 2: Ch 3 **(counts as first dc, now and throughout)**,
2 dc in same st, 3 dc in next sc and in each sc around; join with
slip st to first dc, finish off: 18 dc.

PETALS

Rnd 1: With **right** side facing and working in Back Loops Only
(Fig. 22, page 138), join MC with slip st in any dc; ch 3, dc
in same st, 2 dc in each of next 2 dc, ch 1, (2 dc in each of next
3 dc, ch 1) around; join with slip st to both loops of first dc:
36 dc.

Rnd 2: Working in both loops, ch 3, dc in same st, 2 dc in
each of next 5 dc, ch 1, (2 dc in each of next 6 dc, ch 1)
around; join with slip st to first dc: 72 dc.

Rnd 3: Ch 3, dc in same st and in next 10 dc, 2 dc in next dc,
ch 1, ★ 2 dc in next dc, dc in next 10 dc, 2 dc in next dc, ch 1;
repeat from ★ around; join with slip st to first dc: 84 dc.

Rnd 4: Slip st in next 3 dc, ch 1, sc in same st, (ch 2, sc in next
dc) 3 times, ch 8 (hanger), sc in next dc, (ch 2, sc in next dc)
3 times, skip next 6 dc, ★ sc in next dc, (ch 2, sc in next dc) 7
times, skip next 6 dc; repeat from ★ around; join with slip st to
first sc, finish off.

FOUR-SEASON FRIDGIES

Celebrate the joys of the seasons with this cute collection of magnets. Worked with worsted weight yarn, these attention-getters are ideal for posting notes and reminders or simply perking up the refrigerator door.

MATERIALS

Worsted Weight Yarn, approximately:
    15 to 30 yards **total** assorted colors for **each** Fridgie
Crochet hook, size F (3.75 mm)
Yarn needle
Finishing materials: Adhesive magnetic strips, glue, 6 mm and 3 mm black beads, paper clip or wire, 3" chenille stem, black and white embroidery floss, black buttons, and black felt

Note: Gauge is not important. Fridgies can be smaller or larger without changing the overall effect.

PATTERN STITCH
DECREASE
Pull up a loop in next 2 sts, YO and draw through all 3 loops on hook **(counts as one sc)**.

STRAWBERRY

BERRY (Make 2)
With Red, ch 4 **loosely**.
Row 1 (Right side)**:** Sc in second ch from hook and in each ch across: 3 sc.
Note: Loop a short piece of yarn around any stitch to mark last row as **right** side.
Row 2: Ch 1, turn; sc in each sc across.
Row 3: Ch 1, turn; 2 sc in first sc, sc in next sc, 2 sc in last sc: 5 sc.
Row 4: Ch 1, turn; 2 sc in first sc, sc in next 3 sc, 2 sc in last sc: 7 sc.
Rows 5-7: Ch 1, turn; sc in each sc across.
Row 8: Ch 1, turn; decrease, sc in next 3 sc, decrease: 5 sc.
Edging: Ch 1, turn; sc evenly around entire piece; join with slip st to first sc, finish off leaving a long end for sewing.

STEM AND LEAVES

With Green, ch 3 **loosely**, sc in second ch from hook and in next ch (Stem), ★ ch 4 **loosely**, slip st in second ch from hook, sc in next 2 chs; repeat from ★ 4 times **more**; finish off leaving a long end for sewing: 5 Leaves.

Whipstitch Berries together *(Fig. 28b, page 140)*.
Sew Stem and Leaves to top of Berry.

With Yellow, add straight stitches to front of Berry for seeds *(Fig. 33, page 141)*.
Attach a long magnetic strip to back.

BUTTERFLY
BODY

With Black, ch 3 **loosely**; being careful not to twist ch, join with slip st to form a ring.
Rnd 1 (Right side)**:** Ch 1, 2 sc in each ch around; do **not** join, place marker *(see Markers, page 138)*: 6 sc.
Rnds 2-9: Sc in each sc around.
Rnd 10: (Slip st in next sc, skip next sc) 3 times; join with slip st to first slip st, finish off.

WING (Make 8)
With Yellow, ch 3 **loosely**.
Row 1 (Right side)**:** Sc in second ch from hook and in next ch: 2 sc.
Note: Loop a short piece of yarn around any stitch to mark last row as **right** side.
Row 2: Ch 1, turn; 2 sc in each sc across: 4 sc.
Row 3: Ch 1, turn; sc in each sc across.
Row 4: Ch 1, turn; 2 sc in first sc, sc in next 2 sc, 2 sc in last sc: 6 sc.
Row 5: Ch 1, turn; sc in each sc across.
Row 6: Ch 1, turn; decrease, sc in next 2 sc, decrease: 4 sc.
Row 7: Ch 1, turn; sc in each sc across.
Row 8: Ch 1, turn; decrease twice; finish off: 2 sc.
Edging: With **right** side facing, join Black with slip st in any st; ch 1, sc evenly around entire piece; join with slip st to first sc, finish off leaving a long end for sewing.

Whipstitch 2 Wing pieces together *(Fig. 28b, page 140)*.
Repeat for remaining Wings.
Using photo as a guide for placement, flatten Body and sew Wings to side of Body; tack 1" of top and bottom Wings together beginning at Body.
With black embroidery floss, embroider veins on Wings using Outline Stitch *(Figs. 32a & b, page 141)*.
With white embroidery floss, add French knots around outer edges of Wings *(Fig. 37, page 142)*.
Fold chenille stem in half and insert it into top of Body; tack in place and bend top of stem to form curves.
Attach a long magnetic strip to back.

Shovel driveway!

rake leaves!

BROWN-EYED SUSAN
FLOWER (Make 2)
With Brown, ch 3 **loosely**; being careful not to twist ch, join with slip st to form a ring.

Rnd 1 (Right side)**:** Ch 1, 2 sc in each ch around; do **not** join, place marker *(see Markers, page 138)*: 6 sc.

Note: Loop a short piece of yarn around any stitch to mark last round as **right** side.

Rnd 2: 2 Sc in each sc around; slip st in next sc, finish off: 12 sc.

Rnd 3: With **right** side facing, join Yellow with slip st in same st as slip st, ★ ch 8 **loosely**, slip st in second ch from hook, sc in next ch, hdc in last 5 chs, slip st in next sc on Rnd 2; repeat from ★ around working last slip st in first sc; finish off leaving a long end for sewing: 12 petals.

LEAF (Make 2)
With Green, ch 9 **loosely**; 2 dc in third ch from hook and in each of next 2 chs, hdc in next 2 chs, sc in next ch, (sc, ch 2, sc) in last ch; working in free loops of beginning ch *(Fig. 23b, page 138)*, sc in next ch, hdc in next 2 chs, 2 dc in each of next 2 chs, 3 dc in next ch; join with slip st to top of beginning ch, finish off leaving a long end for sewing.

Whipstitch Brown-eyed Susan together *(Fig. 28b, page 140)*. Using photo as a guide for placement, sew Leaves to back of Flower.
Attach a long magnetic strip to back.

WATERMELON
With Pink, ch 3 **loosely**; being careful not to twist ch, join with slip st to form a ring.

Rnd 1 (Right side)**:** Ch 1, 2 sc in each ch around; join with slip st to first sc: 6 sc.

Note: Loop a short piece of yarn around any stitch to mark last round as **right** side.

Rnds 2 and 3: Ch 1, turn; 2 sc in each sc around; join with slip st to first sc: 24 sc.

Rnd 4: Ch 1, turn; sc in first sc, 2 sc in next sc, (sc in next sc, 2 sc in next sc) around; join with slip st to first sc: 36 sc.

Rnds 5 and 6: Ch 1, turn; sc in each sc around; join with slip st to first sc.

Rnd 7: Ch 1, turn; sc in first 2 sc, 2 sc in next sc, (sc in next 2 sc, 2 sc in next sc) around; join with slip st to first sc: 48 sc.

Rnd 8: Ch 1, turn; sc in each sc around; join with slip st to first sc, finish off.

Rnd 9: With **wrong** side facing, join Light Green with slip st in first sc; ch 1, 2 sc in same st, sc in next 11 sc, (2 sc in next sc, sc in next 11 sc) around; join with slip st to first sc, finish off: 52 sc.

Rnd 10: With **right** side facing, join Dark Green with slip st in first sc; ch 1, 2 sc in same st, sc in next 3 sc, (2 sc in next sc, sc in next 3 sc) around; join with slip st to first sc, finish off leaving a long end for sewing: 65 sc.

Fold piece in half with **wrong** side to the inside and whipstitch edge together *(Fig. 28b, page 140)*.
Glue 3 mm beads to front.
Attach a long magnetic strip to back.

APPLE
BODY (Make 2)
With Red, ch 3 **loosely**; being careful not to twist ch, join with slip st to form a ring.

Rnd 1 (Right side)**:** Ch 1, 2 sc in each ch around; do **not** join, place marker *(see Markers, page 138)*: 6 sc.

Note: Loop a short piece of yarn around any stitch to mark last round as **right** side.

Rnd 2: 2 Sc in each sc around: 12 sc.

Rnd 3: Sc in next 2 sc, (2 hdc in each of next 3 sc, sc in next 2 sc) twice: 18 sts.

Rnd 4: Sc in next 2 sc, 2 hdc in each of next 3 hdc, (sc in next 2 sts, 2 sc in next hdc) twice, sc in next 2 hdc, 2 hdc in each of next 3 hdc, sc in next 2 sc: 26 sts.

Rnd 5: Sc in next 2 sc, 2 hdc in each of next 3 hdc, sc in next 4 sts, (2 sc in each of next 2 sc, sc in next 4 sts) twice, 2 hdc in each of next 3 hdc, sc in next 2 sc; slip st in next sc, finish off leaving a long end for sewing: 36 sts.

STEM
With Brown, ch 4 **loosely**; 2 sc in second ch from hook, slip st in last 2 chs; finish off leaving a long end for sewing.

LEAF
With Green, ch 6 **loosely**; 2 hdc in third ch from hook, hdc in next ch, sc in next ch, (sc, ch 2, sc) in last ch; working in free loops of beginning ch *(Fig. 23b, page 138)*, sc in next ch, hdc in next ch, 2 hdc in next ch, slip st in next ch, ch 2 (stem); finish off leaving a long end for sewing.

Whipstitch Apple together *(Fig. 28b, page 140)*.
Sew Stem and Leaf to top of Apple.
Attach a long magnetic strip to back.

JACK-O'-LANTERN
PUMPKIN (Make 2)
With Orange, ch 3 **loosely**; being careful not to twist ch, join with slip st to form a ring.

Rnd 1 (Right side)**:** Ch 1, 2 sc in each ch around; do **not** join, place marker *(see Markers, page 138)*: 6 sc.

Note: Loop a short piece of yarn around any stitch to mark last round as **right** side.

Rnd 2: 2 Sc in each sc around: 12 sc.
Rnd 3: (Sc in next 3 sc, 2 hdc in each of next 3 sc) twice: 18 sts.
Rnd 4: (Sc in next 3 sc, 2 sc in each of next 6 hdc) twice: 30 sc.
Rnd 5: ★ Sc in next 3 sc, (hdc in next sc, 2 hdc in next sc) 6 times; repeat from ★ once **more**; slip st in next sc, finish off leaving a long end for sewing: 42 sts.

STEM

With **right** side of one Pumpkin facing (front), join Green with slip st in same st as last slip st; ch 3, (2 dc, ch 3, slip st) in same st; finish off.

LEAF (Make 1 **each**: Yellow, Green, Red, and Brown)

Ch 7 **loosely**; slip st in second ch from hook and in next ch, (ch 2, slip st in second ch from hook and in next ch of beginning ch) 4 times; working in free loops of beginning ch *(Fig. 23b, page 138)*, slip st in next ch, (ch 2, slip st in second ch from hook and in next ch of beginning ch) 3 times; finish off leaving a long end for sewing.

Whipstitch Pumpkin together *(Fig. 28b, page 140)*.
Cut facial features from black felt using patterns and glue to front.
Using photo as a guide for placement, sew Leaves to Jack-O'-Lantern. Attach a long magnetic strip to back.

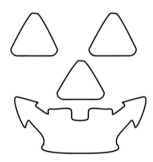

SKI HAT

Rnd 1 (Right side): With Green, ch 4, 9 dc in fourth ch from hook; join with slip st in top of beginning ch changing to White, do **not** cut Green *(Fig. 24b, page 138)*: 10 sts.
Rnd 2: Ch 3 (**counts as first dc, now and throughout**), dc in same st, 2 dc in next dc and in each dc around; join with slip st to first dc changing to Green: 20 dc.
Rnd 3: Ch 3, dc in next dc and in each dc around; join with slip st to first dc changing to White.
Rnd 4: Ch 3, dc in next 2 dc, 2 dc in next dc, (dc in next 3 dc, 2 dc in next dc) around; join with slip st to first dc changing to Green: 25 dc.
Rnd 5: Ch 3, dc in next dc and in each dc around; join with slip st to first dc.
Rnd 6: Ch 1, turn; sc in Back Loop Only of each dc around *(Fig. 22, page 138)*; join with slip st to first sc, finish off.

Using Green and White, make a 1¹/₂" pom-pom *(Figs. 29a & b, page 140)*. Sew pom-pom to top of Hat.

Flatten Hat and stitch opening closed.
Attach a long magnetic strip to back.

SNOWMAN

BODY (Make 2)

With White, ch 3 **loosely**; being careful to not twist ch, join with slip st to form a ring.
Rnd 1 (Right side): Ch 1, 2 sc in each ch around; do **not** join, place marker *(see Markers, page 138)*: 6 sc.
Rnds 2 and 3: 2 Sc in each sc around: 24 sc.
Rnd 4: (Sc in next sc, 2 sc in next sc) around; slip st in next sc, finish off leaving a long end for sewing: 36 sc.

HEAD (Make 2)

Work same as Body through Rnd 3; at end of Rnd 3, slip st in next sc, finish off: 24 sc.

ARM (Make 2)

With Brown, ch 5 **loosely**, slip st in second ch from hook and in next ch, (ch 3, slip st in second ch from hook and in next ch) twice, slip st in last 2 chs of beginning ch-5; finish off leaving a long end for sewing.

NOSE

With Orange, ch 2, slip st in second ch from hook; finish off leaving a long end for sewing.

SCARF

With Red, ch 32 leaving 1¹/₂" of yarn at each end; finish off. Fray ends of yarn and trim.

EARMUFF (Make 2)

With Green, ch 3 **loosely**; being careful not to twist ch, join with slip st to form a ring.
Rnd 1 (Right side): Ch 1, 2 sc in each ch around; do **not** join, place marker: 6 sc.
Rnd 2: 2 Sc in each sc around: 12 sc.
Rnd 3: Decrease 6 times; slip st in next sc, finish off leaving a long end for sewing: 6 sc.

Whipstitch Head together *(Fig. 28b, page 140)*.
Whipstitch Body together.
Using photo as a guide for placement, sew Head and Arms to Body.
Sew Nose and Earmuffs to Head.
Glue 6 mm beads to Head and buttons to Body.
Cut paper clip or wire to measure approximately 3". Insert ends of wire into top of each Earmuff and glue in place curving wire approximately ¹/₄" above Head.
Tie Scarf around neck.
Attach a long magnetic strip to back.

rock-a-bye collection

Celebrate a little one's arrival with precious crocheted gifts and accessories. Our sweet collection includes booties to keep tiny toes toasty warm, snuggly afghans to wrap an infant in love, and a precious little lamb to guide baby to dreamland. Whether stitched for a boy or a girl, these creations are sure to become keepsakes of this wonderful occasion.

CUDDLY SET

Snuggly soft, this precious set will surround a little one with love. The gently textured afghan, worked in worsted weight brushed acrylic yarn, features cluster stitch variations and a delicate picot finish. The sweet lamb makes a cuddly bedtime buddy for baby.

Finished Size: Afghan - approximately 35" x 35"
Lamb - approximately 7" tall

MATERIALS
Worsted Weight Brushed Acrylic Yarn, approximately:
Afghan
19 ounces, (540 grams, 855 yards)
Lamb
MC (White) - 2 ounces, (60 grams, 90 yards)
Color A (Black) - ½ ounce, (15 grams, 25 yards)
Color B (Lilac) - 7 yards
Crochet hooks, sizes E (3.50 mm) **and** H (5.00 mm) **or** sizes needed for gauge
½ yard of ⅜" ribbon
Polyester fiberfill
Yarn needle

AFGHAN

> **PATTERN STITCHES**
> **5-DC CLUSTER**
> ★ YO, insert hook in dc indicated, YO and pull up a loop, YO and draw through 2 loops on hook; repeat from ★ 4 times **more**, YO and draw through all 6 loops on hook **(Figs. 10a & b, page 134)**.
> **PICOT**
> Ch 3, slip st in last sc worked.

GAUGE: With larger size hook, 12 dc = 4" and 5 rows = 3"

With larger size hook, ch 10; being careful not to twist ch, join with slip st to form a ring.
Rnd 1 (Right side): Ch 6 **(counts as first dc plus ch 3, now and throughout)**, (5 dc in ring, ch 3) 3 times, 4 dc in ring; join with slip st to first dc: 20 dc.

Rnd 2: Slip st in first ch-3 sp, ch 6, 2 dc in same sp, dc in next 2 dc, work 5-dc Cluster in next dc, dc in next 2 dc, ★ (2 dc, ch 3, 2 dc) in next ch-3 sp, dc in next 2 dc, work 5-dc Cluster in next dc, dc in next 2 dc; repeat from ★ 2 times **more**, dc in same sp as first dc; join with slip st to first dc: 4 5-dc Clusters.

Rnd 3 AND ALL ODD NUMBERED RNDS THROUGH RND 25: Slip st in first ch-3 sp, ch 6, 2 dc in same sp, dc in each st across to next corner ch-3 sp, ★ (2 dc, ch 3, 2 dc) in corner ch-3 sp, dc in each st across to next corner ch-3 sp; repeat from ★ 2 times **more**, dc in same sp as first dc; join with slip st to first dc.

Rnd 4: Slip st in first ch-3 sp, ch 6, 2 dc in same sp, dc in next 3 dc, work 5-dc Cluster in next dc, dc in next 5 dc, work 5-dc Cluster in next dc, dc in next 3 dc, ★ (2 dc, ch 3, 2 dc) in next corner ch-3 sp, dc in next 3 dc, work 5-dc Cluster in next dc, dc in next 5 dc, work 5-dc Cluster in next dc, dc in next 3 dc; repeat from ★ 2 times **more**, dc in same sp as first dc; join with slip st to first dc: 8 5-dc Clusters.

Rnd 6: Slip st in first ch-3 sp, ch 6, 2 dc in same sp, dc in next 3 dc, work 5-dc Cluster in next dc, dc in next 13 dc, work 5-dc Cluster in next dc, dc in next 3 dc, ★ (2 dc, ch 3, 2 dc) in next corner ch-3 sp, dc in next 3 dc, work 5-dc Cluster in next dc, dc in next 13 dc, work 5-dc Cluster in next dc, dc in next 3 dc; repeat from ★ 2 times **more**, dc in same sp as first dc; join with slip st to first dc.

Rnd 8: Slip st in first ch-3 sp, ch 6, 2 dc in same sp, dc in next 3 dc, work 5-dc Cluster in next dc, (dc in next 10 dc, work 5-dc Cluster in next dc) twice, dc in next 3 dc, ★ (2 dc, ch 3, 2 dc) in next corner ch-3 sp, dc in next 3 dc, work 5-dc Cluster in next dc, (dc in next 10 dc, work 5-dc Cluster in next dc) twice, dc in next 3 dc; repeat from ★ 2 times **more**, dc in same sp as first dc; join with slip st to first dc: 12 5-dc Clusters.

Rnd 10: Slip st in first ch-3 sp, ch 6, 2 dc in same sp, ★ † dc in next 3 dc, work 5-dc Cluster in next dc, dc in next 11 dc, work 5-dc Cluster in next dc, dc in next 5 dc, work 5-dc Cluster in next dc, dc in next 11 dc, work 5-dc Cluster in next dc, dc in next 3 dc †, (2 dc, ch 3, 2 dc) in next corner ch-3 sp; repeat from ★ 2 times **more**, then repeat from † to † once, dc in same sp as first dc; join with slip st to first dc: 16 5-dc Clusters.

Rnd 12: Slip st in first ch-3 sp, ch 6, 2 dc in same sp, ★ † dc in next 3 dc, work 5-dc Cluster in next dc, dc in next 11 dc, work 5-dc Cluster in next dc, dc in next 13 dc, work 5-dc Cluster in next dc, dc in next 11 dc, work 5-dc Cluster in next dc, dc in next 3 dc †, (2 dc, ch 3, 2 dc) in next corner ch-3 sp; repeat from ★ 2 times **more**, then repeat from † to † once, dc in same sp as first dc; join with slip st to first dc.

Rnd 14: Slip st in first ch-3 sp, ch 6, 2 dc in same sp, ★ † dc in next 3 dc, work 5-dc Cluster in next dc, dc in next 11 dc, work 5-dc Cluster in next dc, (dc in next 10 dc, work 5-dc Cluster in next dc) twice, dc in next 11 dc, work 5-dc Cluster in next dc, dc in next 3 dc †, (2 dc, ch 3, 2 dc) in next corner ch-3 sp; repeat from ★ 2 times **more** then repeat from † to † once, dc in same sp as first dc; join with slip st to first dc: 20 5-dc Clusters.

Rnd 16: Slip st in first ch-3 sp, ch 6, 2 dc in same sp, ★ † dc in next 3 dc, work 5-dc Cluster in next dc, (dc in next 11 dc, work 5-dc Cluster in next dc) twice, dc in next 5 dc, work 5-dc Cluster in next dc, (dc in next 11 dc, work 5-dc Cluster in next dc) twice, dc in next 3 dc †, (2 dc, ch 3, 2 dc) in next corner ch-3 sp; repeat from ★ 2 times **more**, then repeat from † to † once, dc in same sp as first dc; join with slip st to first dc: 24 5-dc Clusters.

Rnd 18: Slip st in first ch-3 sp, ch 6, 2 dc in same sp, ★ † dc in next 3 dc, work 5-dc Cluster in next dc, dc in next 18 dc, work 5-dc Cluster in next dc, (dc in next 11 dc, work 5-dc Cluster in next dc) twice, dc in next 18 dc, work 5-dc Cluster in next dc, dc in next 3 dc †, (2 dc, ch 3, 2 dc) in next corner ch-3 sp; repeat from ★ 2 times **more**, then repeat from † to † once, dc in same sp as first dc; join with slip st to first dc: 20 5-dc Clusters.

Rnd 20: Slip st in first ch-3 sp, ch 6, 2 dc in same sp, ★ † dc in next 3 dc, work 5-dc Cluster in next dc, dc in next 27 dc, work 5-dc Cluster in next dc, dc in next 13 dc, work 5-dc Cluster in next dc, dc in next 27 dc, work 5-dc Cluster in next dc, dc in next 3 dc †, (2 dc, ch 3, 2 dc) in next corner ch-3 sp; repeat from ★ 2 times **more**, then repeat from † to † once, dc in same sp as first dc; join with slip st to first dc: 16 5-dc Clusters.

Rnd 22: Slip st in first ch-3 sp, ch 6, 2 dc in same sp, ★ † dc in next 3 dc, work 5-dc Cluster in next dc, dc in next 35 dc, work 5-dc Cluster in next dc, dc in next 5 dc, work 5-dc Cluster in next dc, dc in next 35 dc, work 5-dc Cluster in next dc, dc in next 3 dc †, (2 dc, ch 3, 2 dc) in next corner ch-3 sp; repeat from ★ 2 times **more**, then repeat from † to † once, dc in same sp as first dc; join with slip st to first dc.

Rnd 24: Slip st in first ch-3 sp, ch 6, 2 dc in same sp, dc in next 3 dc, work 5-dc Cluster in next dc, (dc in next 42 dc, work 5-dc Cluster in next dc) twice, dc in next 3 dc, ★ (2 dc, ch 3, 2 dc) in next corner ch-3 sp, dc in next 3 dc, work 5-dc Cluster in next dc, (dc in next 42 dc, work 5-dc Cluster in next dc) twice, dc in next 3 dc; repeat from ★ 2 times **more**, dc in same sp as first dc; join with slip st to first dc: 12 5-dc Clusters.

Rnd 26: Slip st in first ch-3 sp, ch 1, ★ (2 sc, work Picot, 2 sc) in corner ch-3 sp, sc in next dc, work Picot, (sc in next 3 dc, work Picot) across to within one dc of next corner ch-3 sp, sc in next dc; repeat from ★ around; join with slip st to first sc, finish off.

Continued on page 84.

Quick BABY'S BIBLE COVER

*Enhanced with tiny pearls, this dainty cover is designed for holding baby's first Bible.
The lacy jacket features a pretty shell pattern stitched in bedspread weight cotton thread.*

Finished Size: Approximately 4³/₄" x 7"

MATERIALS

Bedspread Weight Cotton Thread (size 10), approximately
85 yards

Steel crochet hook, size 7(1.65 mm) **or** size needed for
gauge

2 - 5" lengths of 1¹/₂" satin ribbon

Straight pins

Sewing needle and thread

35 - 3 mm pearls

Bible: 3" wide x 4¹/₂" long x ⁵/₈" deep

GAUGE: 6 Shells and 10 rows = 2"

PATTERN STITCH

SHELL

(2 Dc, ch 2, sc) in st or sp indicated.

Ch 58 **loosely**.

Row 1 (Right side): (Dc, ch 2, sc) in fourth ch from hook,
(skip next 2 chs, work Shell in next ch) across: 19 ch-2 sps.

Note: Loop a short piece of thread around any stitch to mark
last row as **right** side.

Row 2: Turn; slip st in first ch-2 sp, ch 3 **(counts as first dc,
now and throughout)**, (dc, ch 2, sc) in same sp, work Shell
in each Shell (ch-2 sp) across: 19 Shells.

Rows 3-22: Repeat Row 2, 20 times.

Edging: Turn; slip st in first ch-2 sp, ch 3, (dc, ch 2, sc) in
same sp, work Shell in each Shell across; working in end of
rows, work Shell in first row, (skip next row, work Shell in next
row) across to last row, work Shell in last row; working over
beginning ch, work Shell in each ch-2 sp across; working in
end of rows, work Shell in first row, (skip next row, work Shell
in next row) across to last row, work Shell in last row; join with
slip st to first dc, finish off: 62 Shells.

Fold cut ends of ribbons under ¹/₄" and pin ribbons to wrong
side of Cover with folded edges on Rows 1 and 22 and long edge
along outer edge of Cover. Sew ribbons in place, stitching along
folded edges and outer edges, leaving inside edge of each
ribbon free.

Using photo as a guide for placement, sew pearls randomly to
Cover.

Insert Bible.

CUDDLY SET

Continued from page 82.

LAMB

PATTERN STITCHES

DECREASE

Pull up a loop in next 2 sts, YO and draw through all 3 loops on hook **(counts as one sc)**.

3-DC CLUSTER

★ YO, insert hook in st indicated, YO and pull up a loop, YO and draw through 2 loops on hook; repeat from ★ 2 times **more**, YO and draw through all 4 loops on hook.

GAUGE: With smaller size hook, 10 sc and 10 rows = 2"

HEAD

Rnd 1 (Right side)**:** With smaller size hook and MC, ch 2, 8 sc in second ch from hook; do **not** join, place marker *(see Markers, page 138)*.

Rnd 2: 2 Sc in each sc around: 16 sc.

Rnd 3: (Sc in next sc, 2 sc in next sc) around: 24 sc.

Rnd 4: (Sc in next 2 sc, 2 sc in next sc) around: 32 sc.

Rnds 5-11: Sc in each sc around.

Rnd 12: Decrease around: 16 sc.

Rnd 13: Sc in each sc around; slip st in next sc, finish off leaving a long end for sewing.

Stuff **firmly**.

BODY

Rnds 1-4: Work same as Head: 32 sc.

Rnd 5: (Sc in next sc, work 3-dc Cluster in next sc) around to last 2 sc, decrease: 15 3-dc Clusters.

Rnd 6: Work 3-dc Cluster in next sc, (sc in next st, work 3-dc Cluster in next sc) around: 16 3-dc Clusters.

Rnd 7: Sc in next 3-dc Cluster, (work 3-dc Cluster in next sc, sc in next 3-dc Cluster) around: 15 3-dc Clusters.

Rnds 8-13: Repeat Rnds 6 and 7, 3 times.

Rnd 14: Sc in next 3 sts, (decrease, sc in next 2 sts) around: 24 sc.

Rnd 15: (Decrease, sc in next sc) around: 16 sc.

Stuff **firmly**.

Rnd 16: Decrease around: 8 sc.

Rnd 17: Decrease around; slip st in next sc, finish off leaving a long end for sewing: 4 sc.

Thread needle with end and weave through remaining sts; gather tightly and secure.

LEG (Make 4)

Rnd 1 (Right side)**:** With smaller size hook and Color A, ch 2, 6 sc in second ch from hook; do **not** join, place marker.

Rnd 2: 2 Sc in each sc around: 12 sc.

Rnd 3: Sc in next 2 sc, work 3-dc Cluster in each of next 2 sc (hoof), sc in each sc around: 12 sts.

Rnds 4 and 5: Sc in each st around.

Rnd 6: Sc in next 10 sc, decrease changing to MC *(Fig. 24a, page 138)*: 11 sc.

Rnds 7 and 8: Repeat Rnds 6 and 7 of Body: 5 3-dc Clusters.

Rnd 9: Sc in each st around.

Stuff **firmly**.

Rnd 10: Decrease, (sc in next sc, decrease) around; slip st in next sc, finish off leaving a long end for sewing: 7 sc.

MUZZLE

Rnd 1 (Right side)**:** With smaller size hook and Color A, ch 2, 6 sc in second ch from hook; do **not** join, place marker.

Rnd 2: 2 Sc in each sc around: 12 sc.

Rnd 3: Sc in each sc around.

Rnd 4: (Sc in next sc, 2 sc in next sc) around: 18 sc.

Rnd 5: Sc in each sc around; slip st in next sc, finish off leaving a long end for sewing.

EAR (Make 2)

With smaller size hook and Color A, ch 7 **loosely**.

Rnd 1 (Right side)**:** Sc in second ch from hook and in next ch, hdc in next 3 chs, 8 dc in last ch; working in free loops of beginning ch *(Fig. 23b, page 138)*, hdc in next 3 chs, sc in next 2 chs, ch 1; join with slip st to first sc, finish off leaving a long end for sewing.

TAIL

With smaller size hook and MC, ch 7 **loosely**.

Rnd 1 (Right side)**:** Sc in second ch from hook and in next ch, work 3-dc Cluster in next 3 chs, work 3-dc Cluster 3 times in last ch; working in free loops of beginning ch, work 3-dc Cluster in next 3 chs, sc in next 2 chs, ch 1; join with slip st to first sc, finish off leaving a long end for sewing.

FLOWER (Make 2)

Rnd 1: With smaller size hook and Color B, ch 4, 5 dc in fourth ch from hook; join with slip st to top of beginning ch: 6 sts.

Rnd 2 (Wrong side)**:** Ch 1, (2 dc, ch 1, slip st) in same st as joining, (slip st, ch 1, 2 dc, ch 1, slip st) in next dc and in each dc around pushing center to front; finish off leaving a long end for sewing.

FINISHING

Using photo as a guide for placement, sew Head to Body.

Sew Muzzle to Head stuffing lightly before closing.

Sew Ears to Head. Sew Tail and Flowers to Body.

With MC, add Turkey Loop Stitch to top of Head between Ears *(Fig. 31, page 141)*.

With Color A, add French Knot eyes *(Fig. 37, page 142)*.

Sew Legs to Body with hooves facing forward.

Tie ribbon in a bow around neck.

Quick FOR TINY TOES

Tiny toes will appreciate the warmth of these cozy booties. Ideal for shower gifts,
both styles are made using baby fingering weight yarn for softness. The booties
are trimmed with satin ribbons woven through eyelet rounds on the cuffs.

Finished Size: 3 to 6 months

MATERIALS
Baby Fingering Weight Yarn, approximately:
Solid
1½ ounces, (40 grams, 262 yards)
Striped
MC (White) - 1½ ounces, (40 grams, 262 yards)
CC (Blue) - 11 yards
Crochet hook, size D (3.25 mm) **or** size needed for gauge
1 yard of ¼" ribbon for **each** pair

GAUGE: 12 dc and 6 rows = 2"

PATTERN STITCH
CLUSTER
★ YO, insert hook in sp indicated, YO and pull up a loop, YO and draw through 2 loops on hook; repeat from ★ once **more**, YO and draw through all 3 loops on hook **(Figs. 10a & b, page 134)**.

SOLID BOOTIE
SOLE
With MC, ch 14 **loosely**.

Rnd 1 (Right side): 3 Sc in second ch from hook, sc in next 3 chs, hdc in next 3 chs, dc in next 5 chs, 7 dc in last ch; working in free loops of beginning ch **(Fig. 23b, page 138)**, dc in next 5 chs, hdc in next 3 chs, sc in next 3 chs; join with slip st to first sc: 32 sts.

Note: Loop a short piece of yarn around any stitch to mark last round as **right** side.

Rnd 2: Ch 3 **(counts as first dc, now and throughout)**, turn; dc in same st and in next 11 sts, 2 dc in each of next 7 dc, dc in next 11 sts, 2 dc in each of last 2 sc; join with slip st to first dc: 42 dc.

Rnd 3: Ch 3, turn; 2 dc in next dc, dc in next dc, 2 dc in next dc, dc in next 12 dc, 2 dc in next dc, (dc in next dc, 2 dc in next dc) 6 times, dc in next 12 dc, 2 dc in last dc; join with slip st to Back Loop Only of first dc **(Fig. 22, page 138)**: 52 dc.

SIDES

Rnd 1: Ch 3, do **not** turn; dc in Back Loop Only of next dc and in each dc around; join with slip st to both loops of first dc.

Rnd 2: Ch 3, turn; dc in both loops of next dc and in each dc around; join with slip st to first dc.

Rnd 3: Ch 3, turn; dc in next 33 dc, place marker around last dc worked for Instep placement, dc in last 18 dc; join with slip st to first dc, finish off.

INSTEP

Row 1: With **wrong** side facing, join MC with slip st in marked dc; ch 3, dc in next 9 dc, leave remaining dc unworked: 10 dc.

Rows 2-4: Ch 3, turn; dc in next dc and in each dc across. Finish off leaving a long end for sewing.

With **right** side of Instep and Side together and beginning in seventh dc from Instep, sew Instep to Sides.

CUFF

Fold Bootie in half to find center back stitch.

Rnd 1: With **right** side facing, join MC with slip st in dc at center back; ch 1, sc in same st and in each dc across to Instep seam, sc in seam and in next 10 dc of Instep, sc in seam and in each dc around; join with slip st to first sc: 40 sc.

Rnd 2 (Eyelet rnd)**:** Ch 4, skip next sc, (dc in next sc, ch 1, skip next sc) around; join with slip st to third ch of beginning ch-4: 20 ch-1 sps.

Rnd 3: Ch 6, dc in same st, ch 2, skip next dc, ★ (dc, ch 3, dc) in next dc, ch 2, skip next dc; repeat from ★ around; join with slip st to third ch of beginning ch-6: 10 ch-3 sps.

Rnd 4: (Slip st, ch 2, dc, ch 3, work Cluster) in first ch-3 sp, ch 1, dc in next ch-2 sp, ch 1, ★ work (Cluster, ch 3, Cluster) in next ch-3 sp, ch 1, dc in next ch-2 sp, ch 1; repeat from ★ around; skip beginning ch-2 and join with slip st to first dc.

Rnd 5: Ch 1, ★ (hdc, 3 dc, hdc) in next ch-3 sp, ch 1, sc in next dc, ch 1; repeat from ★ around; join with slip st to first hdc, finish off.

Weave ribbon tie through Eyelet rnd.

STRIPED BOOTIE

Work same as Solid Bootie through Rnd 2 of Cuff.

Rnd 3: Ch 1, sc in same st, (ch 5, skip next dc, sc in next dc) around to last dc, ch 2, skip last dc, dc in first sc to form last loop: 10 loops.

Rnd 4: Ch 1, (sc, ch 2, 3 dc) in same loop, (sc in center ch of next loop, ch 2, 3 dc in same loop) around; join with slip st to first sc, finish off.

Rnd 5: With **wrong** side facing, join CC with slip st in first ch-2 sp; ch 2, 4 dc in same sp, (slip st, ch 2, 4 dc) in next ch-2 sp and in each ch-2 sp around; join with slip st to first slip st, finish off.

Rnd 6: With **right** side facing, join MC with slip st in first ch-2 sp; ch 4, slip st in third ch from hook, 4 dc in same ch-2 sp, ★ slip st in next ch-2 sp, ch 4, slip st in third ch from hook, 4 dc in same ch-2 sp; repeat from ★ around; join with slip st to first slip st, finish off.

Weave ribbon tie through Eyelet rnd.

~~Quick~~ DOWNY-SOFT AFGHANS

Baby is sure to have sweet dreams when covered with one of these downy-soft afghans. Worked holding two strands of baby fingering weight yarn, both feature a pretty "V" design that's created with front post treble crochets.

Finished Size: Approximately 30" x 40"

MATERIALS

Baby Fingering Weight Yarn, approximately:

Solid

   15 ounces, (430 grams, 2,140 yards)

Striped

   MC (White) - 11 ounces, (310 grams, 1,570 yards)

   Color A (Blue) - 2 ounces, (60 grams, 285 yards)

   Color B (Pink) - 2 ounces, (60 grams, 285 yards)

Crochet hook, size K (6.50 mm) **or** size needed for gauge

Note: Entire Afghan is worked holding 2 strands of yarn together.

GAUGE: In pattern, 13 dc = 4" and 12 rows (1 repeat) = 4¹/₂"

BODY

*Note: For Striped Afghan, work in the following Color Sequence: 2 Rows using two strands MC (Fig. 24a, page 138), ★ 2 rows using one strand MC **and** one strand Color A, 2 rows using one strand MC **and** one strand Color B, 2 rows using two strands MC; repeat from ★ throughout.*

Ch 96 **loosely.**

Row 1 (Right side)**:** Dc in fourth ch from hook and in each ch across: 94 sts.

Row 2: Ch 1, turn; sc in each st across.
Row 3: Ch 3 **(counts as first dc, now and throughout)**, turn; dc in next sc, (ch 2, skip next 2 sc, dc in next 2 sc) across: 23 ch-2 sps.
Row 4: Ch 1, turn; sc in first 2 dc, (ch 2, sc in next 2 dc) across.
Row 5: Ch 1, turn; sc in first 2 sc, ★ working in **front** of ch-2 sps of previous 2 rows, work 2 FPtr around center sc in row **below** *(Fig. 18, page 136)*, sc in next 2 sc; repeat from ★ across: 46 FPtr.
Row 6: Ch 1, turn; sc in each sc and in each FPtr across.
Row 7: Ch 3, turn; dc in next sc and in each sc across.
Row 8: Ch 1, turn; sc in each dc across.
Row 9: Ch 3, turn; dc in next 3 sc, ch 2, (skip next 2 sc, dc in next 2 sc, ch 2) across to last 6 sc, skip next 2 sc, dc in last 4 sc: 22 ch-2 sps.
Row 10: Ch 1, turn; sc in first 4 dc, ch 2, (sc in next 2 dc, ch 2) across to last 4 dc, sc in last 4 dc.
Row 11: Ch 1, turn; sc in first 4 sc, working in **front** of ch-2 sps of previous 2 rows, work 2 FPtr around center sc in row **below**,

★ sc in next 2 sc, working in **front** of ch-2 sps of previous 2 rows, work 2 FPtr around center sc in row **below**; repeat from ★ across to last 4 sc, sc in last 4 sc: 44 FPtr.
Row 12: Ch 1, turn; sc in each sc and in each FPtr across.
Row 13: Ch 3, turn; dc in next sc and in each sc across.
Rows 14-104: Repeat Rows 2-13, 7 times, then repeat Rows 2-8 once **more**; do **not** finish off.

EDGING

Rnd 1: Ch 1, turn; (sc, ch 2, sc) in first sc, sc in each sc across to last sc, (sc, ch 2, sc) in last sc; work 122 sc evenly spaced across end of rows; working in free loops of beginning ch *(Fig. 23b, page 138)*, (sc, ch 2, sc) in first ch, sc in each ch across to last ch, (sc, ch 2, sc) in last ch; work 122 sc evenly spaced across end of rows; join with slip st to first sc: 436 sc.
Rnd 2: Slip st in first corner ch-2 sp, ch 1, ★ (sc, hdc, dc, hdc, sc) in corner sp, ch 1, [skip next 2 sc, (sc, dc, sc) in next sc, ch 1] across to within 1 sc of next corner ch-2 sp, skip next sc; repeat from ★ around; join with slip st to first sc, finish off.

*E*mbroidered bluebirds and daisies dress up these darling bubble suits for sizes 3, 6, and 12 months. Fashioned with sport weight yarn using simple crochet stitches, the wee wearables are ideal for playtime or outings to Grandma's house.

Finished Size: 3 months   6 months   12 months
Finished Length: 16"   18½"   21"

Size Note: Instructions are written for size 3 months with sizes 6 and 12 months in braces. Instructions will be easier to read if you circle all the numbers pertaining to your size.

MATERIALS
Sport Weight Yarn, approximately:
  MC (Blue or Pink) - 3{4½-5} ounces,
    [100{130-140} grams, 330{425-470} yards]
  CC (White) - 1¼{1½-1¾} ounces
    [35{40-50} grams, 120{140-165} yards]
  For embroidery:
    Pink Suit - small amount **each** Yellow and Green
    Blue Suit - small amount **each** Pink, Green, Gold,
      and Dark Blue
Crochet hook, size F (3.75 mm) **or** size needed for gauge
Yarn needle
6" length of snap tape for **each**
3 - ½" buttons **each**
Sulky® Solvy stabilizer
Sewing needle and thread

GAUGE: 20 dc and 10 rows = 4"
      sc, (ch 1, sc) 10 times and 19 rows = 4"

PATTERN STITCH
DECREASE
Working in sc and ch-1 sps, pull up a loop in next 2 sts, YO and draw through all 3 loops on hook (**counts as one sc**).

YOKE
With CC, ch 53{58-60} **loosely.**
Row 1 (Right side): Sc in second ch from hook and in each ch across: 52{57-59} sc.
Note: Loop a short piece of yarn around any stitch to mark last row as **right** side.
Row 2: Ch 3 (**counts as first dc, now and throughout**), turn; dc in next 2{2-3} sc, 2 dc in next sc, (dc in next 4 sc, 2 dc in next sc) across to last 3{3-4} sc, dc in last 3{3-4} sc: 62{68-70} dc.

Row 3: Ch 3, turn; dc in next 2{0-1} dc, 2 dc in next dc, (dc in next 4 dc, 2 dc in next dc) across to last 3{1-2} dc, dc in last 3{1-2} dc: 74{82-84} dc.
Row 4: Ch 3, turn; dc in next 3{1-2} dc, 2 dc in next dc, (dc in next 5 dc, 2 dc in next dc) across to last 3{1-2} dc, dc in last 3{1-2} dc: 86{96-98} dc.
Row 5: Ch 3, turn; dc in next 3{1-2} dc, 2 dc in next dc, (dc in next 6 dc, 2 dc in next dc) across to last 4{2-3} dc, dc in last 4{2-3} dc: 98{110-112} dc.
Row 6: Ch 3, turn; dc in next 4{2-3} dc, 2 dc in next dc, (dc in next 7 dc, 2 dc in next dc) across to last 4{2-3} dc, dc in last 4{2-3} dc: 110{124-126} dc.
Row 7: Ch 3, turn; dc in next 4{2-3} dc, 2 dc in next dc, (dc in next 8 dc, 2 dc in next dc) across to last 5{3-4} dc, dc in last 5{3-4} dc: 122{138-140} dc.
Row 8: Ch 3, turn; dc in next 5{3-4} dc, 2 dc in next dc, (dc in next 9 dc, 2 dc in next dc) across to last 5{3-4} dc, dc in last 5{3-4} dc: 134{152-154} dc.
Row 9: Ch 3, turn; dc in next 5{3-4} dc, 2 dc in next dc, (dc in next 10 dc, 2 dc in next dc) across to last 6{4-5} dc, dc in last 6{4-5} dc: 146{166-168} dc.
Row 10: Ch 3, turn; dc in next 6{4-5} dc, 2 dc in next dc, (dc in next 11 dc, 2 dc in next dc) across to last 6{4-5} dc, dc in last 6{4-5} dc: 158{180-182} dc.
Row 11: Ch 3, turn; dc in next 6{4-5} dc, 2 dc in next dc, (dc in next 12 dc, 2 dc in next dc) across to last 7{5-6} dc, dc in last 7{5-6} dc: 170{194-196} dc.
Size 12 Months Only - Row 12: Ch 3, turn; dc in next 6 dc, 2 dc in next dc, (dc in next 13 dc, 2 dc in next dc) across to last 6 dc, dc in last 6 dc: 210 dc.
All Sizes: Finish off.

BODY
Rnd 1: With **wrong** side facing, skip first 59{67-73} dc and join MC with slip st in next dc; ch 1, sc in same st, ch 1, (skip next dc, sc in next dc, ch 1) 26{29-31} times, skip next 32{38-42} dc (armhole), (sc in next dc, ch 1, skip next dc) 13{15-16} times; working across sts on left Back, sc in first dc, ch 1, (skip next dc, sc in next dc, ch 1) 13{14-15} times, skip last 32{38-42} dc (armhole); join with slip st to first sc: 54{60-64} sc.

Rnd 2: Ch 1, turn; sc in first ch-1 sp, ch 1, (skip next sc, sc in next ch-1 sp, ch 1) around; join with slip st to first sc.
Repeat Rnd 2 until piece measures approximately 11{13-15}" from beginning ch, ending by working a **wrong** side round.

BACK LEG SHAPING

Note: Begin working in rows.
Row 1: Ch 1, turn; slip st in first ch-1 sp, decrease beginning in next sc, ch 1, (skip next sc, sc in next ch-1 sp, ch 1) 24{27-29} times, skip next sc, decrease, leave remaining sts unworked: 26{29-31} sc.
Row 2 (Decrease row): Ch 1, turn; decrease, ch 1, (skip next sc, sc in next ch-1 sp, ch 1) across to last 2 sc, skip next sc, decrease: 25{28-30} sc.
Repeat Row 2, 6{7-8} times: 19{21-22} sc.
Next 3 Rows: Turn; slip st in first 4 sts, ch 1, sc in same ch-1 sp, (ch 1, skip next sc, sc in next ch-1 sp) across to last 2 sc, leave remaining sts unworked: 10{12-13} sc.
Next Row: Ch 1, turn; sc in first sc, (ch 1, skip next sc, sc in next ch-1 sp) across to last sc, sc in last sc.
Repeat last row until piece measures approximately 15{17½-20}" from beginning ch, ending by working a **wrong** side row, do **not** finish off.

LOWER BAND

Row 1: Ch 1, turn; sc in each sc and in each ch-1 sp across: 18{22-24} sc.
Rows 2-5: Ch 1, turn; sc in each sc across.
Finish off.

FRONT LEG SHAPING

Row 1: With **right** side facing, skip 3{5-7} sc from Back and join MC with slip st in next ch-1 sp; ch 1, sc in same sp, (ch 1, skip next sc, sc in next ch-1 sp) across to last 3{5-7} sc, leave remaining sts unworked: 21{20-18} sc.
Row 2 (Decrease row): Ch 1, turn; decrease, ch 1, (skip next sc, sc in next ch-1 sp, ch 1) across to last 2 sc, skip next sc, decrease: 20{19-17} sc.
Repeat Row 2, 10{7-4} times: 10{12-13} sc.

UPPER BAND

Row 1: Ch 1, turn; sc in first sc, (ch 1, skip next sc, sc in next ch-1 sp) across to last sc, sc in last sc.
Repeat Row 1 until piece measures approximately 15{17½-20}" from beginning ch, ending by working a **wrong** side row; do **not** finish off.

LOWER BAND

Work same as Back.

SLEEVE

Rnd 1: With **wrong** side facing, join MC with slip st in first dc on armhole; ch 1, sc in same st, ch 1, skip next dc, (sc in next dc, ch 1, skip next dc) around; join with slip st to first sc: 16{19-21} sc.
Rnd 2: Ch 1, turn; sc in first ch-1 sp, ch 1, (skip next sc, sc in next ch-1 sp, ch 1) around; join with slip st to first sc.
Repeat Rnd 2 until Sleeve measures approximately 1½{1¾-2}" from Yoke, ending by working a **wrong** side round.
Last Rnd: Ch 1, turn; sc in each sc and in each ch-1 sp around; join with slip st to first sc, finish off.
Repeat for second Sleeve.

FINISHING

LEG BAND

Row 1: With **right** side facing, join MC with slip st in end of last row on either Lower Band; ch 1, work 60{70-75} sc evenly spaced across Leg opening.
Row 2: Ch 1, turn; sc in first 2 sc, decrease, (sc in next 3 sc, decrease) across to last sc, sc in last sc: 48{56-60} sc.
Row 3: Ch 1, turn; sc in each sc across; finish off.
Repeat for second Leg opening.

BACK EDGING

Row 1: With **wrong** side facing; join CC with slip st in corner at left Back neck edge; ch 1, work 21{21-23} sc evenly spaced across end of rows, work 21{21-23} sc evenly spaced across end of rows of right Back: 42{42-46} sc.
For Girl's Only - Row 2: Ch 1, turn; sc in first sc, ch 3, skip next 2 sc (buttonhole), ★ sc in next 6{6-7} sc, ch 3, skip next 2 sc; repeat from ★ once **more**, sc in next sc, decrease, sc in each sc across; finish off.
For Boy's Only - Row 2: Ch 1, turn; sc in first 20{20-22} sc, decrease, sc in next sc, ch 3, skip next 2 sc (buttonhole), ★ sc in next 6{6-7} sc, ch 3, skip next 2 sc; repeat from ★ once **more**, sc in last sc; finish off.

Sew buttons to side opposite buttonholes.
Sew snap tape to each Lower Band, lapping Front over Back.
With MC, sew opening closed between Body and Sleeve.
Trace embroidery diagram of your choice from page 142 onto Sulky® Solvy stabilizer, using manufacturers instructions. Centering design, baste stabilizer to front of Yoke. Embroider design on stabilizer. Remove stabilizer by tearing or cutting away large areas. Remaining stabilizer may be removed by submerging Bubble Suit in water for 30 seconds to 2 minutes, then shape and air dry.

FLORAL ENSEMBLE

As pretty as a spring garden, this floral set will make mother and baby feel extra special. The delightful throw is created holding two strands of yarn and enhanced with rows of dainty flowers that are worked in as you stitch. A matching bottle cover completes the ensemble.

Finished Size: Afghan - approximately 35" x 47"
Bottle Cover - approximately 6½" tall

MATERIALS
Baby Fingering Weight Yarn, approximately:
Afghan
MC (White) - 17 ounces, (480 grams, 2,430 yards)
Color A (Yellow) - 8 ounces,
(230 grams, 1,145 yards)
Color B (Green) - ¾ ounce, (20 grams, 110 yards)

Bottle Cover
MC (White) - ½ ounce, (15 grams, 70 yards)
Color A (Yellow) - 30 yards
Color B (Green) - 3 yards
Crochet hooks, sizes C (2.75 mm) **and** size H (5.00 mm)
or sizes needed for gauge
½ yard of ⅛" ribbon
Yarn needle

PATTERN STITCH

DECREASE

YO, insert hook in **same** sc, YO and pull up a loop, YO and draw through 2 loops on hook, YO, skip next sc, insert hook in next sc, YO and pull up a loop, YO and draw through 2 loops on hook, YO and draw through all 3 loops on hook.

AFGHAN

GAUGE: With larger size hook, 8 sc = 2"

Note: Entire Afghan is worked holding 2 strands of yarn together.

BODY

With MC and larger size hook, ch 133 **loosely**.

Row 1 (Right side): Dc in fourth ch from hook (**3 skipped chs count as first dc**) and in each ch across: 131 dc.

Note: Loop a short piece of yarn around any stitch to mark last row as **right** side.

Row 2: Ch 1, turn; sc in first dc, (dc in next dc, sc in next dc) across.

Row 3: Ch 3 (**counts as first dc, now and throughout**), turn; dc in next st and in each st across.

Rows 4 and 5: Repeat Rows 2 and 3 changing to Color A at end of Row 5 *(Fig. 24a, page 138)*.

Row 6: Ch 1, turn; sc in each st across.

Row 7: Ch 1, turn; sc in first sc, (tr in next sc, sc in next sc pushing tr to right side) across.

Row 8: Ch 1, turn; sc in each st across changing to MC in last sc.

Rows 9 and 10: Ch 1, turn; sc in each sc across.

Row 11: Ch 1, turn; sc in first 8 sc changing to Color B in last sc worked, do **not** cut MC, ★ † sc in next sc, ch 10, slip st in tenth ch from hook, (ch 9, slip st in same ch) twice changing to MC in last st worked †, sc in next 18 sc changing to Color B in last sc worked, do **not** cut MC; repeat from ★ 5 times **more**, then repeat from † to † once, sc in last 8 sc: 21 loops.

Rows 12-14: Ch 1, turn; holding loops to **right** side, sc in each sc across: 131 sc.

Row 15: Ch 1, turn; sc in first 5 sc, ★ † holding next loop in front of next sc, sc in both loop **and** in sc, sc in next 5 sc, skip next loop, holding next loop in front of next sc, sc in both loop **and** in sc †, sc in next 12 sc; repeat from ★ 5 times **more**, then repeat from † to † once, sc in last 5 sc.

Rows 16-18: Ch 1, turn; sc in each sc across.

Row 19: Ch 1, turn; sc in first 8 sc changing to Color A in last sc worked, do **not** cut MC, ★ † dc in center loop, (ch 3, slip st in last dc worked, dc in same loop) 4 times changing to MC in last dc worked, skip next sc †, sc in next 18 sc changing to Color A in last sc worked, do **not** cut MC; repeat from ★ 5 times **more**, then repeat from † to † once, sc in last 8 sc: 7 flowers.

Row 20: Ch 1, turn; sc in first 8 sc, ch 1, skip next flower, (sc in next 18 sc, ch 1, skip next flower) across to last 8 sc, sc in last 8 sc: 124 sc.

Row 21: Ch 1, turn; sc in first 8 sc, holding flower in front of next ch-1 sp, sc in both Back Loop Only of center dc **and** in ch-1 sp *(Fig. 22, page 138)*, ★ sc in next 18 sc, holding flower in front of next ch-1 sp, sc in both Back Loop Only of center dc **and** in ch-1 sp; repeat from ★ across to last 8 sc, sc in last 8 sc: 131 sc.

Rows 22 and 23: Ch 1, turn; sc in each sc across changing to Color A at end of Row 23.

Rows 24-26: Repeat Rows 6-8.

Row 27: Ch 3, turn; dc in next sc and in each sc across.

Rows 28-47: Repeat Rows 2 and 3, 10 times.

Rows 48-157: Repeat Rows 6-47 twice, then repeat Rows 6-31 once **more**.

Finish off.

EDGING

Rnd 1: With **wrong** side facing, join Color A with slip st in any corner st; ch 1, sc evenly around working 3 sc in each corner (total sc must be a multiple of 2); join with slip st to Front Loop Only of first sc.

Rnd 2: Ch 6, turn; dc in fourth ch from hook, working in Back Loops Only, (decrease, ch 4, dc in top of decrease) around to last sc, dc in same st as last decrease, skip last sc; join with slip st to second ch of beginning ch-6, finish off.

Rnd 3: With **right** side facing, holding Rnd 2 forward, and working in free loops of Rnd 1 *(Fig. 23a, page 138)*, join Color A with slip st in first sc; ch 6, dc in fourth ch from hook, (decrease, ch 4, dc in top of decease) around to last sc, dc in same st as last decrease, skip last sc; join with slip st to second ch of beginning ch-6, finish off.

BOTTLE COVER

GAUGE: With smaller size hook, Rnds 1-3 of Bottom = 2"
      11 sc = 2"

BOTTOM

With smaller size hook and MC, ch 2; join with slip st to form a ring.

Rnd 1 (Right side): Ch 3 **(counts as first dc, now and throughout)**, 11 dc in ring; join with slip st to first dc: 12 dc. *Note:* Loop a short piece of yarn around any stitch to mark last round as **right** side.

Rnd 2: Ch 3, dc in same st, 2 dc in each dc around; join with slip st to first dc: 24 dc.

Rnd 3: Ch 3, 2 dc in next dc, (dc in next dc, 2 dc in next dc) around; join with slip st to first dc: 36 dc.

SIDES

Rnd 1: Slip st from **back** to **front** around post of first dc, ch 3, work BPdc around next dc and around each dc around *(Fig. 17, page 136)*; join with slip st to first dc.

Rnd 2: Ch 1, turn; sc in first st, dc in next st, (sc in next st, dc in next st) around; join with slip st to first sc.

Rnd 3: Ch 3, turn; dc in next st and in each st around; join with slip st to first dc.

Rnds 4 and 5: Repeat Rnds 2 and 3 changing to Color A at end of Rnd 5 *(Fig. 24b, page 138)*.

Rnd 6: Ch 1, turn; sc in each st around; join with slip st to first sc.

Rnd 7: Ch 1, turn; sc in first sc, tr in next sc, (sc in next sc pushing tr to right side, tr in next sc) around; join with slip st to first sc.

Rnd 8: Ch 1, turn; sc in each st around; join with slip st to first sc changing to MC.

Rnds 9 and 10: Ch 1, turn; sc in each sc around; join with slip st to first sc.

Rnd 11: Ch 1, turn; sc in first 6 sc changing to Color B in last sc worked, do **not** cut MC, ★ † sc in next sc, ch 10, slip st in tenth ch from hook, (ch 9, slip st in same ch) twice changing to MC in last st worked †, sc in next 11 sc changing to Color B in last sc worked, do **not** cut MC; repeat from ★ once **more**, then repeat from † to † once, sc in last 5 sc; join with slip st to first sc: 9 loops.

Rnds 12-14: Ch 1, turn; holding loops to **right** side, sc in each sc around; join with slip st to first sc: 36 sc.

Rnd 15: Ch 1, turn; sc in first 3 sc, ★ † holding next loop in front of next sc, sc in both loop **and** in sc, sc in next 5 sc, skip next loop, holding next loop in front of next sc, sc in both loop **and** in sc †, sc in next 5 sc; repeat from ★ once **more**, then repeat from † to † once, sc in last 2 sc; join with slip st to first sc.

Rnds 16-18: Ch 1, turn; sc in each sc around; join with slip st to first sc.

Rnd 19: Ch 1, turn; sc in first 6 sc changing to Color A in last sc worked, do **not** cut MC, ★ † dc in center loop, (ch 3, slip st in last dc worked, dc in same loop) 4 times changing to MC in last dc worked, skip next sc †, sc in next 11 sc changing to Color A in last sc worked, do **not** cut MC; repeat from ★ once **more**, then repeat from † to † once, sc in last 5 sc; join with slip st to first sc: 3 flowers.

Rnd 20: Ch 1, turn; sc in first 6 sc, ch 1, skip next flower, (sc in next 11 sc, ch 1, skip next flower) twice, sc in last 5 sc; join with slip st to first sc: 33 sc.

Rnd 21: Ch 1, turn; sc in first 6 sc, holding flower in front of next ch-1 sp, sc in both Back Loop Only of center dc **and** in ch-1 sp *(Fig. 22, page 138)*, ★ sc in next 11 sc, holding flower in front of next ch-1 sp, sc in both Back Loop Only of center dc **and** in ch-1 sp; repeat from ★ once **more**, sc in last 5 sc; join with slip st to first sc: 36 sc.

Rnds 22 and 23: Ch 1, turn; sc in each sc around; join with slip st to first sc changing to Color A at end of Rnd 23.

Rnds 24-26: Repeat Rnds 6-8.

Rnd 27: Ch 3, turn; dc in next sc and in each sc around; join with slip st to first dc.

Rnds 28-31: Repeat Rnds 2-5.

Rnd 32: Ch 1, do **not** turn; sc in each dc around; join with slip st to Front Loop Only of first sc.

Rnd 33: Ch 6, turn; dc in fourth ch from hook, working in Back Loops Only, (decrease, ch 4, dc in top of decrease) around to last sc, dc in same st as last decrease, skip last sc; join with slip st to second ch of beginning ch-6, finish off.

Rnd 34: With **right** side facing, holding Rnd 33 forward, and working in free loops of Rnd 32 *(Fig. 23a, page 138)*, join Color A with slip st in first sc; ch 6, dc in fourth ch from hook, (decrease, ch 4, dc in top of decease) around to last sc, dc in same st as last decrease; join with slip st to second ch of beginning ch-6, finish off.

Weave ribbon through dc on Rnd 31 and tie in a bow.

fashion corner

Wake up your wardrobe with these stylish crocheted wearables. From a light spring cardigan for her or a cozy winter sweater for him to fanciful footwear for children, there's something to brighten everyone's day. This crocheted collection makes a fashion forecast for fun!

DELICATE CARDIGAN

Make a statement for style when you wear this feminine cardigan! The airy cover-up — designed for small, medium, and large sizes — uses clusters to create its delicate motifs. Stitched in neutral with cotton thread, it can be worn during any season.

Size:	Small	Medium	Large
Finished Chest			
Measurement:	36"	42"	48"

Size Note: Instructions are written for size Small with sizes Medium and Large in braces. Instructions will be easier to read if you circle all the numbers pertaining to your size.

MATERIALS

Cotton Crochet Thread (size 5), approximately:
    24{27-29} ounces, [680{770-820} grams,
      2,060{2,315-2,485} yards]
Crochet hook, size E (3.50 mm) **or** size needed for gauge
5 - ³/₈" buttons
Sewing needle and thread

GAUGE: Rnds 1 and 2 of Motif (Flower) = 1³/₄"
      One Motif slightly stretched = 3"

PATTERN STITCHES
BEGINNING CLUSTER
Ch 2, ★ YO, insert hook in same sp, YO and pull up a loop, YO and draw through 2 loops on hook; repeat from ★ once **more**, YO and draw through all 3 loops on hook *(Figs. 10a & b, page 134).*

CLUSTER
★ YO, insert hook in sp indicated, YO and pull up a loop, YO and draw through 2 loops on hook; repeat from ★ 2 times **more**, YO and draw through all 4 loops on hook.
SCALLOP
Slip st in st indicated, ch 3, 2 dc in same st.

MOTIF [Make 134{154-164}]

Ch 6; join with slip st to form a ring.
Rnd 1 (Right side)**:** Ch 6, (dc in ring, ch 3) 7 times; join with slip st to third ch of beginning ch-6: 8 ch-3 sps.
Note: Loop a short piece of thread around any stitch to mark last round as **right** side.
Rnd 2: Slip st in first ch-3 sp, (ch 1, sc, ch 2, 3 dc, ch 2, sc) in same sp and in each ch-3 sp around, sc in first sc to form last sp: 8 Petals.
Rnd 3: Ch 1, sc in same sp, ch 5, (sc in next ch-1 sp between Petals, ch 5) around; join with slip st to first sc: 8 loops.
Rnd 4: Slip st in first loop, work (beginning Cluster, ch 3, Cluster) in same sp, ch 5, sc in next loop, ch 5, ★ work (Cluster, ch 3, Cluster) in next loop, ch 5, sc in next loop, ch 5; repeat from ★ around; join with slip st to top of beginning Cluster.

Rnds 5 and 6: Slip st in first ch-3 sp, work (beginning Cluster, ch 3, Cluster) in same sp, ch 5, ★ (sc in next loop, ch 5) across to next ch-3 sp, work (Cluster, ch 3, Cluster) in ch-3 sp, ch 5; repeat from ★ 2 times **more**, (sc in next loop, ch 5) across; join with slip st to top of beginning Cluster. Finish off.

HALF MOTIF [Make 6{2-6}]

Ch 4; join with slip st to form a ring.

Row 1: Ch 6, dc in ring, (ch 3, dc in ring) 4 times: 5 sps.

Row 2 (Right side)**:** Turn; slip st in first ch-3 sp, (ch 1, sc, ch 2, 3 dc, ch 2, sc) in same sp and in each sp across: 5 Petals.

Note: Mark last row as **right** side.

Row 3: Ch 1, turn; sc in first sc, ch 5, (sc in next ch-1 sp between Petals, ch 5) across, sc in last sc: 5 loops.

Row 4: Turn; slip st in first loop, work (beginning Cluster, ch 3, Cluster) in same loop, ★ ch 5, sc in next loop, ch 5, work (Cluster, ch 3, Cluster) in next loop; repeat from ★ once **more**.

Rows 5 and 6: Turn; slip st in first ch-3 sp, work (beginning Cluster, ch 3, Cluster) in same sp, ★ ch 5, (sc in next loop, ch 5) across to next ch-3 sp, work (Cluster, ch 3, Cluster) in ch-3 sp; repeat from ★ once **more**. Finish off.

ASSEMBLY

Using Placement Diagram as a guide, join Motifs and Half Motifs together forming strips, then join strips, leaving edges of Motifs along dotted lines unjoined.

Join Motifs as follows:

With **right** sides together and working through **both** pieces, join thread with slip st in corner ch-3 sp; ch 1, sc in same sp, ch 4, (sc in next loop, ch 4) across to next corner ch-3 sp, sc in corner ch-3 sp; finish off.

Join strips as follows:

With **right** sides together and working through **both** pieces, join thread with slip st in corner ch-3 sp; ch 1, sc in same sp, ch 4, (sc in next loop, ch 4) across to next corner ch-3 sp, sc in corner ch-3 sp, ★ ch 1, sc in corner ch-3 sp of next Motif, ch 4, (sc in next loop, ch 4) across to next corner ch-3 sp, sc in corner ch-3 sp; repeat from ★ across; finish off.

Small and Large Sizes Only

Join underarm and side seams in same manner as joining strips.

Medium Size Only

Beginning at bottom edge, join Front to Back at side, in the same manner as joining strips. Join underarm from wrist to center of sixth Motif, then join top of last Motif to Sleeve.

Repeat for second side.

96

PLACEMENT DIAGRAMS

Small

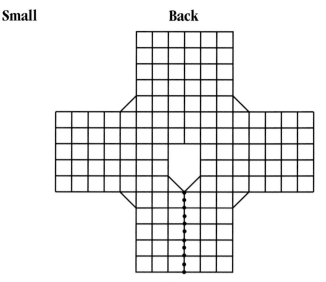

Medium

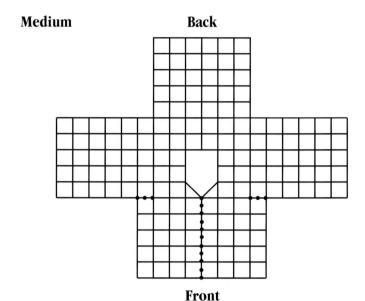

Large

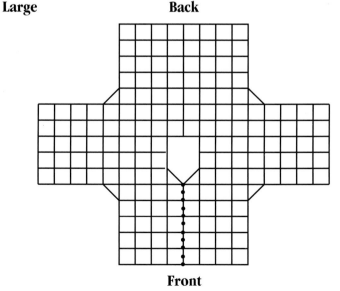

Continued on page 98.

~Quick~ FEMININE SCARF

*Welcome chilly weather with this classy mini muffler! Worked in shell stitches to create
its familiar pineapple pattern, the toasty neck-warmer makes a chic accent. It's fast
to finish, so you can make several to coordinate with all of your outerwear.*

Finished Size: Approximately 5" x 32"

MATERIALS
  Sport Weight Yarn, approximately:
    1¼ ounces, (35 grams, 120 yards)
  Crochet hook, size H (5.00 mm) **or** size needed for gauge

GAUGE: Rows 1-9 = 5"

PATTERN STITCHES
BEGINNING SHELL
Ch 3 **(counts as first dc, now and throughout)**,
(dc, ch 1, 2 dc) in same sp.
SHELL
(2 Dc, ch 1, 2 dc) in sp indicated.
PICOT
Ch 3, slip st in third ch from hook.

FIRST HALF
Ch 17 **loosely**.
Row 1: Sc in second ch from hook, (ch 3, skip next 2 chs, sc
in next ch) across: 5 ch-3 sps.
Row 2 (Right side): Turn; slip st in first ch-3 sp, work
beginning Shell, ch 1, skip next ch-3 sp, 6 tr in next ch-3 sp,
ch 1, skip next ch-3 sp, work Shell in last ch-3 sp.
Note: Loop a short piece of yarn around any stitch to mark last
row as **right** side.
Row 3: Turn; slip st in first 2 dc and in next ch-1 sp, work
beginning Shell, ch 1, sc in next tr, (ch 3, sc in next tr) 5 times,
ch 1, work Shell in next Shell (ch-1 sp).
Row 4: Turn; slip st in first 2 dc and in next ch-1 sp, work
beginning Shell, ch 1, sc in next ch-3 sp, (ch 3, sc in next
ch-3 sp) 4 times, ch 1, work Shell in next Shell.

Row 5: Turn; slip st in first 2 dc and in next ch-1 sp, work beginning Shell, ch 2, sc in next ch-3 sp, (ch 3, sc in next ch-3 sp) 3 times, ch 2, work Shell in next Shell.

Row 6: Turn; slip st in first 2 dc and in next ch-1 sp, work beginning Shell, ch 2, sc in next ch-3 sp, (ch 3, sc in next ch-3 sp) twice, ch 2, work Shell in next Shell.

Row 7: Turn; slip st in first 2 dc and in next ch-1 sp, work beginning Shell, ch 3, (sc in next ch-3 sp, ch 3) twice, work Shell in next Shell.

Row 8: Turn; slip st in first 2 dc and in next ch-1 sp, work beginning Shell, ch 4, skip next ch-3 sp, sc in next ch-3 sp, ch 4, work Shell in next Shell.

Row 9: Turn; slip st in first 2 dc and in next ch-1 sp, work beginning Shell, ch 3, skip next 2 ch-4 sps, work Shell in next Shell.

Row 10: Turn; slip st in first 2 dc and in next ch-1 sp, work beginning Shell, ch 1, 6 tr in next ch-3 sp, ch 1, work Shell in next Shell.

Rows 11-25: Repeat Rows 3-10 once, then repeat Rows 3-9 once **more**.

Row 26: Turn; slip st in first 2 dc and in next ch-1 sp, work beginning Shell, skip next ch-3 sp, work Shell in next Shell.

Row 27: Turn; slip st in first 2 dc and in next ch-1 sp, ch 3, slip st in next Shell.

Row 28: Turn; slip st in ch-3 sp, work beginning Shell, finish off.

SECOND HALF

Row 1: With **right** side facing and working over beginning ch, join yarn with slip st in first ch-3 sp; work beginning Shell in same sp, ch 1, skip next ch-3 sp, 6 tr in next ch-3 sp, ch 1, skip next ch-3 sp, work Shell in last ch-3 sp.

Rows 2-24: Work same as First Half, Rows 3-10 twice, then repeat Rows 3-9 once **more**.

Rows 25-27: Work same as First Half, Rows 26-28.

EDGING

With **right** side facing, join yarn with slip st in first dc on either point; ch 1, sc in same st, work Picot, ★ skip next dc, sc in next ch-1 sp, work Picot 3 times, sc in same sp, work Picot, skip next dc, sc in next dc, work Picot; working in end of rows, (sc in top of next dc, work Picot) across to beginning ch-3 sp, (sc, work Picot) twice in ch-3 sp, (sc in top of next dc, work Picot) across; repeat from ★ once **more**; join with slip st to first sc, finish off.

DELICATE CARDIGAN

Continued from page 96.

EDGING

Rnd 1: With **right** side facing, join thread with slip st in corner ch-3 sp of bottom left front; ch 1, 3 sc in same sp, sc in next Cluster, 3 sc in next loop, (sc in next sc, 3 sc in next loop) 3 times, sc in next Cluster, ★ sc in next 2 ch-3 sps, sc in next Cluster, 3 sc in next loop, (sc in next sc, 3 sc in next loop) 3 times, sc in next Cluster; repeat from ★ across to next corner ch-3 sp, 3 sc in corner ch-3 sp, † sc in next Cluster, 3 sc in next loop, (sc in next sc, 3 sc in next loop) 3 times, sc in next Cluster, sc in next 2 ch-3 sps †, repeat from † to † across to next Half Motif, sc in next Cluster, work 25 sc evenly spaced across end of rows, sc in next Cluster, sc in next 3 ch-3 sps, (repeat from † to † twice, sc in next ch-3 sp) 3 times, sc in next Cluster, work 25 sc evenly spaced across end of rows, sc in next Cluster, sc in next 2 ch-3 sps, repeat from † to † 4 times, sc in next Cluster, 3 sc in next loop, (sc in next sc, 3 sc in next loop) 3 times, sc in next Cluster; join with slip st to first sc: 596{634-672} sc.

Rnd 2: Ch 1, sc in first sc, 2 sc in next sc, sc in each sc across bottom edge to next corner sc, 2{3-2} sc in corner sc, sc in next 17 sc, ch 3 (buttonhole), skip next 3 sc, (sc in next 16 sc, ch 3, skip next 3 sc) 4 times, sc in next sc, 3 sc in next sc, sc in next 174 sc, 3 sc in next sc, sc in each sc across; join with slip st to first sc: 587{626-663} sc.

Rnd 3: Ch 3, 2 dc in same st, (skip next 2 sc, work Scallop in next sc) across to first buttonhole, skip next ch-3 sp, ★ work Scallop in next sc, (skip next 2 sc, work Scallop in next sc) 5 times, skip next ch-3 sp; repeat from ★ 3 times **more**, (work Scallop in next sc, skip next 2 sc) across; join with slip st to base of beginning ch-3, finish off: 199{212-225} Scallops.

CUFF

Rnd 1: With **right** side facing, join thread with slip st in ch-3 sp to **right** of any joining on Sleeve; ch 1, sc in same sp and in next ch-3 sp, 3 sc in each of next 4 loops, (sc in next 2 ch-3 sps, 3 sc in each of next 4 loops) around; join with slip st to first sc: 70 sc.

Rnds 2 and 3: Ch 1, 2 sc in first sc, sc next sc and in each sc around; join with slip st to first sc: 72 sc.

Rnd 4: Ch 3, 2 dc in same st, skip next 2 sc, (work Scallop in next sc, skip next 2 sc) around; join with slip st to base of beginning ch-3, finish off: 24 Scallops.

Repeat for second Cuff.

Sew buttons opposite buttonholes.

HIS-AND-HERS PULLOVERS

*Make one to share and one to wear when you stitch these pullovers for him or her.
Cozy additions to a cool-weather wardrobe, they're fashioned with worsted weight
yarn and finished with classic ribbing. Instructions are given for sizes 32 to 46.*

Size:	32	34	36	38	40	42	44	46
Finished Chest								
Measurement:	36"	38"	40"	42"	44"	46"	48"	50"

Size Note: Instructions are written for sizes 32, 34, 36, and 38
in first braces with sizes 40, 42, 44 and 46 in second braces.
Instructions will be easier to read if you circle all the numbers
pertaining to your size.

MATERIALS
Worsted Weight Yarn, approximately:
{21-22-23-24}{25-26-28-29} ounces,
[{600-620-650-680}{710-740-800-820} grams,
{1,380-1,445-1,510-1,575}
{1,640-1,705-1,840-1,905} yards]
Crochet hook, size I (5.50 mm) **or** size needed for gauge
Yarn needle

GAUGE: In pattern, 14 sts and 10 rows = 4"

PATTERN STITCH
DECREASE
★ YO, insert hook in **next** sc, YO and pull up a loop, YO and draw through 2 loops on hook; repeat from ★ once **more**, YO and draw through all 3 loops on hook **(counts as one dc)**.

BACK

Ch {65-69-73-75}{79-83-87-89} sts **loosely**.

Row 1 (Right side)**:** Dc in fourth ch from hook and in each ch across: {63-67-71-73}{77-81-85-87} sts.

Note: Loop a short piece of yarn around any stitch to mark last row as **right** side.

Row 2: Ch 1, turn; sc in first dc, dc in next dc, (slip st in next dc, dc in next dc) across to last st, sc in last st.

Row 3: Ch 3 **(counts as first dc, now and throughout)**, turn; [YO, insert hook in same st, YO and pull up a loop, YO and draw through 2 loops on hook, YO, insert hook in next dc, YO and pull up a loop, YO and draw through 2 loops on hook, YO and draw through all 3 loops on hook **(counts as one dc)**], dc in next st and in each st across.

Repeat Rows 2 and 3 for pattern until Back measures approximately {21-21½-22-22½}{23-23½-24-24½}", ending by working a **wrong** side row.

RIGHT NECK SHAPING

Row 1: Work in pattern across {19-21-23-23}{25-27-29-29} sts, leave remaining sts unworked.

Rows 2-4: Work across in pattern.
Finish off.

LEFT NECK SHAPING

Row 1: With **right** side facing, skip {25-25-25-27}{27-27-27-29} sts from Right Neck Shaping and join yarn with slip st in next st; work across in pattern: {19-21-23-23}{25-27-29-29} sts.

Rows 2-4: Work across in pattern.
Finish off.

FRONT

Work same as Back until Front measures approximately {19½-20-20½-21}{21½-22-22½-23}", ending by working a **wrong** side row.

LEFT NECK SHAPING

Row 1: Work in pattern across {19-21-23-23}{25-27-29-29} sts, leave remaining sts unworked.

Rows 2-8: Work across in pattern.
Finish off.

RIGHT NECK SHAPING

Row 1: With **right** side facing, skip {25-25-25-27}{27-27-27-29} sts from Left Neck Shaping and join yarn with slip st in next st; work across in pattern: {19-21-23-23}{25-27-29-29} sts.

Rows 2-8: Work across in pattern.
Finish off.

SLEEVE (Make 2)

Ch {39-39-41-41}{43-43-45-45} sts **loosely**.

Row 1 (Right side)**:** Dc in fourth ch from hook and in each ch across: {37-37-39-39}{41-41-43-43} sts.

Note: Mark last row as **right** side.

Row 2: Ch 1, turn; sc in first dc, dc in next dc, (slip st in next dc, dc in next dc) across to last st, sc in last st.

Row 3 (Increase row)**:** Ch 3, dc in same st and in each st across to last sc, 2 dc in last sc: {39-39-41-41}{43-43-45-45} sts.

Repeat Rows 2 and 3, {15-15-16-16}{16-16-17-17} times: {69-69-73-73}{75-75-79-79} sts.

Work even until Sleeve measures approximately {15¼-15¼-16¼-16¼}{16¼-16¼-16¾-16¾}", ending by working a **wrong** side row; finish off.

FINISHING

Whipstitch shoulder seams *(Fig. 28a, page 140)*.
Whipstitch Sleeves to Pullover, matching center of Sleeve to shoulder seam and beginning {10-10-10½-10½}{10¾-10¾-11¼-11¼}" down from shoulder seam.
Whipstitch underarm and side in one continuous seam.

BOTTOM RIBBING

Rnd 1: With **right** side facing and working in free loops of beginning ch *(Fig. 23b, page 138)*, join yarn with slip st in first ch on Back; ch 1, sc in same st and in each ch around; join with slip st to first sc: {126-134-142-146}{154-162-170-174} sc.

Rnd 2: Ch 3, dc in next sc and in each sc around; join with slip st to first dc.

Rnds 3-5: Ch 3, work FPdc around next st *(Fig. 16, page 136)*, ★ work BPdc around next st *(Fig. 17, page 136)*, work FPdc around next st; repeat from ★ around; join with slip st to first dc. Finish off.

SLEEVE RIBBING

Rnd 1: With **right** side facing and working in free loops of beginning ch, join yarn with slip st in first ch; ch 1, work {36-36-39-39}{39-39-42-42} sc evenly spaced around; join with slip st to first sc.

Rnd 2: Ch 2, dc in next 2 sc, (decrease, dc in next sc) around; skip beginning ch-2 and join with slip st to first dc: {24-24-26-26}{26-26-28-28} dc.

Rnds 3-5: Work same as Bottom Ribbing.
Finish off.

NECK RIBBING

Rnd 1: With **right** side facing, join yarn with slip st at right shoulder seam; ch 1, work 3 sc evenly spaced across end of rows, place marker, work {23-23-23-25}{25-25-25-27} sc evenly spaced across Back, place marker, work 11 sc evenly spaced across end of rows, place marker, work {23-23-23-25}{25-25-25-27} sc evenly spaced across Front, place marker, work 8 sc evenly spaced across end of rows; join with slip st to first sc: {68-68-68-72}{72-72-72-76} sc.

Rnd 2: Ch 3, (dc in each sc across to within one st of marker, decrease) 4 times, dc in each sc across; join with slip st to first dc: {64-64-64-68}{68-68-68-72} dc.

Rnds 3-5: Work same as Bottom Ribbing.

Finish off.

Quick SLIPPERS FOR KIDS

Easy to stitch, these sassy slippers for kids are as much fun to wear as they are to make! Pom-poms and long single and double crochets worked in black create a bold accent on the booties. Soft and comfortable, they're made of long-wearing worsted weight yarn.

Size:	Small	Medium	Large
Sole length:	6¹/₂"	7"	7¹/₂"

Size Note: Instructions are written for size Small with sizes Medium and Large in braces. Instructions will be easier to read if you circle all the numbers pertaining to your size. If only one number is given, it applies to all sizes.

MATERIALS

Worsted Weight Yarn, approximately:
  MC (Red) - 3{3¹/₂-4} ounces,
    [90{100-110} grams, 170{200-225} yards]
  CC (Black) - 40 yards
Crochet hook, size G (4.00 mm) **or** size needed for gauge
Yarn needle

PATTERN STITCHES

DECREASE

Pull up a loop in next 2 sts, YO and draw through all 3 loops on hook **(counts as one sc)**.

LONG DOUBLE CROCHET (abbreviated Long dc)

YO, insert hook in st on row below next st, YO and pull up a loop **even** with loop on hook **(Fig. 5, page 133)**, (YO and draw through 2 loops on hook) twice.

LONG SINGLE CROCHET (abbreviated Long sc)

Insert hook in st on row below next st, YO and pull up a loop **even** with loop on hook, YO and draw through both loops on hook.

SOLE

Holding 2 strands of MC together, ch 16{18-21} **loosely**.

Rnd 1 (Right side): 3 Sc in second ch from hook, sc in each ch across to last ch, 3 sc in last ch; working in free loops of beginning ch **(Fig. 23b, page 138)**, sc in each ch across; join with slip st to first sc: 32{36-42} sc.

Note: Loop a short piece of yarn around any stitch to mark last round as **right** side.

Rnd 2: Ch 1, turn; sc in next 7{7-8} sc, hdc in next 5{7-9} sc, 2 hdc in each of next 5 sc, hdc in next 5{7-9} sc, sc in next 7{7-8} sc, 2 sc in each of last 3 sc; join with slip st to first sc: 40{44-50} sts.

Rnd 3: Ch 1, turn; 2 sc in each of next 5 sc, sc in next 8{8-9} sc, hdc in next 7{9-11} hdc, 2 hdc in each of next 5 hdc, hdc in next 7{9-11} hdc, sc in last 8{8-9} sts; join with slip st to first sc: 50{54-60} sts.

Rnd 4: Ch 1, turn; sc in next 8 sc, hdc in next 10{11-14} hdc, 2 hdc in each of next 3{5-5} hdc, hdc in next 10{11-14} hdc, sc in next 12{12-11} sts, 2 sc in each of next 3{4-5} sc, sc in last 4{3-3} sc; finish off: 56{63-70} sts.

TOP

Rnd 1: With **right** side facing and working in Back Loops Only **(Fig. 22, page 138)**, join 1 strand of MC with slip st in center back sc; ch 2 **(counts as first hdc, now and throughout)**, hdc in next sc and in each st around; join with slip st to first hdc.

Rnd 2: Ch 2, do **not** turn; working in both loops, hdc in next hdc and in each hdc around; join with slip st to first hdc, finish off.

Rnd 3: With **right** side facing, join 1 strand of CC with slip st in same st as joining; ch 1, sc in same st and in next 2 hdc, work Long dc, sc in next 2 hdc, work Long sc, ★ sc in next 3 hdc, work Long dc, sc in next 2 hdc, work Long sc; repeat from ★ around; join with slip st to first sc, finish off.

Rnd 4: With **right** side facing, join 1 strand of MC with slip st in Back Loop Only of first sc; ch 2, hdc in Back Loop Only of next 2 sc, hdc in **both** loops of next st, hdc in Back Loop Only of next 2 sc, hdc in **both** loops of next st, ★ hdc in Back Loop Only of next 3 sc, hdc in **both** loops of next st, hdc in Back Loop Only of next 2 sc, hdc in **both** loops of next st; repeat from ★ around; join with slip st to first hdc.

Rnd 5: Ch 2, working in both loops, hdc in next hdc and in each hdc around; join with slip st to first hdc.

Rnd 6: Ch 2, hdc in next 25{28-33} hdc, decrease 5 times, hdc in each hdc around; join with slip st to first hdc: 51{58-65} sts.

Rnd 7: Ch 2, hdc in next 23{26-31} hdc, decrease 5 times, hdc in each hdc around; join with slip st to first hdc: 46{53-60} sts.

Rnd 8: Ch 2, hdc in next 11{13-13} hdc, dc in next 5{6-7} hdc, hdc in next 7{7-11} hdc, decrease 3 times, hdc in next 7{7-10} hdc, dc in next 5{6-7} hdc, hdc in each hdc around; join with slip st to first hdc: 43{50-57} sts.

Rnd 9: Ch 2, hdc in next 15{18-20} sts, 2 dc in next dc, skip next 17{17-24} sts, 2 dc in next dc, hdc in each st around; join with slip st to first hdc, finish off: 28{35-35} sts.

TRIM

Rnd 1: With **right** side facing, join 1 strand of CC with slip st in center back hdc; ch 1, sc in same st and in next 2 hdc, work Long dc, sc in next 2 sts, work Long sc, ★ sc in next 3 sts, work Long dc, sc in next 2 sts, work Long sc; repeat from ★ around; join with slip st to first sc.

Rnd 2: Ch 1, sc in each st around; join with slip st to Front Loop Only of first sc.

Rnd 3: Ch 3, turn; (slip st in Back Loop Only of next sc, ch 3) around; join with slip st to base of first slip st.

Rnd 4: Turn; working in free loops on Rnd 2 **(Fig. 23a, page 138)**, slip st in each st around; join with slip st to first slip st, finish off.

Sew seam.

With CC, make two 1¹/₂" pom-poms **(Figs. 29a & b, page 140)** and attach to Slippers.

~~Quick~~ TULIP GARDEN SWEATSHIRT

A garden of pretty tulips blooms on this cozy crewneck that's just right for early spring weather. It's created by inserting a panel of crocheted flowers in the front of a sweatshirt and adding single crochet ribbing along the neck, sleeves, and bottom.

MATERIALS

Worsted Weight Yarn, approximately:
   6 ounces, (170 grams, 405 yards) (for size Medium)
Crochet hooks, sizes E (3.50 mm) **and** G (4.00 mm) **or**
   sizes needed for gauge
Adult sweatshirt
Seam ripper
Tape measure
Yarn needle
Erasable marking pen
Straight pins
Sewing needle and thread
Sewing machine

GAUGE: With larger size hook, 8 sts = 2"
        Panel = 5^1/$_4$" wide

SWEATSHIRT PREPARATION

Use seam ripper to remove ribbing from bottom, neck, and sleeves of sweatshirt. Try on sweatshirt. Crocheted Sleeve Ribbing will extend approximately 2³/₄" below edge of sleeve and Bottom Ribbing will extend approximately 3¹/₄" below edge of body. If sleeves and body will be too long, determine desired length of body and sleeves, and place a pin to mark each length.

PATTERN STITCHES

FRONT POST DOUBLE CROCHET *(abbreviated FPdc)*
YO, insert hook from **front** to **back** around post of st indicated *(Fig. 13, page 135)*, YO and pull up a loop **even** with loop on hook, (YO and draw through 2 loops on hook) twice. Skip st behind FPdc.

DECREASE
Pull up a loop in each of next 2 dc, YO and draw through all 3 loops on hook (**counts as one sc**).

PANEL

With larger size hook, ch 22 **loosely**.

Row 1 (Right side)**:** Sc in second ch from hook and in each ch across: 21 sc.

Note: Loop a short piece of yarn around any stitch to mark last row as **right** side.

Row 2: Ch 2, turn; dc in first 11 sts, (ch 10, dc) 3 times in same st as last dc, dc in last 10 sts: 24 dc.

Row 3: Ch 1, turn; sc in first 2 dc, work FPdc around st in row **below** next dc, sc in next dc, work FPdc around st in row **below** next dc, sc in next 4 dc, decrease 3 times working **behind** ch-10 loops, sc in next 4 dc, work FPdc around st in row **below** next dc, sc in next dc, work FPdc around st in row **below** next dc, sc in last 2 dc, leave turning ch unworked (**now and throughout**): 21 sts.

Row 4: Ch 2, turn; dc in each st across.

Row 5: Ch 1, turn; sc in first 2 dc, work FPdc around FPdc below next dc, sc in next dc, work FPdc around FPdc below next dc, sc in next 2 dc, holding next loop in front of next dc, sc in both loop **and** in next dc, sc in next 5 dc, skip next loop, holding next loop in front of next dc, sc in both loop **and** in next dc, sc in next 2 dc, work FPdc around FPdc below next dc, sc in next dc, work FPdc around FPdc below next dc, sc in last 2 dc.

Row 6: Ch 2, turn; dc in each st across.

Row 7: Ch 1, turn; sc in first 2 dc, work FPdc around FPdc below next dc, sc in next dc, work FPdc around FPdc below next dc, sc in next 5 dc, holding center loop in front of next dc, 6 dc in both loop **and** in next dc, drop loop from hook, insert hook in first dc of 6-dc group, hook dropped loop and draw through, ch 1 to close, sc in next 5 dc, work FPdc around FPdc below next dc, sc in next dc, work FPdc around FPdc below next dc, sc in last 2 dc.

Row 8: Ch 2, turn; dc in first 10 sts, dc in next ch, dc in last 10 sts.

Row 9: Ch 1, turn; sc in first 2 dc, work FPdc around FPdc below next dc, sc in next dc, work FPdc around FPdc below next dc, sc in next 11 dc, work FPdc around FPdc below next dc, sc in next dc, work FPdc around FPdc below next dc, sc in last 2 dc.

Repeat Rows 2-9 until Panel measures approximately same as determined length of sweatshirt front, ending by working Row 9; finish off. Adjust length of sweatshirt if needed.

ASSEMBLY

1. Lay sweatshirt flat; draw lines across sweatshirt bottom and sleeves at determined lengths, adding ¼" for seam allowances.
2. Cut sweatshirt bottom and sleeves off at drawn lines.
3. Cut strip from center front of sweatshirt, ½" less than width of Panel.
4. Zigzag stitch **all** raw edges.
5. With right sides together, sew Panel to sweatshirt using a ¼" seam.

SLEEVE RIBBING (Make 2)

With smaller size hook, ch 14 **loosely**.

Row 1 (Right side)**:** Sc in second ch from hook and in each ch across: 13 sc.

Note: Mark last row as **right** side.

Row 2: Ch 1, turn; sc in Back Loop Only of each sc across *(Fig. 22, page 138)*; do **not** finish off.

On **right** side of sweatshirt, measure around sleeve opening. Multiply this measurement by .667. Repeat Row 2 until Ribbing is approximately the same length as determined measurement, ending by working a **wrong** side row.

Joining Row: With **right** sides together and working in Back Loops Only of last row **and** in free loops of beginning ch *(Fig. 23b, page 138)*, slip st in each st across; finish off.

BOTTOM RIBBING

With smaller size hook, ch 16 **loosely**.

Row 1 (Right side)**:** Sc in second ch from hook and in each ch across: 15 sc.

Note: Mark last row as **right** side.

Row 2: Ch 1, turn; sc in Back Loop Only of each sc across; do **not** finish off.

On **right** side of sweatshirt, measure around bottom opening. Multiply this measurement by .667. Repeat Row 2 until Ribbing is approximately the same length as determined measurement, ending by working a **wrong** side row.

Joining Row: With **right** sides together and working in Back Loops Only of sc on last row **and** in free loops of beginning ch, slip st in each st across; finish off.

Continued on page 107.

TOPS FOR TODDLERS

*T*oddlers will look precious in these pullovers for girls or boys. Splashed with color, the sweaters have rich texture that's created using treble crochet clusters. They're stitched in baby fingering weight yarn for softness next to a little one's sensitive skin.

Size:	2	4	6
Finished Chest			
Measurement:	25"	27"	29"

Size Note: Instructions are written for size 2 with sizes 4 and 6 in braces. Instructions will be easier to read if you circle all the numbers pertaining to your size.

MATERIALS

Baby Fingering Weight Yarn, approximately:

2-Color

MC (Navy) - 6{7-8} ounces,
[170{200-230} grams, 860{1,000-1,145} yards]

CC (Red) - 1¼{1½-1¾} ounces,
[35{40-50} grams, 180{215-250} yards]

4-Color

MC (Light Blue) - 4{5-5½} ounces,
[110{140-160} grams, 570{715-785} yards]

Color A (White) - ¾{1-1} ounce,
[20{30-30} grams, 110{145-145} yards]

Color B (Red) - 1½{1¾-2} ounces,
[40{50-60} grams, 215{250-285} yards]

Color C (Navy) - 1{1¼-1½} ounces,
[30{35-40} grams, 145{180-215} yards]

Crochet hooks, sizes C (2.75 mm) **and** D (3.25 mm) **or** sizes needed for gauge

Yarn needle

GAUGE: With larger size hook, in pattern,
(ch 2, tr) 4 times = 2" and 8 rows = 1¾"

PATTERN STITCHES

TR CLUSTER

★ YO twice, insert hook in st or sp indicated, YO and pull up a loop, (YO and draw through 2 loops on hook) twice; repeat from ★ once **more**, YO and draw through all 3 loops on hook *(Figs. 10a & b, page 134)*.

DC CLUSTER

★ YO, insert hook in sp indicated, YO and pull up a loop, YO and draw through 2 loops on hook; repeat from ★ once **more**, YO and draw through all 3 loops on hook.

Note: Instructions are written for 2-Colored Pullover. If making the 4-Colored Pullover, work all Ribbings with Color B; at end of Ribbing, change to next color *(Fig. 24a, page 138)*. Work Body of Back and Right Sleeve with MC. Work Body of Front with MC and Color A. Work Body of Left Sleeve with Color C.

BACK

RIBBING

With smaller size hook and MC, ch 15 **loosely**.

Row 1: Sc in second ch from hook and in each ch across: 14 sc.

Row 2: Ch 1, turn; sc in Back Loop Only of each sc across *(Fig. 22, page 138)*.

Repeat Row 2 until 38{41-44} ribs [76{82-88} rows] are complete; do **not** finish off.

BODY

Change to larger size hook.

Row 1 (Right side)**:** Ch 1, work 76{82-88} sc evenly spaced across end of rows.

Note: Loop a short piece of yarn around any stitch to mark last row as **right** side.

Row 2: Ch 6 **(counts as first tr plus ch 2, now and throughout)**, turn; skip next 2 sc, tr in next sc, (ch 2, skip next 2 sc, tr in next sc) across: 25{27-29} ch-2 sps.

Row 3: Ch 1, turn; sc in first tr, ★ working **behind** next ch-2 sp, work tr Cluster in each of next 2 skipped sc on row **below**, sc in next tr; repeat from ★ across: 50{54-58} tr Clusters.

Row 4: Ch 6, turn; skip next 2 sts, tr in next sc, (ch 2, skip next 2 sts, tr in next sc) across: 25{27-29} ch-2 sps.

Row 5: Ch 1, turn; sc in first tr, ★ working **behind** next ch-2 sp, work 2 tr Clusters in ch-2 sp **below**, sc in next tr; repeat from ★ across: 50{54-58} tr Clusters.

Repeat Rows 4 and 5 for pattern, 21{23-25} times; do **not** finish off.

LEFT NECK SHAPING

Row 1: Ch 6, turn; skip next 2 sts, tr in next sc, (ch 2, skip next 2 sts, tr in next sc) 7{8-9} times, ch 3, skip next 2 sts, slip st in next sc, leave remaining sts unworked: 9{10-11} sps.

Row 2: Ch 1, turn; working **behind** first ch-3 sp, work (dc Cluster, tr Cluster) in ch-2 sp **below**, sc in next tr, ★ working **behind** next ch-2 sp, work 2 tr Clusters in ch-2 sp **below**, sc in next tr; repeat from ★ across: 18{20-22} Clusters.

Row 3: Ch 6, turn; skip next 2 sts, tr in next sc, ★ ch 2, skip next 2 sts, tr in next sc; repeat from ★ across to last sc, ch 3, slip st in last sc: 8{9-10} sps.

Row 4: Repeat Row 2; finish off: 16{18-20} Clusters.

RIGHT NECK SHAPING

Row 1: With **wrong** side facing, skip 6 sc from Left Neck Shaping and join MC with slip st in next sc; ch 3, skip next 2 sts, tr in next sc, (ch 2, skip next 2 sts, tr in next sc) across: 9{10-11} sps.

Row 2: Ch 1, turn; sc in first tr, ★ working **behind** next ch-2 sp, work 2 tr Clusters in ch-2 sp **below**, sc in next tr; repeat from ★ across to last ch-3 sp, working **behind** last ch-3 sp, work (tr Cluster, dc Cluster) in ch-2 sp **below**, slip st in last st: 18{20-22} Clusters.

Row 3: Ch 1, turn; slip st in first 2 Clusters and in next sc, ch 3, skip next 2 sts, tr in next sc, (ch 2, skip next 2 sts, tr in next sc) across: 8{9-10} sps.

Row 4: Repeat Row 2; finish off: 16{18-20} Clusters.

FRONT

Work same as Back through Row 3 of Body.

Row 4: Ch 6, turn; skip next 2 sts, tr in next sc, ★ ch 2, skip next 2 sts, tr in next sc; repeat from ★ across to last 3 sts changing to CC in last tr worked *(Fig. 24a, page 138)*, drop MC, do **not** cut yarn unless otherwise instructed, ch 2, skip next 2 sts, tr in last sc: 25{27-29} ch-2 sps.

Row 5: Ch 1, turn; sc in first tr, working **behind** next ch-2 sp, work 2 tr Clusters in ch-2 sp **below**, sc in next tr changing to MC, drop CC, ★ working **behind** next ch-2 sp, work 2 tr Clusters in ch-2 sp **below**, sc in next tr; repeat from ★ across.

Row 6: Ch 6, turn; skip next 2 sts, tr in next sc, ★ ch 2, skip next 2 sts, tr in next sc; repeat from ★ across to last 2 MC Clusters changing to CC in last tr worked, drop MC, (ch 2, skip next 2 sts, tr in next sc) across.

Row 7: Ch 1, turn; sc in first tr, (working **behind** next ch-2 sp, work 2 tr Clusters in ch-2 sp **below**, sc in next tr) across to first MC ch-2 sp changing to MC in last sc worked, drop CC, ★ working **behind** next ch-2 sps, work 2 tr Clusters in ch-2 sp **below**, sc in next tr; repeat from ★ across.

Repeat Rows 6 and 7, 18{20-22} times; do **not** finish off.

RIGHT NECK SHAPING

Note: Continue to work in established diagonal pattern.

Row 1: Ch 6, turn; skip next 2 sts, tr in next sc, (ch 2, skip next 2 sts, tr in next sc) 8{9-10} times, ch 3, skip next 2 sts, slip st in next sc, leave remaining sts unworked: 10{11-12} sps.

Rows 2-6: Repeat Rows 2 and 3 of Back Left Neck Shaping twice, then repeat Row 2 once **more**: 16{18-20} Clusters.

Rows 7 and 8: Repeat Rows 4 and 5 of Back Body: 14{16-18} Clusters.

Finish off.

LEFT NECK SHAPING

Row 1: With **wrong** side facing, skip 4 sc from Right Neck Shaping and join CC with slip st in next sc; ch 3, skip next 2 sts, tr in next sc, (ch 2, skip next 2 sts, tr in next sc) across: 10{11-12} sps.

Rows 2-6: Repeat Rows 2 and 3 of Back Right Neck Shaping twice, then repeat Row 2 once **more**: 16{18-20} Clusters.

Row 7: Ch 1, turn; slip st in first 2 Clusters and in next sc, ch 6, skip next 2 sts, tr in next sc, (ch 2, skip next 2 sts, tr in next sc) across: 7{8-9} sps.

Row 8: Repeat Row 5 of Back Body: 14{16-18} Clusters. Finish off.

SLEEVE (Make 2)
RIBBING

With smaller size hook and MC, ch 11 **loosely**.

Row 1: Sc in second ch from hook and in each ch across: 10 sc.

Row 2: Ch 1, turn; sc in Back Loop Only of each sc across.

Repeat Row 2 until Ribbing measures approximately 5¹⁄₄{5¹⁄₂ -5¹⁄₂}".

BODY

Change to larger size hook.

Row 1 (Right side)**:** Ch 1, work 37{37-43} sc evenly spaced across end of rows.

Note: Mark last row as **right** side.

Row 2: Ch 6, turn; skip next 2 sc, tr in next sc, (ch 2, skip next 2 sc, tr in next sc) across: 12{12-14} ch-2 sps.

Row 3: Ch 1, turn; sc in first tr, ★ working **behind** next ch-2 sp, work tr Cluster in each of next 2 skipped sc on row **below**, sc in next tr; repeat from ★ across: 24{24-28} tr Clusters.

Row 4: Ch 6, turn; skip next 2 sts, tr in next sc, (ch 2, skip next 2 sts, tr in next sc) across: 12{12-14} ch-2 sps.

Row 5: Ch 1, turn; sc in first tr, ★ working **behind** next ch-2 sp, work 2 tr Clusters in ch-2 sp **below**, sc in next tr; repeat from ★ across: 24{24-28} tr Clusters.

Rows 6-9: Repeat Rows 4 and 5, twice.

Row 10 (Increase row)**:** Ch 6, turn; tr in first sc, ch 2, skip next 2 sts, (tr in next sc, ch 2, skip next 2 sts) across to last sc, (tr, ch 2, tr) in last sc: 14{14-16} ch-2 sps.

Row 11: Ch 1, turn; sc in first tr, working **behind** first ch-2 sp, work 2 tr Clusters in first sc on row **below**, sc in next tr, ★ working **behind** next ch-2 sp, work 2 tr Clusters in ch-2 sp **below**, sc in next tr; repeat from ★ across to last ch-2 sp, working **behind** last ch-2 sp, work 2 tr Clusters in last sc on row **below**, sc in last tr: 28{28-32} tr Clusters.

Repeat Rows 6-11, 4{5-5} times: 44{48-52} tr Clusters.

Repeat Rows 4 and 5 for pattern until Sleeve measures approximately 9¹⁄₂{10¹⁄₂-11¹⁄₂}" from bottom edge, ending by working Row 5; finish off.

FINISHING

Sew shoulder seams.

NECK RIBBING

Foundation Rnd: With **right** side facing and using smaller size hook, join MC with slip st at right shoulder seam; ch 1, work 8 sc evenly spaced along Right Back Neck edge, work 22 sc evenly spaced across Back, work 8 sc evenly spaced along Left Back Neck edge, work 16 sc evenly spaced along Left Front Neck edge, work 16 sc evenly spaced across Front, work 16 sc evenly spaced along Right Front Neck edge; join with slip st to first sc: 86 sc.

Ch 6{6-8} **loosely**.

Row 1: Sc in second ch from hook and in each ch across, slip st in first 2 sc on Foundation Rnd: 7{7-9} sts.

Row 2: Turn; skip first 2 slip sts, sc in Back Loop Only of each sc across: 5{5-7} sc.

Row 3: Ch 1, turn; sc in Back Loop Only of each sc across, slip st in next 2 sc on Foundation Rnd: 7{7-9} sts.

Repeat Rows 2 and 3 around, ending by working Row 2.

Last Row: Ch 1, turn; sc in Back Loop Only of each sc across, slip st in last sc on Foundation Rnd; finish off leaving a long end for sewing.

Whipstitch seam on Neck Ribbing *(Fig. 28a, page 140)*. Whipstitch Sleeves to Top, matching center of Sleeve to shoulder seam and beginning 5¹⁄₂{6-6¹⁄₂}" down from shoulder seam. Whipstitch underarm and side in one continuous seam.

TULIP GARDEN SWEATSHIRT

Continued from page 104.

NECK RIBBING

With smaller size hook, ch 8 **loosely**.

Row 1 (Right side)**:** Sc in second ch from hook and in each ch across: 7 sc.

Note: Mark last row as **right** side.

Row 2: Ch 1, turn; sc in Back Loop Only of each sc across; do **not** finish off.

On **right** side of sweatshirt, measure around neck opening. Multiply this measurement by .667. Repeat Row 2 until Ribbing is approximately the same length as determined measurement, ending by working a **wrong** side row.

Joining Row: With **right** sides together and working in Back Loops Only of sc on last row **and** in free loops of beginning ch, slip st in each st across; finish off.

With **right** sides together and stretching each Ribbing to fit opening, sew Ribbings to sweatshirt using a ¹⁄₄" seam.

hooked on holidays

*Celebrate a year of holidays with these festive projects!
Our fun-filled assortment includes delightful decorations and
great gift ideas, too. For Valentine's Day, cute frames surround
special photos with love, and a pair of patriotic mascots brings
spirit to the Fourth of July. Wheat-sheaf patterns enrich
a Thanksgiving doily, and a three-dimensional Christmas tree
makes a charming centerpiece. With these unique projects — and
so many more — it's easy to become hooked on holidays!*

VALENTINE'S DAY

*You'll love displaying your sweetheart's photo in one of these frilly magnetic frames. Stitched in
bedspread weight cotton thread, they're just the right size to take to the office or place on the refrigerator
door. With three styles from which to choose, you can always keep your loved one close to your heart!*

Quick SWEETHEART FRAMES

Finished Size: Heart - approximately 4³/₄" wide x 4¹/₂" high
Oval - approximately 4¹/₂" wide x 5" high
Round - approximately 4¹/₂" in diameter

MATERIALS
Bedspread Weight Cotton Thread (size 10), approximately:
Heart or Round - 35 yards **each**
Oval - 45 yards
Steel crochet hook, size 7 (1.65 mm) **or** size needed
for gauge
Magnetic strips
Cardboard
Heart: ¹/₂ yard of ¹/₈" ribbon

GAUGE: 9 sc = 1"

PATTERN STITCHES
DC DECREASE (uses next 2 sts)
★ YO, insert hook in **next** st, YO and pull up a loop, YO and
draw through 2 loops on hook; repeat from ★ once **more**,
YO and draw through all 3 loops on hook (**counts as
one dc**).
DOUBLE DECREASE (uses next 3 sts)
★ YO, insert hook in **next** st, YO and pull up a loop, YO and
draw through 2 loops on hook; repeat from ★ 2 times
more, YO and draw through all 4 loops on hook.
SC DECREASE
Pull up a loop in next 2 sts, YO and draw through all 3 loops
on hook (**counts as one sc**).
SHELL
(2 Dc, ch 4, 2 dc) in st indicated.
V-ST
(Dc, ch 1, dc) in st indicated.

HEART FRAME

Ch 9 **loosely**.

Rnd 1: 2 Hdc in third ch from hook, sc in next ch, slip st in next ch, skip next ch, slip st in next ch, sc in next ch, 5 hdc in last ch; working in free loops of beginning ch *(Fig. 23b, page 138)*, sc in next 2 chs, 3 sc in next ch, sc in next 2 chs, 2 hdc in next ch; join with slip st to top of beginning ch: 21 sts.

Note: Loop a short piece of thread around any stitch to mark last round as back.

Rnd 2: Ch 2, hdc in same st, hdc in next hdc, sc in next 2 sts, slip st in next 2 slip sts, sc in next 2 sts, hdc in next hdc, 2 hdc in next hdc, 3 dc in next hdc, 2 hdc in next hdc, sc in next 3 sc, 3 hdc in next sc, sc in next 3 sc, 2 hdc in next hdc, 3 dc in last hdc; join with slip st top of beginning ch-2: 31 sts.

Rnd 3: Ch 3 **(counts as first dc, now and throughout)**, dc in same st, 3 dc in next hdc, hdc in next hdc, sc in next sc, slip st in next sc, skip next 2 slip sts, slip st in next sc, sc in next sc, hdc in next hdc, 3 dc in next hdc, 2 dc in each of next 5 sts, dc in next 5 sts, (dc, tr, dc) in next hdc, dc in next 5 sts, 2 dc in each of last 4 sts; join with slip st to first dc: 45 sts.

Rnd 4: Ch 3, dc in same st and in next dc, 2 dc in each of next 2 dc, hdc in next 2 sts, sc in next sc, skip next 2 slip sts, sc in next sc, hdc in next 2 sts, 2 dc in each of next 2 dc, dc in next dc, 2 dc in next dc, 3 dc in next dc, (dc in next dc, 2 dc in next dc) 3 times, dc in next 7 dc, (dc, tr, dc) in next tr, dc in next 7 dc, (2 dc in next dc, dc in next dc) 3 times, 3 dc in last dc; join with slip st to first dc: 61 sts.

Rnd 5: Ch 3, dc in same st, (dc in next dc, 2 dc in next dc) twice, hdc in next 2 dc, sc in next 2 sts, skip next 2 sc, sc in next 2 hdc, hdc in next 2 dc, 2 dc in next dc, (dc in next dc, 2 dc in next dc) 5 times, dc in next 2 dc, 2 dc in next dc, dc in next 11 dc, (dc, tr, dc) in next tr, dc in next 11 dc, 2 dc in next dc, dc in next 2 dc, (2 dc in next dc, dc in next dc) 3 times; join with slip st to first dc: 75 sts.

Rnd 6: Ch 1, **turn**; working in Back Loops Only *(Fig. 22, page 138)*, sc in first 63 sts, skip next 2 sc, sc in last 10 sts; join with slip st to first sc: 73 sc.

Rnd 7 (Eyelet rnd): Ch 5, skip next sc, working in both loops, dc in next sc, (ch 2, skip next sc, dc in next sc) 11 times, ch 1, skip next sc, (dc, ch 1, tr, ch 1, dc) in next sc, ch 1, (skip next sc, dc in next sc, ch 2) 16 times, skip next sc, dc in next sc, ch 1, skip next sc, dc decrease, ch 1, skip next sc, (dc in next sc, ch 2, skip next sc) 4 times; join with slip st to third ch of beginning ch-5: 38 sps.

Rnd 8: Ch 1, sc in same st, ch 3, (sc in next dc, ch 3) 13 times, (sc, ch 3, sc) in next tr, (ch 3, sc in next dc) around, ch 1, hdc in first sc to form last sp: 39 sps.

Rnd 9: Ch 1, sc in same sp, ch 4, (sc in next ch-3 sp, ch 4) 14 times, (sc, ch 4, sc) in next ch-3 sp, (ch 4, sc in next ch-3 sp) around, ch 1, dc in first sc to form last sp: 40 sps.

Rnd 10: Ch 1, sc in same sp, ch 5, slip st in third ch from hook, ch 2, (sc in next ch-4 sp, ch 5, slip st in third ch from hook, ch 2) around; join with slip st to first sc, finish off.

FRONT EDGING

With back facing, Rnds 6-10 forward, and working in free loops on Rnd 5 *(Fig. 23a, page 138)*, join thread with slip st in same st as joining; ch 2, dc in next st, dc decrease 5 times, (dc, tr, dc) in same st as last decrease worked, dc decrease 7 times, dc in next dc, (dc decrease, dc in next dc) 7 times, work double decrease, (dc in next dc, dc decrease) 8 times; skip beginning ch-2 and join with slip st to first dc, finish off.

OVAL FRAME

Ch 5 **loosely**.

Rnd 1: Sc in third ch from hook and in next ch, (hdc, dc, hdc) in last ch; working in free loops of beginning ch *(Fig. 23b, page 138)*, sc in next ch, (sc, hdc, dc) in next ch; join with slip st to top of beginning ch: 10 sts.

Note: Loop a short piece of thread around any stitch to mark last round as back.

Rnd 2: Ch 2 **(counts as first hdc, now and throughout)**, hdc in same st and in next 2 sc, 2 hdc in next hdc, 3 dc in next dc, 2 hdc in next hdc, hdc in next 2 sc, 2 hdc in next hdc, 3 dc in last dc; join with slip st to first hdc: 18 sts.

Rnd 3: Ch 2, hdc in same st and in next 4 hdc, 2 hdc in next hdc, dc in next dc, 3 dc in next dc, dc in next dc, 2 hdc in next hdc, hdc in next 4 hdc, 2 hdc in next hdc, dc in next dc, 3 dc in next dc, dc in last dc; join with slip st to first hdc: 26 sts.

Rnd 4: Ch 2, hdc in same st and in next 6 hdc, 2 hdc in next hdc, dc in next dc, (2 dc in next dc, dc in next dc) twice, 2 hdc in next hdc, hdc in next 6 hdc, 2 hdc in next hdc, dc in next dc, (2 dc in next dc, dc in next dc) twice; join with slip st to first hdc: 34 sts.

Rnd 5: Ch 3 **(counts as first dc, now and throughout)**, hdc in same st and in next hdc, † 2 hdc in next hdc, hdc in next 4 hdc, 2 hdc in next hdc, hdc in next hdc, (hdc, dc) in next hdc, dc in next dc, (2 dc in next dc, dc in next dc) 3 times †, (dc, hdc) in next hdc, hdc in next hdc, repeat from † to † once; join with slip st to first dc: 48 sts.

Rnd 6: Ch 3, dc in same st and in next hdc, † 2 hdc in next hdc, hdc in next 8 hdc, 2 hdc in next hdc, dc in next hdc, (2 dc in next dc, dc in next dc) twice, 2 dc in each of next 4 dc, dc in next dc †, (2 dc in next dc, dc in next st) twice, repeat from † to † once, 2 dc in next dc, dc in last dc; join with slip st to first dc: 68 sts.

Rnd 7: Ch 2, hdc in next st and in each st around; join with slip st to first hdc.

Rnd 8: Ch 2, hdc in next 19 hdc, dc in next hdc, (2 dc in next hdc, dc in next hdc) 6 times, hdc in next 21 hdc, dc in next hdc, (2 dc in next hdc, dc in next hdc) 6 times, hdc in last hdc; join with slip st to first hdc: 80 sts.

Rnd 9: Ch 1, **turn**; working in Back Loops Only *(Fig. 22, page 138)*, sc in each st around; join with slip st to first sc.

Rnd 10: Ch 4, working in both loops, dc in same st, ch 3, skip next 3 sc, work Shell in next sc, ch 3, skip next 3 sc, (work V-St in next sc, ch 3, skip next 3 sc, work Shell in next sc, ch 3, skip next 3 sc) around; join with slip st to third ch of beginning ch-4: 10 Shells.

Rnd 11: Ch 1, sc in same st, sc in next ch-1 sp and in next dc, skip next ch-3 sp, dc in next Shell (ch-4 sp), (ch 1, dc) 7 times in same sp, skip next ch-3 sp, ★ sc in next dc, sc in next ch-1 sp and in next dc, skip next ch-3 sp, dc in next Shell, (ch 1, dc) 7 times in same sp, skip next ch-3 sp; repeat from ★ around; join with slip st to first sc.

Rnd 12: Slip st in next sc, ch 1, sc in same st and in next sc, (sc in next ch-1 sp, ch 3, slip st in sc just worked, sc in next dc) 7 times, skip next sc, ★ sc in next 2 sc, (sc in next ch-1 sp, ch 3, slip st in sc just worked, sc in next dc) 7 times, skip next sc; repeat from ★ around; join with slip st to first sc, finish off.

FRONT EDGING

Rnd 1: With back facing, Rnds 9-12 forward, and working in free loops on Rnd 8 *(Fig. 23a, page 138)*, join thread with slip st in same st as joining; ch 2, dc in next 15 hdc, dc decrease, (dc in next st, dc decrease) 8 times, dc in next 14 hdc, (dc decrease, dc in next st) 8 times; skip beginning ch-2 and join with slip st to first dc: 62 dc.

Rnd 2: Ch 1, sc in first 18 dc, sc decrease, (sc in next dc, sc decrease) 3 times, sc in next 20 dc, sc decrease, (sc in next dc, sc decrease) 3 times, sc in last 2 dc; join with slip st to first sc, finish off: 54 sc.

ROUND FRAME

Rnd 1: Ch 2, 6 sc in second ch from hook; do **not** join, place marker *(see Markers, page 138)*.

Note: Loop a short piece of thread around any stitch to mark last round as back.

Rnd 2: 2 Sc in each sc around: 12 sc.

Rnd 3: (Sc in next sc, 2 sc in next sc) around: 18 sc.

Rnd 4: (Sc in next 2 sc, 2 sc in next sc) around: 24 sc.

Rnd 5: (Sc in next 3 sc, 2 sc in next sc) around: 30 sc.

Rnd 6: (Sc in next 4 sc, 2 sc in next sc) around: 36 sc.

Rnd 7: (Sc in next 5 sc, 2 sc in next sc) around: 42 sc.

Rnd 8: (Sc in next 6 sc, 2 sc in next sc) around: 48 sc.

Rnd 9: (Sc in next 5 sc, 2 sc in next sc) around: 56 sc.

Rnd 10: (Sc in next 3 sc, 2 sc in next sc) around; slip st in next sc: 70 sc.

Rnd 11: Ch 1, **turn**; working in Back Loops Only *(Fig. 22, page 138)*, sc in each sc around; join with slip st to first sc.

Rnd 12: Ch 1, working in both loops, 2 sc in same st, sc in next 6 sc, (2 sc in next sc, sc in next 6 sc) around; join with slip st to first sc: 80 sc.

Rnd 13: Ch 1, sc in same st, ch 4, skip next 4 sc, 4 dc in next sc, ch 4, skip next 4 sc, ★ sc in next sc, ch 4, skip next 4 sc, 4 dc in next sc, ch 4, skip next 4 sc; repeat from ★ around; join with slip st to first sc: 8 sc.

Rnd 14: Ch 4, dc in same st, ch 1, 3 dc in each of next 4 dc, ch 1, ★ work V-St in next sc, ch 1, 3 dc in each of next 4 dc, ch 1; repeat from ★ around; join with slip st to third ch of beginning ch-4.

Rnd 15: Ch 1, ★ sc in next ch-1 sp, ch 4, slip st in sc just worked, skip next dc, sc in next 5 dc, hdc in next dc, ch 3, slip st in hdc just worked, dc in next dc, ch 4, slip st in dc just worked, hdc in next dc, ch 3, slip st in hdc just worked, sc in next 4 dc, skip next dc; repeat from ★ around; join with slip st to first sc, finish off.

FRONT EDGING

With back facing, Rnds 11-15 forward, and working in free loops on Rnd 10 *(Fig. 23a, page 138)*, join thread with slip st in same st as joining; ch 2, dc in next st, dc decrease around; skip beginning ch-2 and join with slip st to first dc, finish off: 35 sts.

FINISHING

See Washing and Blocking, page 140.
Cut cardboard to fit inside of Front Edging of each Frame.
Cut photo to fit and insert into frame.
Attach a long magnetic strip to back of each Frame.
Heart: Weave ribbon through Eyelet round and tie in a bow.

These inspirational bookmarks are thoughtful reminders of the Easter story. Perfect for marking a special scripture, they're fashioned with white cotton thread and gold metallic braid.

Quick CROSS BOOKMARKS

Finished Size: Cross #1 - approximately 5" long
Cross #2 - approximately 5¹/₂" long
Cross #3 - approximately 5³/₄" long

MATERIALS
Cotton Crochet Thread (size 20), approximately:
Cross #1 (White) - 13 yards
Cross #2 (White) - 21 yards
Cross #3 (White) - 37 yards
Metallic Braid (size 8), approximately:
Cross #1 (Gold) - 28 yards
Cross #2 (Gold) - 12 yards
Cross #3 (Gold) - 3 yards
Steel crochet hook, size 8 (1.50 mm)

GAUGE: Gauge is not important. Crosses can be smaller or larger without changing the overall effect.

PATTERN STITCHES
CLUSTER
★ YO, insert hook in dc indicated, YO and pull up a loop, YO and draw through 2 loops on hook; repeat from ★ once **more**, YO and draw through all 3 loops on hook *(Figs. 10a & b, page 134)*.
PICOT
Ch 3, slip st in sc just worked.

CROSS #1
FIRST MOTIF
With Gold, ch 5; join with slip st to form a ring.
Rnd 1 (Right side)**:** Ch 3 **(counts as first dc, now and throughout)**, 2 dc in ring, ch 3, (3 dc in ring, ch 3) 3 times; join with slip st to first dc: 12 dc.
Note: Loop a short piece of thread around any stitch to mark last round as **right** side.
Rnd 2: Ch 3, dc in same st and in next dc, 2 dc in next dc, ch 2, dc in next ch-3 sp, ch 2, ★ 2 dc in next dc, dc in next dc, 2 dc in next dc, ch 2, dc in next ch-3 sp, ch 2; repeat from ★ around; join with slip st to first dc: 24 dc.
Rnd 3: Ch 3, working in Back Loops Only *(Fig. 22, page 138)*, dc in same st and in next 3 dc, 2 dc in next dc, ch 2, work (Cluster, ch 3, Cluster) in next dc, ch 2, ★ 2 dc in next dc,

dc in next 3 dc, 2 dc in next dc, ch 2, work (Cluster, ch 3, Cluster) in next dc, ch 2; repeat from ★ around; join with slip st to first dc, finish off.

REMAINING 5 MOTIFS
Work same as First Motif through Rnd 2.
Refer to Assembly Diagram for joining sequence.
Rnd 3 (Joining rnd)**:** Ch 3, working in Back Loops Only, dc in same st and in next 3 dc, 2 dc in next dc, ch 2, ★ work (Cluster, ch 3, Cluster) in next dc, ch 2, 2 dc in next dc, dc in next 3 dc, 2 dc in next dc, ch 2; repeat from ★ once **more**, work Cluster in next dc, ch 1, slip st in center ch of corner ch-3 on **previous Motif**, ch 1, work Cluster in same dc on **new Motif**, ch 2, dc in next dc, slip st in adjacent dc on **previous Motif**, dc in same dc on **new Motif**, dc in next 3 dc, 2 dc in next dc, slip st in adjacent dc on **previous Motif**, ch 2, work Cluster in next dc on **new Motif**, ch 1, slip st in center ch of corner ch-3 on **previous Motif**, ch 1, work Cluster in same dc on **new Motif**, ch 2; join with slip st to first dc, finish off.

ASSEMBLY DIAGRAM

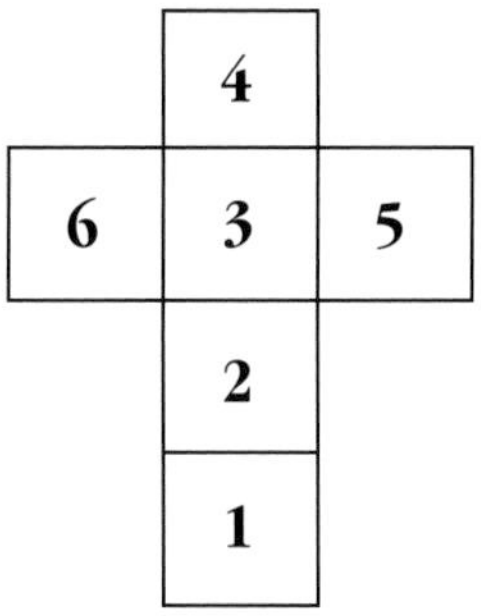

	4	
6	3	5
	2	
	1	

EDGING
Rnd 1: With **right** side facing, join White with slip st in any st, ch 1, sc evenly around working 3 sc in corners (total sc must be a multiple of 2); join with slip st to first sc.
Rnd 2: Ch 1, sc in same st, work Picot, skip next sc, ★ sc in next sc, work Picot, skip next sc; repeat from ★ around; join with slip st to first sc, finish off.

CROSS #2
CENTER
With White, ch 8; join with slip st to form a ring.
Rnd 1: Ch 3 **(counts as first dc, now and throughout)**, 4 dc in ring, ch 3, (5 dc in ring, ch 3) 3 times; join with slip st to first dc: 20 dc.

TOP

Row 1: Ch 3, dc in same st and in next 3 dc, 2 dc in next dc, leave remaining sts unworked: 7 dc.

Rows 2-5: Ch 3, turn; dc in same st and in each dc across to last dc, 2 dc in last dc: 15 dc.

Row 6 (Right side)**:** Ch 3, turn; dc in same st, 2 dc in next dc, 2 tr in each of next 2 dc, tr in next 7 dc, 2 tr in each of next 2 dc, 2 dc in each of last 2 dc: 23 sts.

Note: Loop a short piece of thread around any stitch to mark last row as **right** side.

Row 7: Ch 1, turn; slip st in first 8 sts, ch 4 **(counts as first tr, now and throughout)**, tr in next 8 tr, leave remaining 7 sts unworked: 9 tr.

Row 8: Ch 3, turn; ★ YO twice, insert hook in **next** tr, YO and pull up a loop, (YO and draw through 2 loops on hook) twice; repeat from ★ 7 times **more**, YO and draw through all 9 loops on hook, ch 1 to close, finish off.

LEFT SIDE

Row 1: With **right** side facing, join White with slip st in first dc of next 5-dc group on Center; ch 3, dc in same st, 2 dc in next dc, dc in next dc, 2 dc in each of next 2 dc, leave remaining sts unworked: 9 dc.

Row 2: Ch 3, turn; dc in same st and in next dc, 2 dc in next dc, dc in next 3 dc, 2 dc in next dc, dc in next dc, 2 dc in last dc: 13 dc.

Row 3: Ch 3, turn; dc in same st and in next 11 dc, 2 dc in last dc: 15 dc.

Row 4: Ch 1, turn; slip st in first 5 dc, ch 4, tr in next 6 dc, leave remaining 4 sts unworked: 7 tr.

Row 5: Ch 3, turn; ★ YO twice, insert hook in **next** tr, YO and pull up a loop, (YO and draw through 2 loops on hook) twice; repeat from ★ 5 times **more**, YO and draw through all 7 loops on hook, ch 1 to close, finish off.

113

BOTTOM

Row 1: With **wrong** side facing, skip next 5-dc group and join White with slip st in next dc on Center (opposite Top); ch 3, dc in same st and in next 3 dc, 2 dc in last dc: 7 dc.

Row 2: Ch 3, turn; dc in next dc and in each dc across.

Row 3: Ch 3, turn; dc in same st and in each dc across to last dc, 2 dc in last dc: 9 dc.

Rows 4-9: Repeat Rows 2 and 3, 3 times: 15 dc.

Rows 10-13: Ch 3, turn; dc in next dc and in each dc across.

Rows 14-16: Work same as Rows 6-8 of Top.

RIGHT SIDE

Row 1: With **right** side facing, join White with slip st in first dc of remaining 5-dc group on Center; ch 3, dc in same st, 2 dc in next dc, dc in next dc, 2 dc in each of last 2 dc: 9 dc.

Rows 2-5: Work same as Left Side.

EDGING

Rnd 1: With **right** side facing, join Gold with slip st in any st; ch 1, sc evenly around (total sc must be a multiple of 2); join with slip st to first sc.

Rnd 2: Ch 2, sc in second ch from hook, skip next sc, ★ slip st in next sc, ch 2, sc in second ch from hook, skip next sc; repeat from ★ around; join with slip st to first slip st, finish off.

CROSS #3

CENTER

Rnd 1 (Right side)**:** With Gold, ch 5; (2 dc, ch 1) 3 times in fifth ch from hook, dc in same ch; join with slip st to top of beginning ch: 4 ch-1 sps.

Note: Loop a short piece of thread around any stitch to mark last round as **right** side.

Rnd 2: Slip st in first ch-1 sp, ch 10 **loosely**, dc in fourth ch from hook and in next 6 chs (bottom of Cross), skip next 2 dc, ★ slip st in next ch-1 sp, ch 6 **loosely**, dc in fourth ch from hook and in next 2 chs, skip next 2 dc; repeat from ★ 2 times **more**; join with slip st to first st.

Rnd 3: Ch 16, slip st around skipped chs on end of bottom ch-10, ch 12, ★ tr in next ch-1 sp on Rnd 1, ch 5, slip st around skipped chs on end of next ch-6, ch 5; repeat from ★ around; join with slip st to fourth ch of beginning ch-16, finish off: 8 sps.

BOTTOM

Row 1: With **right** side facing, skip next 5 chs and join White with slip st in next ch, ch 1, 6 sc in same loop, sc in next slip st, 6 sc in next loop: 13 sc.

Row 2: Ch 3 **(counts as first dc, now and throughout)**, turn; skip next sc, (2 dc, ch 1, 2 dc) in next sc, skip next 3 sc, (dc, ch 2, dc) in next sc, skip next 3 sc, (2 dc, ch 1, 2 dc) in next sc, skip next sc, dc in last sc: 12 dc.

Row 3: Ch 3, turn; (dc, ch 2, dc) in next ch-1 sp, (2 dc, ch 1, 2 dc) in next ch-2 sp, (dc, ch 2, dc) in next ch-1 sp, skip next 2 dc, dc in last dc: 10 dc.

Row 4: Ch 3, turn; (2 dc, ch 1, 2 dc) in next ch-2 sp, (dc, ch 2, dc) in next ch-1 sp, (2 dc, ch 1, 2 dc) in next ch-2 sp, skip next dc, dc in last dc: 12 dc.

Rows 5-8: Repeat Rows 3 and 4, twice.

Row 9: Ch 3, turn; dc in same st, (dc, ch 2, dc) in next ch-1 sp, (2 dc, ch 1, 2 dc) in next ch-2 sp, (dc, ch 2, dc) in next ch-1 sp, skip next 2 dc, 2 dc in last dc: 12 dc.

Row 10: Ch 3, turn; dc in next dc, (2 dc, ch 1, 2 dc) in next ch-2 sp, (dc, ch 2, dc) in next ch-1 sp, (2 dc, ch 1, 2 dc) in next ch-2 sp, skip next dc, dc in last 2 dc: 14 dc.

Row 11: Ch 3, turn; dc in same st and in next dc, (dc, ch 2, dc) in next ch-1 sp, (2 dc, ch 1, 2 dc) in next ch-2 sp, (dc, ch 2, dc) in next ch-1 sp, skip next 2 dc, dc in next dc, 2 dc in last dc: 14 dc.

Row 12: Ch 3, turn; dc in next 2 dc, (2 dc, ch 1, 2 dc) in next ch-2 sp, (dc, ch 2, dc) in next ch-1 sp, (2 dc, ch 1, 2 dc) in next ch-2 sp, skip next dc, dc in last 3 dc: 16 dc.

Row 13: Ch 3, turn; dc in same st and in next 2 dc, (dc, ch 2, dc) in next ch-1 sp, (2 dc, ch 1, 2 dc) in next ch-2 sp, (dc, ch 2, dc) in next ch-1 sp, skip next 2 dc, dc in next 2 dc, 2 dc in last dc: 16 dc.

Rnd 14: Ch 3, turn; skip next dc, (dc, ch 2, dc) in next dc, (2 dc, ch 1, 2 dc) in next ch-2 sp, (dc, ch 2, dc) in next ch-1 sp, (2 dc, ch 1, 2 dc) in next ch-2 sp, skip next 2 dc, (dc, ch 2, dc) in next dc, skip next dc, dc in last dc: 16 dc.

Rnd 15: Ch 3, turn; (2 dc, ch 1, 2 dc) in next ch-2 sp, ★ (dc, ch 2, dc) in next ch-1 sp, (2 dc, ch 1, 2 dc) in next ch-2 sp; repeat from ★ once **more**, skip next dc, dc in last dc; finish off.

RIGHT SIDE

Row 1: With **right** side facing, join White with slip st in next ch-5 sp on Center; ch 1, 6 sc in same sp, sc in next slip st, 6 sc in next ch-5 sp: 13 sc.

Rows 2-4: Work same as Rows 2-4 of Bottom.

Rows 5-7: Work same as Rows 9-11 of Bottom.

Row 8: Ch 3, turn; dc in same st and in next 2 dc, (2 dc, ch 1, 2 dc) in next ch-2 sp, (dc, ch 2, dc) in next ch-1 sp, (2 dc, ch 1, 2 dc) in next ch-2 sp, skip next dc, dc in next 2 dc, 2 dc in last dc; finish off: 18 dc.

TOP AND LEFT SIDE

Work same as Right Side.

EDGING

Rnd 1: With **right** side facing, join White with slip st in any st; ch 1, sc evenly around working 3 sc in each corner (total sc must be a multiple of 3); join with slip st to first sc.

Rnd 2: Ch 1, sc in first 2 sc, ch 3, skip next sc, ★ sc in next 2 sc, ch 3, skip next sc; repeat from ★ around; join with slip st to first sc, finish off.

PATRIOTIC DAYS

*S*how your patriotic pride with these popular political mascots. Wearing spirited ribbons, the Democratic donkey and the Republican elephant are Yankee-Doodle dandies!

POLITICAL MASCOTS

Finished Size: Approximately 7¹/₂" tall

MATERIALS
Worsted Weight Yarn, approximately:
  Donkey
    MC (Brown) - 1¹/₄ ounces, (35 grams, 70 yards)
    CC (Dark Brown) - 15 yards
  Elephant
    MC (Grey) - 3 ounces, (90 grams, 170 yards)
    CC (Light Grey) - 4 yards
Crochet hook, size I (5.50 mm) **or** size needed for gauge

Polyester fiberfill
Yarn needle
Donkey: 2 - 6 mm buttons for eyes
    Black embroidery floss
    Cardboard
    ¹/₂ yard of ³/₄" ribbon
Elephant: 2 - 8 mm eyes
    ³/₄ yard of 1" ribbon

GAUGE: 7 sc and 7 rows = 2"

PATTERN STITCHES

DECREASE

Pull up a loop in next 2 sc, YO and draw through all 3 loops on hook **(counts as one sc)**.

POPCORN

3 Sc in Back Loop Only of next sc, drop loop from hook, insert hook in first sc of 3-sc group, hook dropped loop and draw through; drop CC, with MC ch 1 to close.

DONKEY

BODY

Rnd 1 (Right side): With MC, ch 2, 6 sc in second ch from hook; do **not** join, place marker **(see Markers, page 138)**.

Rnd 2: 2 Sc in each sc around: 12 sc.

Rnd 3: (Sc in next sc, 2 sc in next sc) around: 18 sc.

Rnd 4: (Sc in next 5 sc, 2 sc in next sc) around: 21 sc.

Rnds 5-7: Sc in each sc around.

Rnd 8: (Sc in next 5 sc, decrease) around: 18 sc.

Rnds 9-13: Sc in each sc around.

Rnd 14: (Sc in next 5 sc, 2 sc in next sc) around: 21 sc.

Rnds 15-17: Sc in each sc around.

Rnd 18: (Sc in next 5 sc, decrease) around: 18 sc.

Stuff Body as needed.

Rnd 19: (Sc in next sc, decrease) around: 12 sc.

Rnd 20: Decrease around: 6 sc.

Add additional stuffing, if necessary.

Rnd 21: (Skip next sc, slip st in next sc) around; finish off.

HEAD

Rnd 1 (Right side): With MC, ch 2, 6 sc in second ch from hook; do **not** join, place marker.

Rnd 2: (Sc in next sc, 2 sc in next sc) around: 9 sc.

Rnds 3 and 4: Sc in each sc around.

Rnd 5: (Sc in next 2 sc, 2 sc in next sc) around: 12 sc.

Rnd 6: Sc in each sc around.

Rnd 7: (Sc in next 3 sc, 2 sc in next sc) around: 15 sc.

Rnd 8: Sc in each sc around.

Rnd 9: (Sc in next 4 sc, 2 sc in next sc) around: 18 sc.

Rnd 10: (Sc in next 5 sc, 2 sc in next sc) around: 21 sc.

Rnd 11: (Sc in next 6 sc, 2 sc in next sc) around: 24 sc.

Rnd 12: Sc in each sc around.

Stuff Head as needed.

Rnds 13 and 14: Decrease around: 6 sc.

Add additional stuffing, if necessary.

Rnd 15: (Skip next sc, slip st in next sc) around; finish off.

NECK

With MC and leaving a long end for sewing, ch 18 **loosely**; being careful not to twist ch, join with slip st to form a ring.

Rnd 1 (Right side): Ch 1, sc in each ch around; do **not** join, place marker: 18 sc.

Rnds 2 and 3: Sc in each sc around; at end of Rnd 3, slip st in next sc, finish off leaving a long end for sewing.

LEG (Make 4)

Rnd 1 (Right side): With CC, ch 2, 6 sc in second ch from hook; do **not** join, place marker.

Rnd 2: (Sc in next 2 sc, 2 sc in next sc) twice changing to MC in last sc **(Fig. 24a, page 138)**: 8 sc.

Rnds 3-8: Sc in each sc around.

Rnd 9: (Sc in next 3 sc, 2 sc in next sc) twice: 10 sc.

Rnds 10-12: Sc in each sc around.

Rnd 13: (Decrease, sc in next 3 sc) twice: 8 sc.

Rnds 14 and 15: Sc in each sc around.

Rnd 16: (Sc in next 3 sc, 2 sc in next sc) twice: 10 sc.

Rnd 17: (Sc in next 4 sc, 2 sc in next sc) twice; slip st in next sc, finish off leaving a long end for sewing: 12 sc.

Stuff **firmly**.

EAR (Make 2)

With MC, ch 8 **loosely**; sc in second ch from hook, hdc in each ch across; finish off leaving a long end for sewing.

TAIL

With MC, ch 11 **loosely**; slip st in back ridge of second ch from hook and in each ch across **(Fig. 2a, page 133)**; finish off leaving a long end for sewing.

Cut 3 strands of CC each 2" long. Hold strands together and fold in half. With crochet hook, draw the folded end up through end of Tail and pull the loose ends through the folded end; draw the knot up **tightly**. Trim to 1".

FINISHING

Sew Neck to Body and stuff lightly. Sew Head to Neck, with nose pointing down.

Sew Ears to Head.

With embroidery floss, add straight stitch nostrils **(Fig. 33, page 141)**.

Add eyes. Sew Legs and Tail to Body.

Mane

Cut a piece of cardboard 1 1/2" x 4". Wind CC **loosely** and evenly around the cardboard until the card is filled, then cut across one end; repeat as needed.

Thread yarn needle with a long strand of CC. Holding 6 strands of CC together at a time, sew each group to Head and Neck, forming 2 rows. Trim to desired length.

Tie ribbon in a knot around neck and trim ends.

ELEPHANT

TRUNK AND HEAD

Rnd 1 (Right side): With MC, ch 2, 6 sc in second ch from hook; join with slip st to Back Loop Only of first sc *(Fig. 22, page 138)*.

Rnd 2: Ch 1, sc in Back Loop Only of each sc around; do **not** join, place marker *(see Markers, page 138)*.

Note: Stuff as needed while working entire piece.

Rnds 3-10: Sc in both loops of each sc around.

Rnd 11: (Sc in next 2 sc, 2 sc in next sc) twice: 8 sc.

Rnds 12-18: Sc in each sc around.

Rnd 19: (Sc in next 3 sc, 2 sc in next sc) twice: 10 sc.

Rnds 20-22: Sc in each sc around.

Rnd 23: (Sc in next 4 sc, 2 sc in next sc) twice: 12 sc.

Rnd 24: (Sc in next sc, 2 sc in next sc) around: 18 sc.

Rnds 25 and 26: Sc in each sc around.

Rnd 27: (Sc in next 2 sc, 2 sc in next sc) around: 24 sc.

Rnd 28: (Sc in next 3 sc, 2 sc in next sc) around: 30 sc.

Rnd 29: (Sc in next 4 sc, 2 sc in next sc) around: 36 sc.

Rnds 30-34: Sc in each sc around.

Rnd 35: (Sc in next 4 sc, decrease) around: 30 sc.

Rnd 36: (Sc in next 3 sc, decrease) around: 24 sc.

Rnd 37: (Sc in next 2 sc, decrease) around: 18 sc.

Rnd 38: (Sc in next sc, decrease) around: 12 sc.

Rnd 39: Decrease around: 6 sc.

Rnd 40: (Skip next sc, slip st in next sc) around; finish off.

BODY

Rnd 1 (Right side): With MC, ch 2, 6 sc in second ch from hook; do **not** join, place marker.

Rnd 2: 2 Sc in each sc around: 12 sc.

Rnd 3: (Sc in next sc, 2 sc in next sc) around: 18 sc.

Rnd 4: (Sc in next 2 sc, 2 sc in next sc) around: 24 sc.

Rnd 5: (Sc in next 3 sc, 2 sc in next sc) around: 30 sc.

Rnd 6: (Sc in next 4 sc, 2 sc in next sc) around: 36 sc.

Rnds 7-22: Sc in each sc around.

Rnd 23: (Sc in next 4 sc, decrease) around: 30 sc.

Rnd 24: (Sc in next 3 sc, decrease) around: 24 sc.

Rnd 25: (Sc in next 2 sc, decrease) around: 18 sc.

Stuff Body as needed.

Rnd 26: (Sc in next sc, decrease) around: 12 sc.

Rnd 27: Decrease around: 6 sc.

Add additional stuffing, if necessary.

Rnd 28: (Skip next sc, slip st in next sc) around; finish off.

LEG (Make 4)

Rnd 1 (Right side): With MC, ch 2, 6 sc in second ch from hook; do **not** join, place marker.

Rnd 2: 2 Sc in each sc around: 12 sc.

Rnd 3: (Sc in next sc, 2 sc in next sc) around; slip st in Back Loop Only of next sc: 18 sc.

Rnd 4: Ch 1, working in Back Loops Only, sc in first 5 sc changing to CC in last sc worked, drop MC *(Fig. 24a, page 138)*, work Popcorn (toe), ★ sc in next sc changing to CC, drop MC, work Popcorn; repeat from ★ 3 times **more**; cut CC, sc in last 4 sc; do **not** join, place marker.

Rnd 5: Sc in each sc and in each Popcorn around: 18 sc.

Rnd 6: Sc in next 6 sc, decrease 3 times, sc in next 6 sc: 15 sc.

Rnds 7-13: Sc in each sc around.

Rnd 14: (Sc in next 4 sc, 2 sc in next sc) around: 18 sc.

Rnd 15: (Sc in next 5 sc, 2 sc in next sc) around: 21 sc.

Rnd 16: (Sc in next 6 sc, 2 sc in next sc) around; slip st in next sc, finish off leaving a long end for sewing: 24 sc.

Stuff Leg **firmly**.

EAR (Make 4)

With MC, ch 4 **loosely**.

Row 1 (Right side): Sc in second ch from hook and in each ch across: 3 sc.

Note: Loop a short piece of yarn around any stitch to mark last row as **right** side.

Row 2: Ch 1, turn; 2 sc in first sc, sc in next sc, 2 sc in last sc: 5 sc.

Rows 3 and 4: Ch 1, turn; sc in each sc across.

Row 5: Ch 1, turn; 2 sc in first sc, sc in next 3 sc, 2 sc in last sc: 7 sc.

Rows 6-11: Ch 1, turn; sc in each sc across.

Rows 12 and 13: Ch 1, turn; decrease, sc in each sc across to last 2 sc, decrease: 3 sc.

Edging: Ch 1, do **not** turn; sc evenly around; join with slip st to first sc, finish off.

TAIL

With MC, ch 15 **loosely**; slip st in back ridge of second ch from hook and in each ch across *(Fig. 2a, page 133)*; finish off leaving a long end for sewing.

Cut 3 strands of MC each 2" long. Hold strands together and fold in half. With crochet hook, draw the folded end up through end of Tail and pull the loose ends through the folded end; draw the knot up **tightly**. Trim to 1".

FINISHING

Beginning at side, whipstitch 2 Ears together, matching shaping *(Fig. 28b, page 140)*; leave a long end for sewing.
Repeat for second Ear.

Sew Head to Body with Trunk pointing down. Sew Ears to Head. Add eyes.
Sew Legs to Body, with toes pointing forward.
Sew Tail to Body.
Tie ribbon in a bow around neck.

Brew up some Halloween fun with this "spook-tacular" black cat and the magnets shown on page 121! More delightful than frightful, our green-eyed kitty will add mischief to your celebration. The cat is crocheted in worsted weight yarn and then stuffed to be extra cuddly.

BOO KITTY

Finished Size: Approximately 6½" tall x 8" long

MATERIALS
Worsted Weight Yarn, approximately:
MC (Black) - 3 ounces, (90 grams, 170 yards)
Color A (Pink) - 3 yards
Color B (Green) - 1 yard
Crochet hook, size H (5.00 mm) **or** size needed for gauge
Yarn needle
Polyester fiberfill
Purchased whiskers
¾ yard of 1½" ribbon

GAUGE: Rnds 1-4 of Body = 2"

PATTERN STITCH
DECREASE
Pull up a loop in next 2 sc, YO and draw through all 3 loops on hook **(counts as one sc)**.

BODY
With MC, ch 3 **loosely**; being careful not to twist ch, join with slip st to form a ring.
Rnd 1 (Right side)**:** Ch 1, 2 sc in each ch around; do **not** join, place marker *(see Markers, page 138)*: 6 sc.
Rnd 2: 2 Sc in each sc around: 12 sc.
Rnd 3: (Sc in next sc, 2 sc in next sc) around: 18 sc.
Rnd 4: (Sc in next 2 sc, 2 sc in next sc) around: 24 sc.
Rnd 5: (Sc in next 3 sc, 2 sc in next sc) around: 30 sc.
Rnd 6: (Sc in next 4 sc, 2 sc in next sc) around: 36 sc.
Rnd 7: (Sc in next 5 sc, 2 sc in next sc) around: 42 sc.
Rnds 8-21: Sc in each sc around.
Stuff Body as needed.
Rnd 22: (Sc in next 5 sc, decrease) around: 36 sc.
Rnd 23: (Sc in next 4 sc, decrease) around: 30 sc.
Rnd 24: (Sc in next 3 sc, decrease) around: 24 sc.
Rnd 25: (Sc in next 2 sc, decrease) around: 18 sc.
Add additional stuffing, if necessary.
Rnd 26: (Sc in next sc, decrease) around: 12 sc.
Rnd 27: Decrease around: 6 sc.
Rnd 28: (Slip st in next sc, skip next sc) 3 times; slip st in next sc, finish off.

HEAD
Work same as Body through Rnd 7: 42 sc.
Rnds 8-12: Sc in each sc around.
Rnd 13: (Sc in next 5 sc, decrease) around: 36 sc.
Rnd 14: Decrease around; slip st in next sc, finish off leaving a long end for sewing: 18 sc.
Stuff Head as needed.

LEG (Make 4)
With MC, ch 3 **loosely**; being careful not to twist ch, join with slip st to form a ring.
Rnd 1 (Right side)**:** Ch 1, 2 sc in each ch around; do **not** join, place marker: 6 sc.
Rnd 2: 2 Sc in each sc around: 12 sc.
Rnd 3: (Sc in next sc, 2 sc in next sc) around: 18 sc.
Rnd 4: (Sc in next 2 sc, 2 sc in next sc) around: 24 sc.
Rnds 5-7: Sc in each sc around.
Rnd 8: Sc in next 6 sc, decrease 6 times, sc in next 6 sc: 18 sc.
Rnds 9-14: Sc in each sc around; at end of Rnd 14, slip st in next sc, finish off leaving a long end for sewing.
Stuff Leg **firmly**.

EAR (Make 2)
INNER
Row 1 (Right side)**:** With Color A, ch 2, 2 sc in second ch from hook.
Note: Loop a short piece of yarn around any stitch to mark last row as **right** side.
Row 2: Ch 1, turn; 2 sc in each sc across: 4 sc.
Rows 3 and 4: Ch 1, turn; sc in each sc across.
Row 5: Ch 1, turn; 2 sc in first sc, sc in next 2 sc, 2 sc in last sc; finish off.

OUTER
With MC, work same as Inner Ear; at end of Row 5, do **not** finish off.

EDGING
With **wrong** side of Inner and Outer Ears together, with Inner Ear facing, and working through both pieces, ch 1, sc evenly around entire Ear working 2 sc in each corner; join with slip st to first sc, finish off leaving a long end for sewing.

CHEEK (Make 2)
With MC, ch 3 **loosely**; being careful not to twist ch, join with slip st to form a ring.

Rnd 1 (Right side)**:** Ch 1, 2 sc in each ch around; do **not** join, place marker: 6 sc.

Rnd 2: 2 Sc in each sc around: 12 sc.

Rnd 3: (Sc in next 2 sc, 2 sc in next sc) around: 16 sc.

Rnd 4: Sc in each sc around; slip st in next sc, finish off leaving a long end for sewing.

TAIL
With MC, ch 3 **loosely**; being careful not to twist ch, join with slip st to form a ring.

Rnd 1 (Right side)**:** Ch 1, 2 sc in each ch around; do **not** join, place marker: 6 sc.

Rnd 2: 2 Sc in each sc around: 12 sc.

Note: Stuff as needed while working entire Tail.

Rnds 3-22: Sc in each sc around; at end of Rnd 22, slip st in next sc, finish off leaving a long end for sewing.

FINISHING
Using photo as a guide for placement, sew Head, Legs, and Tail to Body.

Sew Cheeks to Head, stuffing lightly before closing.

Sew Ears to top of Head, placing 2 sts apart.

With Color A, add Satin Stitch nose *(Fig. 34, page 141)*.

With Color B and MC, add Satin Stitch eyes.

Add 2 whiskers to each side of Head at Cheek, attaching in same manner as fringe *(Figs. 30a & b, page 140)*.

Tie ribbon in a bow around neck.

HAUNTING MAGNETS

Finished Size: Ghost - approximately 4"
Jack-O'-Lantern - approximately 3"
Witch - approximately 4¹/4"

MATERIALS
Worsted Weight Yarn, approximately:
Ghost
White - 7 yards
Jack-O'-Lantern
Orange - 7 yards
Green - 1 yard
Witch
Green - 6 yards
Black - 4 yards
Orange - 2 yards
Crochet hook, size G (4.00 mm) **or** size needed for gauge
Yarn needle
Black felt - small amount
Magnetic strip - 1" **each**
Glue gun
Ghost: 2 - 10 mm oval wiggle eyes
Witch: 1 - 15 mm oval wiggle eye

GAUGE: 8 sc and 8 rows = 2"

GHOST
HEAD
With White, ch 5; join with slip st to form a ring.
Rnd 1 (Right side)**:** Ch 1, (sc, hdc, dc, 3 tr, dc, hdc, sc) in ring; do **not** join or finish off.

BODY
Row 1: Ch 7 **loosely**, slip st in second ch from hook, sc in each ch across, slip st in ring: 5 sc.
Row 2: Ch 1, turn; skip first slip st, sc in each sc across, leave last slip st unworked.
Row 3: Ch 2, turn; slip st in second ch from hook, sc in each sc across, slip st in ring.
Row 4: Ch 1, turn; skip first slip st, sc in each sc across, leave last slip st unworked.
Row 5: Ch 7 **loosely**, turn; slip st in second ch from hook, sc in each ch and in each sc across, slip st in ring: 10 sc.
Row 6: Ch 1, turn; skip first slip st, sc in each sc across, leave last slip st unworked.
Rows 7-9: Repeat Rows 3 and 4 once, then repeat Row 3 once **more**.
Row 10: Ch 1, turn; skip first slip st, sc in next 5 sc, leave remaining 5 sc unworked: 5 sc.

Rows 11-13: Repeat Rows 3 and 4 once, then repeat Row 3 once **more**.
Finish off.

JACK-O'-LANTERN
PUMPKIN
With Orange, ch 4 **loosely**; being careful not to twist ch, join with slip st to form a ring.
Rnd 1 (Right side)**:** Ch 1, 2 sc in each ch around; do **not** join, place marker *(see Markers, page 138)*: 8 sc.
Rnd 2: 2 Sc in each sc around: 16 sc.
Rnd 3: (Sc in next sc, 2 sc in next sc) around: 24 sc.
Rnd 4: (Sc in next 2 sc, 2 sc in next sc) around: 32 sc.
Rnd 5: Hdc in each sc around; slip st in next hdc, finish off.

STEM AND LEAVES
With Green, ch 6 **loosely**; slip st in second ch from hook and in next 3 chs (Stem), leave last ch unworked, ★ ch 3, slip st in second ch from hook, skip last ch, slip st in last ch of Stem (Leaf); repeat from ★ 2 times **more**; finish off leaving a long end for sewing.

WITCH
HEAD
With Green, ch 4 **loosely**; being careful not to twist ch, join with slip st to form a ring.
Rnd 1 (Right side)**:** Ch 1, 2 sc in same ch, 4 sc in next ch, 2 sc in next ch, 4 sc in last ch; do **not** join, place marker *(see Markers, page 138)*: 12 sc.
Note: Loop a short piece of yarn around any stitch to mark last round as **right** side.
Rnd 2: 2 Sc in each sc around: 24 sc.
Rnd 3: Sc in each sc around.
Rnd 4: Sc in next 5 sc, ch 4 **loosely**, slip st in second ch from hook, hdc in next 2 chs, sc in same st as last sc made (nose), sc in next 3 sc, ch 2, hdc in second ch from hook, sc in same st as last sc made (chin), sc in each sc around; slip st in next sc, finish off.

HAIR
With **wrong** side facing, join Orange with slip st in same st as last slip st; work Loop St in first 6 sc pulling loop to measure approximately 1" *(Figs. 12a-c, page 135)*, work Loop St in next 7 sc pulling loop to measure approximately 1³/4", slip st in next sc; finish off.

HAT
Row 1: With Black, ch 3, 3 hdc in third ch from hook.
Row 2 (Right side)**:** Ch 2 **(counts as first hdc, now and throughout)**, turn; hdc in next 2 hdc, leave turning ch unworked.
Note: Mark last row as **right** side.

Embellished with wiggle eyes and felt facial features, these magnets are sure to scare up lots of smiles!

Row 3: Ch 2, turn; hdc in same st and in next hdc, 2 hdc in last hdc: 5 hdc.

Row 4: Ch 2, turn; hdc in next hdc and in each hdc across.

Row 5: Ch 2, turn; hdc in same st and in next 3 hdc, 2 hdc in last hdc: 7 hdc.

Row 6: Ch 2, turn; hdc in next hdc and in each hdc across.

Row 7: Ch 3, turn; working in Back Loops Only *(Fig. 22, page 138)*, dc in same st, 2 dc in next hdc and in each hdc across; finish off leaving a long end for sewing.

FINISHING

Using photo as guide for placement:
Add black felt facial features.
Ghost: Attach eyes.
Jack-O'-Lantern: Sew on Stem and Leaves.
Witch: Sew Hat to Head and attach eye.
Attach magnetic strip to back.

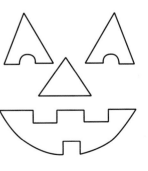

121

Swaying fields of golden grain signal the beginning of the harvest season. During this time of thanksgiving, enrich your celebration with our beautiful doily. It's worked in bedspread weight cotton thread and features a pattern resembling sheaves of wheat.

WHEAT DOILY

Finished Size: Approximately 14" in diameter

MATERIALS

Bedspread Weight Cotton Thread (size 10), approximately 215 yards

Steel crochet hook, size 6 (1.80 mm) **or** size needed for gauge

GAUGE: Rnds 1-8 = 3¼"

PATTERN STITCHES

BEGINNING CLUSTER (uses first 3 dc)
Ch 2, ★ YO, insert hook in **next** dc, YO and pull up a loop, YO and draw through 2 loops on hook; repeat from ★ once **more**, YO and draw through all 3 loops on hook *(Figs. 11a &b, page 134)*.

CLUSTER (uses next 3 dc)
★ YO, insert hook in **next** dc, YO and pull up a loop, YO and draw through 2 loops on hook; repeat from ★ 2 times **more**, YO and draw through all 4 loops on hook.

BODY

Rnd 1 (Right side): Ch 2, 6 sc in second ch from hook; join with slip st to first sc.

Rnds 2 and 3: Ch 1, 2 sc in each sc around; join with slip st to first sc: 24 sc.

Rnd 4: Ch 1, sc in same st, ch 3, skip next sc, (sc in next sc, ch 3, skip next sc) around; join with slip st to first sc: 12 ch-3 sps.

Rnd 5: Slip st in first ch-3 sp, ch 1, sc in same sp, ch 3, (sc in next ch-3 sp, ch 3) around; join with slip st to first sc.

Rnd 6: Slip st in first ch-3 sp, ch 1, (sc, ch 3) twice in same sp and in each ch-3 sp around; join with slip st to first sc: 24 ch-3 sps.

Rnd 7: Repeat Rnd 5.

Rnd 8: Slip st in first ch-3 sp, ch 1, (2 sc, ch 2, 2 sc) in same sp and in each ch-3 sp around; join with slip st to first sc: 24 ch-2 sps.

Rnd 9: Slip st in next sc and in next ch-2 sp, ch 8, (dc in next ch-2 sp, ch 5) around; join with slip st to third ch of beginning ch-8: 24 loops.

Rnd 10: Ch 3 **(counts as first dc, now and throughout)**, (2 dc, ch 3, tr, ch 3, 3 dc) in same st, ch 3, sc in next dc, ch 3, ★ (3 dc, ch 3, tr, ch 3, 3 dc) in next dc, ch 3, sc in next dc, ch 3; repeat from ★ around; join with slip st to first dc: 12 tr.

Rnd 11: Work beginning Cluster, ch 3, (3 dc, ch 3, tr, ch 3, 3 dc) in next tr, ch 3, ★ (work Cluster, ch 3) twice, (3 dc, ch 3, tr, ch 3, 3 dc) in next tr, ch 3; repeat from ★ around to last 3 dc, work Cluster, ch 1, hdc in top of beginning Cluster to form last sp: 24 Clusters.

Rnd 12: Ch 7, work Cluster, ch 3, (3 dc, ch 3, tr, ch 3, 3 dc) in next tr, ch 3, work Cluster, ch 3, skip next ch-3 sp, ★ tr in next ch-3 sp, ch 3, work Cluster, ch 3, (3 dc, ch 3, tr, ch 3, 3 dc) in next tr, ch 3, work Cluster, ch 3, skip next ch-3 sp; repeat from ★ around; join with slip st to fourth ch of beginning ch-7.

Rnd 13: Ch 7, work Cluster, ch 3, (3 dc, ch 3, tr, ch 3, 3 dc) in next tr, ch 3, work Cluster, ch 3, ★ tr in next tr, ch 3, work Cluster, ch 3, (3 dc, ch 3, tr, ch 3, 3 dc) in next tr, ch 3, work Cluster, ch 3; repeat from ★ around; join with slip st to fourth ch of beginning ch-7.

Rnd 14: Ch 3, (2 dc, ch 3, tr, ch 3, 3 dc) in same st, ch 3, work Cluster, ch 3, ★ (3 dc, ch 3, tr, ch 3, 3 dc) in next tr, ch 3, work Cluster, ch 3; repeat from ★ around; join with slip st to first dc.

Rnd 15: Work beginning Cluster, ch 5, 3 dc in next tr, ch 5, ★ (work Cluster, ch 5) twice, 3 dc in next tr, ch 5; repeat from ★ around to last 3 dc, work Cluster, ch 2, dc in top of beginning Cluster to form last loop.

Rnd 16: Ch 1, sc in same loop, ch 5, sc in next loop, ch 5, work Cluster, ch 5, ★ (sc in next loop, ch 5) 3 times, work Cluster, ch 5; repeat from ★ around to last loop, sc in last loop, ch 2, dc in first sc to form last loop.

Rnds 17-19: Ch 1, sc in same loop, (ch 5, sc in next loop) around, ch 2, dc in first sc to form last loop: 96 loops.

Rnd 20: Ch 3, 2 dc in same st, ch 3, sc in next loop, ch 3, ★ 3 dc in center ch of next loop, ch 3, sc in next loop, ch 3; repeat from ★ around; join with slip st to first dc.

Rnd 21: Work beginning Cluster, ch 3, sc in next ch-3 sp, ch 4, slip st in third ch from hook, ch 1, sc in next ch-3 sp, ch 3, ★ work Cluster, ch 3, sc in next ch-3 sp, ch 4, slip st in third ch from hook, ch 1, sc in next ch-3 sp, ch 3; repeat from ★ around; join with slip st to top of beginning Cluster, finish off.

See Washing and Blocking, page 140.

One of the joys of the holiday season is decorating our homes with handmade pieces we've grown to cherish. Sure to be added to those treasured keepsakes are the colorful creations in this collection. Our ruffled miniature tree is stitched with cotton thread and then stiffened. Sprigs of holly and shimmering trims provide a festive finish.

RUFFLED MINI TREE

Finished Size: Approximately 16" tall x 10" in diameter at base

MATERIALS

Bedspread Weight Cotton Thread (size 10),
   approximately 635 yards

Steel crochet hook, size 7 (1.65 mm) **or** size needed for gauge

Starching materials: Commercial fabric stiffener,
   17" x 27½" heavy cardboard, transparent tape, plastic wrap,
   resealable plastic bag, terry towel, paper towels, and
   stainless steel pins

Protective coating materials: Porcelain glaze gloss finish,
   disposable plastic or rubber gloves, stiff paint brush, and
   waxed paper

Finishing materials: Glue gun, glass ornaments, holly sprigs,
   ribbon, and braid

GAUGE: Rnds 1-3 = 1½"

INNER CONE

Rnd 1 (Right side)**:** Ch 4, 5 dc in fourth ch from hook; join with slip st to top of beginning ch: 6 sts.

Note: Loop a short piece of thread around any stitch to mark last round as **right** side.

Rnd 2: Ch 4, tr in next dc and in each dc around; join with slip st to top of beginning ch-4.

Rnd 3: Ch 6, (dtr in next tr, ch 1) around; join with slip st to fifth ch of beginning ch-6.

Rnd 4: Ch 5 **(counts as first dtr, now and throughout)**, dtr in same st, ch 1, (2 dtr in next dtr, ch 1) around; join with slip st to first dtr: 12 dtr.

Rnd 5: Ch 6, (dtr in next dtr, ch 1) around; join with slip st to fifth ch of beginning ch-6.

Rnds 6 and 7: Ch 7, (dtr in next dtr, ch 2) around; join with slip st to fifth ch of beginning ch-7.

Rnd 8: Ch 5, dtr in same st, ch 2, (2 dtr in next dtr, ch 2) around; join with slip st to first dtr: 24 dtr.

Rnds 9 and 10: Ch 6, (dtr in next dtr, ch 1) around; join with slip st to fifth ch of beginning ch-6.

Rnds 11-14: Ch 7, (dtr in next dtr, ch 2) around; join with slip st to fifth ch of beginning ch-7.

Rnd 15: Ch 5, dtr in same st, ch 2, (dtr in next dtr, ch 2) twice, ★ 2 dtr in next dtr, ch 2, (dtr in next dtr, ch 2) twice; repeat from ★ around; join with slip st to first dtr: 32 dtr.

Rnds 16 and 17: Ch 7, (dtr in next dtr, ch 2) around; join with slip st to fifth ch of beginning ch-7.

Rnds 18-20: Ch 8, (dtr in next dtr, ch 3) around; join with slip st to fifth ch of beginning ch-8.

Rnd 21: Ch 9, (dtr in next dtr, ch 4) around; join with slip st to fifth ch of beginning ch-9; do **not** finish off.

Note: Layers are worked from bottom of Inner Cone to top.

FIRST LAYER (Bottom)

Rnd 1: Slip st in first ch-4 sp, ch 3, 3 dc in same sp, 4 dc in next ch-4 sp and in each ch-4 sp around; join with slip st to top of beginning ch-3: 128 sts.

Rnd 2: Ch 6, (dtr in next dc, ch 1) around; join with slip st to fifth ch of beginning ch-6.

Rnd 3: Slip st in first ch-1 sp, ch 1, sc in same sp, (ch 4, sc in next ch-1 sp) around, ch 1, dc in first sc to form last sp.

Rnds 4-6: Ch 1, sc in same sp, (ch 4, sc in next ch-4 sp) around, ch 1, dc in first sc to form last sp.

Rnd 7: Ch 7, dc in fourth ch from hook, dc in same sp, ★ dc in next ch-4 sp, ch 4, dc in fourth ch from hook, dc in same sp; repeat from ★ around; join with slip st to third ch of beginning ch-7, finish off.

SECOND LAYER

Rnd 1: With **right** side facing, join thread with slip st in any ch-3 sp on Rnd 18; ch 3, 3 dc in same sp, 4 dc in next ch-3 sp and in each ch-3 sp around; join with slip st to top of beginning ch-3: 128 sts.

Rnds 2-7: Repeat Rnds 2-7 of First Layer.

THIRD LAYER

Rnd 1: With **right** side facing, join thread with slip st in any ch-2 sp on Rnd 15; ch 3, 3 dc in same sp, 4 dc in next ch-2 sp and in each ch-2 sp around; join with slip st to top of beginning ch-3: 96 sts.

Rnds 2-7: Repeat Rnds 2-7 of First Layer.

FOURTH LAYER

Rnd 1: With **right** side facing, join thread with slip st in any ch-2 sp on Rnd 12; ch 3, 3 dc in same sp, 4 dc in next ch-2 sp and in each ch-2 sp around; join with slip st to top of beginning ch-3: 96 sts.

Rnds 2-7: Repeat Rnds 2-7 of First Layer.

FIFTH LAYER

Rnd 1: With **right** side facing, join thread with slip st in any ch-1 sp on Rnd 10; ch 5, (tr, ch 1) twice in same sp, (tr, ch 1) 3 times in next ch-1 sp and in each ch-1 sp around; join with slip st to fourth ch of beginning ch-5: 72 ch-1 sps.

Rnd 2: Slip st in first ch-1 sp, ch 1, sc in same sp, (ch 4, sc in next ch-1 sp) around, ch 1, dc in first sc to form last sp.

Rnds 3 and 4: Ch 1, sc in same sp, (ch 4, sc in next ch-4 sp) around, ch 1, dc in first sc to form last sp.
Rnd 5: Repeat Rnd 7 of First Layer.

SIXTH LAYER

Rnd 1: With **right** side facing, join thread with slip st in any ch-2 sp on Rnd 8; ch 5, (tr, ch 1) 3 times in same sp, (tr, ch 1) 4 times in next ch-2 sp and in each ch-2 sp around; join with slip st to fourth ch of beginning ch-5: 48 ch-1 sps.
Rnds 2-5: Repeat Rnds 2-5 of Fifth Layer.

SEVENTH LAYER

Rnd 1: With **right** side facing, join thread with slip st in any ch-2 sp on Rnd 6; ch 5, (tr, ch 1) 3 times in same sp, (tr, ch 1) 4 times in next ch-2 sp and in each ch-2 sp around; join with slip st to fourth ch of beginning ch-5: 48 ch-1 sps.
Rnds 2-5: Repeat Rnds 2-5 of Fifth Layer.

EIGHTH LAYER

Rnd 1: With **right** side facing, join thread with slip st in any ch-1 sp on Rnd 4; ch 5, (tr, ch 1) 3 times in same sp, (tr, ch 1) 4 times in next ch-1 sp and in each ch-1 sp around; join with slip st to fourth ch of beginning ch-5: 24 ch-1 sps.
Rnds 2-5: Repeat Rnds 2-5 of Fifth Layer.

NINTH LAYER (Top)

Rnd 1: With **right** side facing, join thread with slip st in any ch-1 sp on Rnd 3; ch 4, (dc, ch 1) twice in same sp, (dc, ch 1) 3 times in next ch-1 sp and in each ch-1 sp around; join with slip st to third ch of beginning ch-4: 18 ch-1 sps.
Rnds 2-5: Repeat Rnds 2-5 of Fifth Layer.

FINISHING

See Starching and Blocking, page 143.
Decorate as desired.

Quick CHEERY TREE SKIRT

Finished Size: Approximately 18" from top edge to bottom edge.

MATERIALS
Worsted Weight Yarn, approximately:
MC (Red) - 27 ounces, (770 grams, 1,775 yards)
Color A (Green) - 3 ounces, (90 grams, 195 yards)
Color B (White) - 2 ounces, (60 grams, 130 yards)
Crochet hook, size N (9.00 mm) **or** size needed for gauge

Note: Entire Skirt is worked holding 4 strands of yarn together.

GAUGE: 7 sc and 8 rows = 4"

With MC, ch 25 **loosely**.
Row 1 (Right side): Sc in second ch from hook and in each ch across: 24 sc.
Note: Loop a short piece of yarn around any stitch to mark last row as **right** side.
Row 2: Ch 1, turn; 2 sc in first sc, sc in next 3 sc, (2 sc in next sc, sc in next 3 sc) across: 30 sc.
Row 3: Ch 1, turn; 2 sc in first sc, sc in next 4 sc, (2 sc in next sc, sc in next 4 sc) across: 36 sc.
Row 4: Ch 1, turn; 2 sc in first sc, sc in next 5 sc, (2 sc in next sc, sc in next 5 sc) across: 42 sc.
Row 5: Ch 1, turn; 2 sc in first sc, sc in next 6 sc, (2 sc in next sc, sc in next 6 sc) across changing to Color A in last sc *(Fig. 24a, page 138)*: 48 sc.
Row 6: Ch 1, turn; (sc, ch 1, sc) in first sc, ★ (ch 1, skip next sc, sc in next sc) 3 times, ch 1, skip next sc, (sc, ch 1, sc) in next sc; repeat from ★ across to last 7 sc, ch 1, (skip next sc, sc in next sc, ch 1) twice, skip next sc, sc in last 2 sc changing to Color B in last sc: 31 sc and 29 ch-1 sps.
Row 7: Ch 1, turn; sc in first sc, (ch 1, skip next sc, sc in next ch-1 sp) across to last sc, sc in last sc changing to Color A.
Row 8: Ch 1, turn; (sc, ch 1, sc) in first sc, (ch 1, skip next sc, sc in next ch-1 sp) 4 times, ★ ch 1, skip next sc, (sc, ch 1, sc) in next ch-1 sp, (ch 1, skip next sc, sc in next ch-1 sp) 4 times; repeat from ★ across to last sc, sc in last sc changing to MC: 37 sc and 35 ch-1 sps.
Row 9: Ch 1, turn; sc in first sc, (ch 1, skip next sc, sc in next ch-1 sp) across to last sc, sc in last sc.
Row 10: Ch 1, turn; 2 sc in first sc, sc in next sc, (sc in next ch-1 sp, sc in next sc) 5 times, ★ 2 sc in next ch-1 sp, sc in next sc, (sc in next ch-1 sp, sc in next sc) 5 times; repeat from ★ across: 78 sc.
Row 11: Ch 1, turn; 2 sc in first sc, sc in next 12 sc, (2 sc in next sc, sc in next 12 sc) across: 84 sc.
Row 12: Ch 1, turn; 2 sc in first sc, sc in next 13 sc, (2 sc in next sc, sc in next 13 sc) across: 90 sc.
Row 13: Ch 1, turn; 2 sc in first sc, sc in next 14 sc, (2 sc in next sc, sc in next 14 sc) across: 96 sc.
Row 14: Ch 1, turn; 2 sc in first sc, sc in next 15 sc, (2 sc in next sc, sc in next 15 sc) across: 102 sc.
Row 15: Ch 1, turn; 2 sc in first sc, sc in next 16 sc, (2 sc in next sc, sc in next 16 sc) across: 108 sc.
Row 16: Ch 1, turn; 2 sc in first sc, sc in next 17 sc, (2 sc in next sc, sc in next 17 sc) across: 114 sc.
Row 17: Ch 1, turn; 2 sc in first sc, sc in next 18 sc, (2 sc in next sc, sc in next 18 sc) across: 120 sc.
Row 18: Ch 1, turn; 2 sc in first sc, sc in next 19 sc, (2 sc in next sc, sc in next 19 sc) across: 126 sc.
Row 19: Ch 1, turn; 2 sc in first sc, sc in next 20 sc, (2 sc in next sc, sc in next 20 sc) across: 132 sc.

Worked holding four strands of yarn, this colorful striped skirt makes a cheery accent for your Christmas tree.

Row 20: Ch 1, turn; 2 sc in first sc, sc in next 21 sc, (2 sc in next sc, sc in next 21 sc) across: 138 sc.

Row 21: Ch 1, turn; 2 sc in first sc, sc in next 22 sc, (2 sc in next sc, sc in next 22 sc) across: 144 sc.

Row 22: Ch 1, turn; 2 sc in first sc, sc in next 23 sc, (2 sc in next sc, sc in next 23 sc) across: 150 sc.

Row 23: Ch 1, turn; 2 sc in first sc, sc in next 24 sc, (2 sc in next sc, sc in next 24 sc) across: 156 sc.

Row 24: Ch 1, turn; 2 sc in first sc, sc in next 25 sc, (2 sc in next sc, sc in next 25 sc) across: 162 sc.

Row 25: Ch 1, turn; 2 sc in first sc, sc in next 26 sc, (2 sc in next sc, sc in next 26 sc) across: 168 sc.

Row 26: Ch 1, turn; 2 sc in first sc, sc in next 27 sc, (2 sc in next sc, sc in next 27 sc) across: 174 sc.

Row 27: Ch 1, turn; 2 sc in first sc, sc in next 28 sc, (2 sc in next sc, sc in next 28 sc) across: 180 sc.

Row 28: Ch 1, turn; (sc, ch 1, sc) in first sc, ★ (ch 1, skip next sc, sc in next sc) 14 times, ch 1, skip next sc, (sc, ch 1, sc) in next sc; repeat from ★ 4 times **more**, (ch 1, skip next sc, sc in next sc) across to last 3 sc, ch 1, skip next sc, sc in last 2 sc changing to Color A in last sc: 97 sc and 95 ch-1 sps.

Row 29: Ch 1, turn; sc in first sc, (ch 1, skip next sc, sc in next ch-1 sp) across to last sc, sc in last sc changing to Color B.

Row 30: Ch 1, turn; (sc, ch 1, sc) in first sc, (ch 1, skip next sc, sc in next ch-1 sp) 15 times, ★ ch 1, skip next sc, (sc, ch 1, sc) in next ch-1 sp, (ch 1, skip next sc, sc in next ch-1 sp) 15 times; repeat from ★ across to last sc, sc in last sc changing to Color A: 103 sc and 101 ch-1 sps.

Row 31: Ch 1, turn; sc in first sc, (ch 1, skip next sc, sc in next ch-1 sp) across to last sc, sc in last sc changing to MC.

Row 32: Ch 1, turn; sc in first sc, ch 2, skip next sc, sc in next ch-1 sp, ★ (ch 1, skip next sc, sc in next ch-1 sp) 16 times, ch 2, skip next sc, sc in next ch-1 sp; repeat from ★ 4 times **more**, (ch 1, skip next sc, sc in next ch-1 sp) across to last sc, sc in last sc; finish off.

SNOWFLAKE SACHETS

Finished Size: Approximately 4" in diameter

MATERIALS
Bedspread Weight Cotton Thread (size 10), approximately:

Snowflake #1
  MC (Red) - 35 yards
  CC (Ecru) - 13 yards

Snowflake #2
  MC (Red) - 35 yards
  CC (Ecru) - 15 yards

Snowflake #3
  MC (Red) - 35 yards
  CC (Ecru) - 18 yards

Steel crochet hook, size 6 (1.80 mm) **or** size needed
  for gauge
1/2 yard of 1/8" ribbon for **each**
Tapestry needle
Sewing needle and thread
4 - 5" squares of bridal net for **each**
Potpourri

GAUGE: Rnds 1 and 2 of Back = 1 1/4"

PATTERN STITCHES

CLUSTER
Ch 3, ★ YO, insert hook in third ch from hook, YO and pull up a loop, YO and draw through 2 loops on hook; repeat from ★ once **more**, YO and draw through all 3 loops on hook *(Figs. 10a & b, page 134)*.

5-TR CLUSTER (uses next 5 tr)
★ YO twice, insert hook in **next** tr, YO and pull up a loop, (YO and draw through 2 loops on hook) twice; repeat from ★ 4 **more**, YO and draw through all 6 loops on hook *(Figs. 11a & b, page 134)*.

2-TR CLUSTER
Ch 4, ★ YO twice, insert hook in fourth ch from hook, YO and pull up a loop, (YO and draw through 2 loops on hook) twice; repeat from ★ once **more**, YO and draw through all 3 loops on hook.

BEGINNING 3-TR CLUSTER
Ch 3, ★ YO twice, insert hook st or sp indicated, YO and pull up a loop, (YO and draw through 2 loops on hook) twice; repeat from ★ once **more**, YO and draw through all 3 loops on hook.

3-TR CLUSTER
★ YO twice, insert hook st or sp indicated, YO and pull up a loop, (YO and draw through 2 loops on hook) twice; repeat from ★ 2 times **more**, YO and draw through all 4 loops on hook.

2-PICOT LOOP
Ch 6, slip st in fifth ch from hook, ch 8, slip st in fifth ch from hook, ch 2.

4-PICOT LOOP
(Ch 5, slip st in fifth ch from hook) 4 times, ch 1.

BACK
With MC, ch 4; join with slip st to form a ring.

Rnd 1 (Right side): Ch 3, 11 dc in ring; join with slip st to top of beginning ch-3: 12 sts.

Note: Loop a short piece of thread around any stitch to mark last round as **right** side.

Rnd 2: Ch 5 (counts as first dc plus ch 2, now and throughout), dc in same st, ch 2, dc in next dc, ch 2, ★ (dc, ch 2) twice in next dc, dc in next dc, ch 2; repeat from ★ around; join with slip st to first dc: 18 dc.

Rnd 3: Ch 5, dc in next dc, ch 2, (dc, ch 2) twice in next dc, ★ (dc in next dc, ch 2) twice, (dc, ch 2) twice in next dc; repeat from ★ around; join with slip st to first dc: 24 dc.

Rnd 4: Ch 5, dc in same st, ch 2, (dc in next dc, ch 2) 3 times, ★ (dc, ch 2) twice in next dc, (dc in next dc, ch 2) 3 times; repeat from ★ around; join with slip st to first dc: 30 dc.

Rnd 5: Ch 5, dc in next dc, ch 2, (dc, ch 2) twice in next dc, ★ (dc in next dc, ch 2) 4 times, (dc, ch 2) twice in next dc; repeat from ★ around to last 2 dc, (dc in next dc, ch 2) twice; join with slip st to first dc: 36 dc.

Rnd 6: Ch 5, dc in same st, ch 2, (dc in next dc, ch 2) 5 times, ★ (dc, ch 2) twice in next dc, (dc in next dc, ch 2) 5 times; repeat from ★ around; join with slip st to first dc: 42 dc.

Rnd 7: Ch 5, (dc in next dc, ch 2) 3 times, (dc, ch 2) twice in next dc, ★ (dc in next dc, ch 2) 6 times, (dc, ch 2) twice in next dc; repeat from ★ around to last 2 dc, (dc in next dc, ch 2) twice; join with slip st to first dc: 48 dc.

Rnd 8 (Eyelet rnd): Ch 5, (dc in next dc, ch 2) around; join with slip st to first dc, finish off: 48 ch-2 sps.

SNOWFLAKE #1 - FRONT
Rnd 1 (Right side): With CC, ch 2, sc in second ch from hook, (ch 6, sc in same ch) 5 times, ch 2, tr in first sc to form last loop: 6 loops.

Note: Mark last round as **right** side.

Rnd 2: Ch 8, dc in same loop, ch 6, ★ (dc, ch 5, dc) in next loop, ch 6; repeat from ★ around; join with slip st to third ch of beginning ch-8: 12 loops.

Filled with potpourri, these lacy ornaments also make sweet-smelling gifts and package tie-ons.

Rnd 3: Slip st in first loop, ch 6, (tr, ch 5, tr, ch 2, tr) in same loop, ch 1, sc in next ch-6 loop, ch 1, ★ (tr, ch 2, tr, ch 5, tr, ch 2, tr) in next ch-5 loop, ch 1, sc in next ch-6 loop, ch 1; repeat from ★ around; join with slip st to fourth ch of beginning ch-6.

Rnd 4: Ch 1, sc in same st, work Cluster, dc in next tr, work Cluster, (tr, work Cluster) 3 times in next loop, dc in next tr, work Cluster, sc in next tr and in next ch-1 sp, sc in next sc and in next ch-1 sp, ★ sc in next tr, work Cluster, dc in next tr, work Cluster, (tr, work Cluster) 3 times in next loop, dc in next tr, work Cluster, sc in next tr and in next ch-1 sp, sc in next sc and in next ch-1 sp; repeat from ★ around; join with slip st to first sc, finish off: 36 Clusters.

Rnd 5: With **right** side facing, skip first Cluster and join MC with sc in next dc *(see Joining With Sc, page 137)*; ch 9, skip next 4 Clusters, keeping chs **behind** Clusters, sc in next dc, ch 5, ★ skip next 2 Clusters, sc in next dc, ch 9, skip next 4 Clusters, keeping chs **behind** Clusters, sc in next dc, ch 5; repeat from ★ around; join with slip st to first sc: 12 loops.

Rnd 6: Ch 5, (skip next ch, dc in next ch, ch 2) 4 times, dc in next sc, ch 2, (skip next ch, dc in next ch, ch 2) twice, ★ dc in next sc, ch 2, (skip next ch, dc in next ch, ch 2) 4 times, dc in next sc, ch 2, (skip next ch, dc in next ch, ch 2) twice; repeat from ★ around; join with slip st to first dc: 48 ch-2 sps.

Rnd 7 (Eyelet rnd): Ch 5, dc in next dc, ch 2, holding next tip of Snowflake in front of next dc, dc in both center tr on Rnd 4 **and** in dc to join Snowflake, ch 2, ★ (dc in next dc, ch 2) 7 times, holding next tip of Snowflake in front of next dc, dc in both center tr on Rnd 4 **and** in dc, ch 2; repeat from ★ 4 times **more**, (dc in next dc, ch 2) around; join with slip st to first dc: 48 ch-2 sps.

Rnd 8 (Edging): Ch 2, dc in same st, (slip st, ch 2, dc) in next dc and in each dc around; join with slip st to first st, finish off.

SNOWFLAKE #2 - FRONT

Rnd 1 (Right side): With CC, ch 9, dc in ninth ch from hook, (ch 5, dc in same ch) 4 times, ch 2, dc in fourth ch of beginning ch-9 to form last loop: 6 loops.

Note: Mark last round as **right** side.

Rnd 2: Ch 1, (sc, ch 5, sc) in same loop, (ch 5, sc) twice in next loop and in each loop around, ch 2, dc in first sc to form last loop: 12 loops.

Rnd 3: Ch 1, sc in same loop, ch 4, 5 tr in next loop, ★ ch 4, sc in next loop, ch 4, 5 tr in next loop; repeat from ★ around, tr in first sc to form last sp: 30 tr.

Rnd 4: Ch 1, sc in same sp, ch 5, sc in next ch-4 sp, ch 5, work 5-tr Cluster, ★ ch 6, (sc in next ch-4 sp, ch 5) twice, work 5-tr Cluster; repeat from ★ around, ch 2, tr in first sc to form last loop: 6 5-tr Clusters.

Rnd 5: Ch 1, sc in same loop, work 2-tr Cluster, (tr, work 2-tr Cluster twice, tr) in next loop, work 2-tr Cluster, sc in next loop, ch 5, ★ sc in next loop, work 2-tr Cluster, (tr, work 2-tr Cluster twice, tr) in next loop, work 2-tr Cluster, sc in next loop, ch 5; repeat from ★ around; join with slip st to first sc, finish off: 24 2-tr Clusters.

Rnd 6: With **right** side facing, skip next 2-tr Cluster and join MC with slip st in next tr, ch 8, skip next 2 2-tr Clusters, keeping chs **behind** 2-tr Clusters, dc in next tr, ch 2, [tr, ch 2, (dc, ch 2) twice, tr] in next loop, ch 2, ★ skip next 2-tr Cluster, dc in next tr, ch 5, skip next 2 2-tr Clusters, keeping chs **behind** 2-tr Clusters, dc in next tr, ch 2, [tr, ch 2, (dc, ch 2) twice, tr] in next loop, ch 2; repeat from ★ around; join with slip st to third ch of beginning ch-8: 36 sps.

Rnd 7 (Eyelet rnd): Ch 5, (dc, ch 2) twice in next loop, dc in next dc, ch 2, ★ (skip next ch-2 sp, dc in next st, ch 2) 5 times, (dc, ch 2) twice in next loop, dc in next dc, ch 2; repeat from ★ 4 times **more**, (skip next ch-2 sp, dc in next st, ch 2) 4 times; join with slip st to third ch of beginning ch-5: 48 ch-2 sps.

Rnd 8 (Edging): Ch 2, dc in same st, (slip st, ch 2, dc) in next dc and in each dc around; join with slip st to first st, finish off.

SNOWFLAKE #3 - FRONT

Rnd 1 (Right side): With CC, ch 2, 6 sc in second ch from hook; join with slip st to first sc.

Note: Mark last round as **right** side.

Rnd 2: Work beginning 3-tr Cluster in same st, work 2-tr Cluster, ch 1, ★ work 3-tr Cluster in next sc, work 2-tr Cluster, ch 1; repeat from ★ around; join with slip st to top of beginning 3-tr Cluster: 12 Clusters.

Rnd 3: Ch 1, sc in same st, work 2-Picot Loop, skip next 2-tr Cluster, ★ sc in next 3-tr Cluster, work 2-Picot Loop, skip next 2-tr Cluster; repeat from ★ around; join with slip st to first sc: 12 Picots.

Rnd 4: Slip st in first 2 chs, ch 1, working **behind** next Picot, slip st in next ch, ch 1, 3 sc in same sp, ch 10, skip next 2 Picots, ★ 3 sc in next sp, ch 10, skip next 2 Picots; repeat from ★ around; join with slip st to first sc: 6 loops.

Rnd 5: Slip st in next 2 sc and in next loop, in same loop work [beginning 3-tr Cluster, ch 3, 3-tr Cluster, (4-Picot Loop, 3-tr Cluster) twice, ch 3, 3-tr Cluster], in next loop and in each loop around work [3-tr Cluster, ch 3, 3-tr Cluster, (4-Picot Loop, 3-tr Cluster) twice, ch 3, 3-tr Cluster]; join with slip st to top of beginning 3-tr Cluster, finish off: 30 Clusters.

Rnd 6: With **right** side facing, join MC with slip st in first ch-3 sp, ch 10 **(counts as first tr plus ch 6)**, skip next 3-tr Cluster, tr in next 3-tr Cluster, ch 6, tr in next ch-3 sp, ch 4, ★ tr in next ch-3 sp, ch 6, skip next 3-tr Cluster, tr in next 3-tr Cluster, ch 6, tr in next ch-3 sp, ch 4; repeat from ★ around; join with slip st to first tr: 18 tr.

Rnd 7 (Eyelet rnd): Ch 5, [(dc, ch 2) twice in next ch-6 loop, dc in next tr, ch 2] 2 times, dc in next ch-4 sp, ch 2, ★ dc in next tr, ch 2, [(dc, ch 2) twice in next ch-6 loop, dc in next tr, ch 2] 2 times, dc in next ch-4 sp, ch 2; repeat from ★ around; join with slip st to first dc: 48 ch-2 sps.

Rnd 8 (Edging): Ch 2, dc in same st, (slip st, ch 2, dc) in next dc and in each dc around; join with slip st to first st, finish off.

FINISHING

See Washing and Blocking, page 140.

POTPOURRI POUCH

Using Back for pattern, cut four pieces of bridal net, allowing 1/4" seam allowance. Sew seam leaving a 2" opening for turning. Turn right side out having 2 layers for each side. Fill with potpourri and sew opening closed.

JOINING

With **wrong** sides together and matching spaces, weave ribbon through Eyelet rnd, inserting pouch before closing. Tie ribbon in a bow to secure.

Symbolizing bead garlands, ribbons of Christmasy colors make this fringed afghan especially merry!

MERRY AFGHAN

Finished Size: Approximately 49" x 65"

MATERIALS

Worsted Weight Yarn, approximately:
MC (White) - 25 ounces, (710 grams, 1,645 yards)
Color A (Red) - 12 ounces, (340 grams, 790 yards)
Color B (Green) - 11 ounces, (310 grams, 725 yards)
Crochet hook, size I (5.50 mm) **or** size needed for gauge

Note #1: Each row is worked across length of afghan.
Note #2: When changing colors at end of rows, leave a 7" end
for fringe.

COLOR SEQUENCE

2 Rows each Color A *(Fig. 24a, page 138)*, ★ MC, Color B,
MC, Color A; repeat from ★ throughout.

GAUGE: In pattern, 14 sts = 4"

With Color A, ch 229 **loosely**.
Row 1 (Right side): Sc in second ch from hook and in next
3 chs, (dc in next 4 chs, sc in next 4 chs) across: 228 sts.
Note: Loop a short piece of yarn around any stitch to mark last
row as **right** side.
Row 2: Ch 1, turn; sc in first 4 sc, (dc in next 4 dc, sc in next
4 sc) across.
Row 3: Ch 3 **(counts as first dc, now and throughout)**,
turn; dc in next 3 sc, (sc in next 4 dc, dc in next 4 sc) across.
Row 4: Ch 3, turn; dc in next 3 dc, (sc in next 4 sc, dc in next
4 dc) across.
Row 5: Ch 1, turn; sc in first 4 dc, (dc in next 4 sc, sc in next
4 dc) across.
Repeat Rows 2-5 until afghan measures approximately 49",
ending by working Row 2 with Color A.
Finish off.

Add fringe using 2 or 3 strands of matching color, each 15" long
(Figs. 30a & b, page 140); attach in end of each row across
both ends of afghan.

131

general instructions

ABBREVIATIONS

BLO	Back Loop(s) Only
BPdc	Back Post double crochet(s)
BPhdc	Back Post half double crochet(s)
CC	Contrasting Color
ch(s)	chain(s)
dc	double crochet(s)
dtr	double treble crochet(s)
FLO	Front Loop(s) Only
FPdc	Front Post double crochet(s)
FPhdc	Front Post half double crochet(s)
FPtr	Front Post treble crochet(s)
hdc	half double crochet(s)
MC	Main Color
mm	millimeters
Rnd(s)	Round(s)
sc	single crochet(s)
sp(s)	space(s)
st(s)	stitch(es)
tr	treble crochet(s)
YO	yarn over

★ — work instructions following ★ as many **more** times as indicated in addition to the first time.

† to † — work all instructions from first † to second † **as many** times as specified.

( ) or [ ] — work enclosed instructions **as many** times as specified by the number immediately following **or** work all enclosed instructions in the stitch or space indicated **or** contains explanatory remarks.

work even — work without increasing or decreasing in the established pattern.

GAUGE

Correct gauge is essential for proper size or fit. Hook sizes given in instructions are merely guides and should never be used without first making a sample swatch as indicated. Then measure it, counting your stitches and rows or rounds carefully. If your swatch is smaller than specified, try again with a larger size hook; if larger, try again with a smaller size. Keep trying until you find the size that will give you the specified gauge. DO NOT HESITATE TO CHANGE HOOK SIZE TO OBTAIN CORRECT GAUGE. On garments and afghans, once proper gauge is obtained, measure width of piece approximately every 3" to be sure gauge remains consistent.

basic stitch guide

CHAIN

When beginning a first row of crochet in a chain, always skip the first chain from the hook, and work into the second chain from hook (for single crochet), third chain from hook (for half double crochet), or fourth chain from hook (for double crochet), etc. *(Fig. 1)*.

Fig. 1

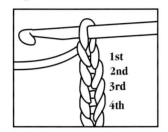

WORKING INTO THE CHAIN

Method 1: Insert hook into back ridge of each chain indicated *(Fig. 2a)*.
Method 2: Insert hook under top two strands of each chain *(Fig. 2b)*.

Fig. 2a   **Fig. 2b**

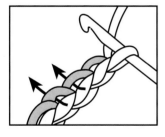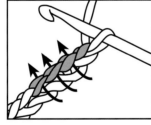

MAKING A BEGINNING RING

Chain amount indicated in instructions. Being careful not to twist chain, slip stitch in first chain to form a ring *(Fig. 3)*.

Fig. 3

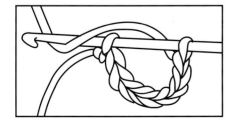

SINGLE CROCHET *(abbreviated sc)*

Insert hook in stitch or space indicated, YO and pull up a loop, YO and draw through both loops on hook *(Fig. 4)*.

Fig. 4

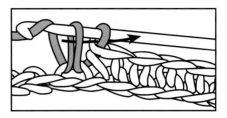

LONG STITCH

Work single crochet *(sc)* or double crochet *(dc)* inserting hook in stitch indicated in instructions *(Fig. 5)* and pulling up a loop even with loop on hook; complete as instructed.

Fig. 5

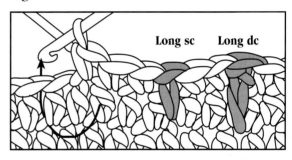

HALF DOUBLE CROCHET
(abbreviated hdc)

YO, insert hook in stitch or space indicated, YO and pull up a loop, YO and draw through all 3 loops on hook *(Fig. 6)*.

Fig. 6

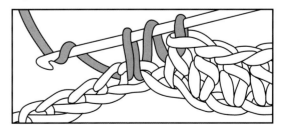

DOUBLE CROCHET *(abbreviated dc)*

YO, insert hook in stitch or space indicated, YO and pull up a loop, YO and draw through 2 loops on hook *(Fig. 7a)*, YO and draw through remaining 2 loops on hook *(Fig. 7b)*.

Fig. 7a

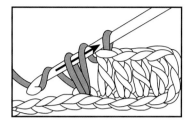

Fig. 7b

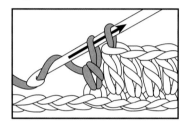

TREBLE CROCHET *(abbreviated tr)*

YO twice, insert hook in stitch or space indicated, YO and pull up a loop *(Fig. 8a)*, (YO and draw through 2 loops on hook) 3 times *(Fig. 8b)*.

Fig. 8a

Fig. 8b

DOUBLE TREBLE CROCHET *(abbreviated dtr)*

YO three times, insert hook in stitch or space indicated, YO and pull up a loop *(Fig. 9a)*, (YO and draw through 2 loops on hook) 4 times *(Fig. 9b)*.

Fig. 9a

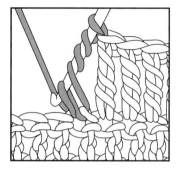

Fig. 9b

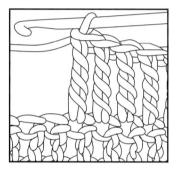

CLUSTER

A Cluster can be worked all in the same stitch or space *(Figs. 10a & b)*, **or** across several stitches *(Figs. 11a & b)*.

Fig. 10a

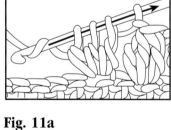

Fig. 10b

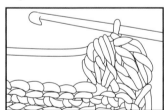

Fig. 11a

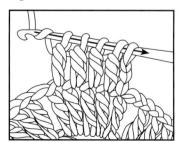

Fig. 11b

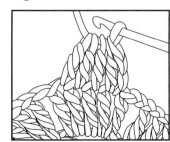

LOOP STITCH

Insert hook in next stitch, wrap yarn around index finger of left hand once **more**, insert hook through both loops on finger following direction indicated by arrow *(Fig. 12a)*, being careful to hook all loops *(Fig. 12b)*, draw through stitch pulling each loop as specified in instructions, remove finger from loop, YO and draw through all 3 loops on hook **(Loop St made, Fig. 12c)**.

Fig. 12a

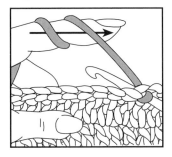

Fig. 12b

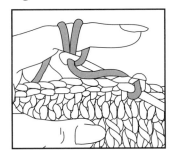

Fig. 12c

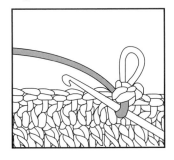

POST STITCH

Work around post of stitch indicated, inserting hook in direction of arrow *(Fig. 13)*.

Fig. 13

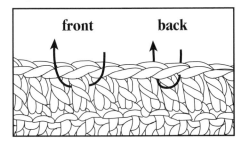

FRONT POST HALF DOUBLE CROCHET
(abbreviated FPhdc)

YO, insert hook from **front** to **back** around post of stitch indicated *(Fig. 13)*, YO and pull up a loop, YO and draw through all 3 loops on hook *(Fig. 14)*.

Fig. 14

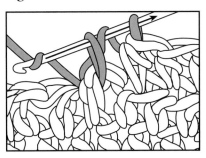

BACK POST HALF DOUBLE CROCHET
(abbreviated BPhdc)

YO, insert hook from **back** to **front** around post of stitch indicated *(Fig. 13)*, YO and pull up a loop, YO and draw through all 3 loops on hook *(Fig. 15)*.

Fig. 15

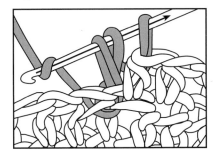

FRONT POST DOUBLE CROCHET
(abbreviated FPdc)
YO, insert hook from **front** to **back** around post of stitch indicated (*Fig. 13, page 135*), YO and pull up a loop (*Fig. 16*), (YO and draw through 2 loops on hook) twice.

Fig. 16

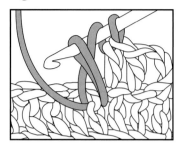

BACK POST DOUBLE CROCHET
(abbreviated BPdc)
YO, insert hook from **back** to **front** around post of stitch indicated (*Fig. 13, page 135*), YO and pull up a loop (*Fig. 17*), (YO and draw through 2 loops on hook) twice.

Fig. 17

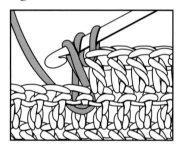

FRONT POST TREBLE CROCHET
(abbreviated FPtr)
YO twice, insert hook from **front** to **back** around post of stitch indicated (*Fig. 13, page 135*), YO and pull up a loop (*Fig. 18*), (YO and draw through 2 loops on hook) 3 times.

Fig. 18

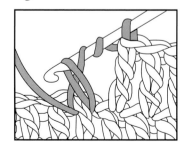

REVERSE SINGLE CROCHET
(abbreviated Reverse sc)
Working from **left** to **right**, insert hook in stitch to right of hook (*Fig. 19a*), YO and draw through, under and to left of loop on hook (2 loops on hook) (*Fig. 19b*), YO and draw through both loops on hook (*Fig. 19c*) (**Reverse sc made, *Fig. 19d***).

Fig. 19a   **Fig. 19b**

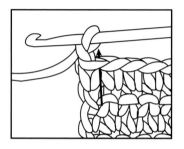   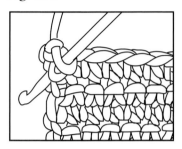

Fig. 19c   **Fig. 19d**

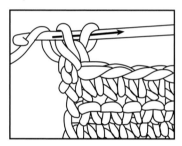   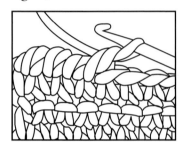

REVERSE HALF DOUBLE CROCHET
(abbreviated Reverse hdc)
Working from **left** to **right**, YO, insert hook in stitch indicated to right of hook (*Fig. 20a*), YO and draw through, under and to left of loops on hook (3 loops on hook) (*Fig. 20b*), YO and draw through all 3 loops on hook (*Fig. 20c*) (**Reverse hdc made, *Fig. 20d***).

Fig. 20a   **Fig. 20b**

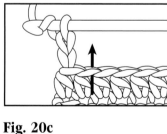   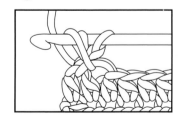

Fig. 20c   **Fig. 20d**

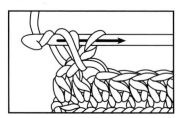   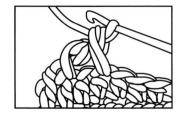

YARN

Yarn weight (type or size) is divided into four basic categories: **Fingering** (baby clothes), **Sport** (light-weight sweaters and afghans), **Worsted** (sweaters, afghans, toys), and **Bulky** (heavy sweaters, potholders, and afghans).

Baby yarn may either be classified as Fingering or Sport - check the label for the recommended gauge.

These weights have absolutely nothing to do with the number of plies. Ply refers to the number of strands that have been twisted together to make the yarn. There are fingering weight yarns consisting of four plies - and there are bulky weight yarns made of a single ply.

SUBSTITUTING YARN

Once you know the **weight** of the yarn specified for a particular pattern, **any** brand of the **same** weight may be used for that pattern.

You may wish to purchase a single skein first, and crochet a gauge swatch. Compare the gauge (remember, it **must** match the gauge in the pattern) and then compare the way the new yarn looks to the photographed item to be sure that you'll be satisfied with the finished results.

How many skeins to buy depends on the **yardage**. Compare the labels and don't hesitate to ask the shop owner for assistance. Ounces and grams can vary from one brand of the same weight yarn to another, but the yardage required to make a garment or item, in the size and pattern you've chosen, will always remain the same provided gauge is met and maintained.

DYE LOTS

Yarn is dyed in "lots" and then numbered. Different lots of the same color will vary slightly in shade and will be noticeable if crocheted in the same piece.

When buying yarn, it is important to check labels for the dye lot number. You should purchase enough of one color, from the same lot, to finish the entire project. It is a good practice to purchase an extra skein to be sure that you have enough to complete your project.

HOOKS

Crochet hooks used for working with **yarn** are made from aluminum, plastic, bone, or wood. They are lettered in sizes ranging from size B (2.25 mm) to the largest size Q (15.00 mm) - **the higher the letter, the larger the hook size**.

Crochet hooks used for **thread** work are most commonly made of steel. They are numbered in sizes ranging from size 00 (3.50 mm) to a very small size 14 (.75 mm) and, unlike aluminum hooks, **the higher the number, the smaller the hook size**.

HOW TO DETERMINE THE RIGHT SIDE

Many designs are made with the **front** of the stitch as the **right** side. Notice that the **front** of the stitches are smooth *(Fig. 21a)* and the **back** of the stitches are bumpy *(Fig. 21b)*. For easy identification, it may be helpful to loop a short piece of yarn, thread, or fabric around any stitch to mark **right** side.

Fig. 21a

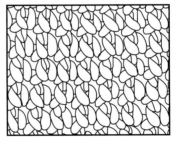

Fig. 21b

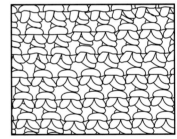

JOINING WITH SC

When instructed to join with sc, begin with a slip knot on hook. Insert hook in stitch or space indicated, YO and pull up a loop, yarn over and draw through both loops on hook.

MARKERS

Markers are used to help distinguish the beginning of each round being worked. Place a 2" scrap piece of yarn or fabric before the first stitch of each round, moving marker after each round is complete. Remove when no longer needed.

BACK OR FRONT LOOP ONLY

Work only in loop(s) indicated by arrow *(Fig. 22)*.

Fig. 22

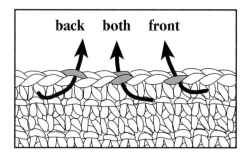

FREE LOOP

After working in Back or Front Loops Only on a row or round, there will be a ridge of unused loops. These are called the free loops. Later, when instructed to work in the free loops of the same row or round, work in these loops *(Fig. 23a)*. When instructed to work in a free loop of a beginning chain, work in loop indicated by arrow *(Fig. 23b)*.

Fig. 23a

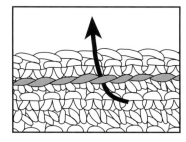

Fig. 23b

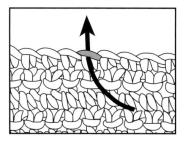

CHANGING COLORS

Work the last stitch to within one step of completion, hook new yarn *(Fig. 24a)* and draw through loops on hook. Cut old yarn and work over both ends unless otherwise specified. When working in rounds, drop old yarn and join with slip stitch to first stitch using new yarn *(Fig. 24b)*.

Fig. 24a

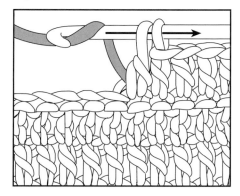

Fig. 24b

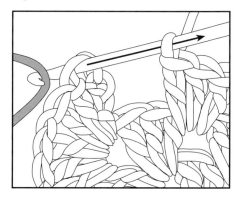

WORKING OVER WIRE

Place wire against chain or row indicated. Work stitches indicated over wire *(Fig. 25)*.

Fig. 25

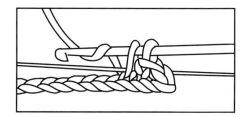

PREPARING FABRIC STRIPS

Fabric selected should be high quality, even weave 100% cotton, such as those sold for piecing quilts. Yardages given are based on fabrics 44/45" wide.

If the fabric is not pre-shrunk, it should be gently machine washed and dried. Straighten your fabric by pulling it across the bias. It may be necessary to lightly press the fabric.

To avoid joining strips often, we recommend that your strips be two yards or longer.

TEARING STRIPS

Tear off selvages, then tear into strips as instructed.

CUTTING STRIPS

1. Fold the fabric in half, short end to short end, as many times as possible, while still being able to cut through all thicknesses *(Fig. 26a)*.

Fig. 26a

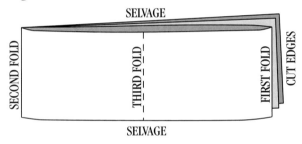

2. Cut off selvages, then cut fabric into 1" wide strips *(Fig. 26b)*. For quick results, a rotary cutter and mat may be used to cut several layers of fabric at one time.

Fig. 26b

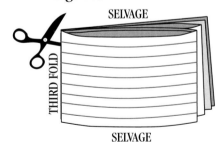

JOINING FABRIC STRIPS

The following is a technique for joining fabric strips without sewing strips together, and eliminates knots or ends to weave in later.

1. To join a new strip of fabric to working strip, cut a ½" slit, about ½" from ends of both fabric strips *(Fig. 27a)*.

Fig. 27a

2. With **right** sides up, place end of new strip over end of working strip and match slits *(Fig. 27b)*.

Fig. 27b

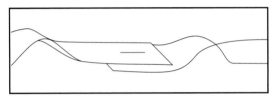

3. Pull free end of new strip through both slits from bottom to top *(Fig. 27c)*.

Fig. 27c

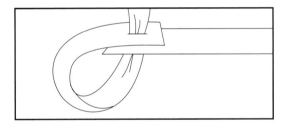

4. Pull new strip firmly to form a small knot *(Fig. 27d)*. Right sides of both strips should be facing up. Continue working with new strip.

Fig. 27d

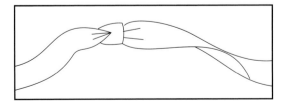

finishing

MAKING PILLOW FORM

Using crocheted piece for pattern, cut two pieces of fabric, allowing 1/4" for seam allowance.

With **right** sides together, sew seam leaving a 2" opening for turning.

Turn form right side out; stuff firmly and sew opening closed.

WASHING AND BLOCKING

For a more professional look, thread projects should be washed and blocked. Using a mild detergent and warm water and being careful not to rub, twist, or wring, gently squeeze suds through the piece. Rinse several times in cool, clear water. Roll piece in a clean terry towel and gently press out the excess moisture. Lay piece on a flat surface and shape to proper size; where needed, pin in place using stainless steel pins. Allow to dry **completely**. Doilies can be spray starched for extra crispness.

WHIPSTITCH

With **wrong** sides together, and beginning in corner stitch, sew through both pieces once to secure the beginning of the seam, leaving an ample yarn end to weave in later. Insert needle from **front** to **back** through **both** loops of **each** piece **(Fig. 28a)** or through **inside** loops **(Fig. 28b)**. Bring needle around and insert it from **front** to **back** through the next loops of **both** pieces. Continue in this manner across to corner, keeping the sewing yarn fairly loose.

Fig. 28a

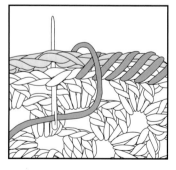

Fig. 28b

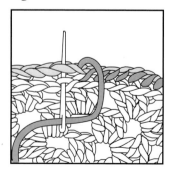

POM-POM

Cut a piece of cardboard 3" wide and as long as the diameter of your finished pom-pom is to be.

Wind the yarn around the cardboard until it is approximately 1/2" thick in the middle **(Fig. 29a)**.

Carefully slip the yarn off the cardboard and firmly tie an 18" length of yarn around the middle **(Fig. 29b)**. Leave yarn ends long enough to attach the pom-pom.

Cut the loops on both ends and trim the pom-pom into a smooth ball.

Fig. 29a

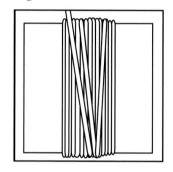

Fig. 29b

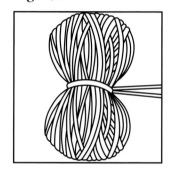

FRINGE

Cut a piece of cardboard 8" wide and half as long as specified in instructions for finished strands. Wind the yarn **loosely** and **evenly** around the cardboard until the card is filled, then cut across one end; repeat as needed. Hold the number of strands specified for one knot together and fold in half.

With **wrong** side facing and using a crochet hook, draw the folded end up through a row or stitch and pull the loose ends through the folded end **(Fig. 30a)**; draw the knot up **tightly** **(Fig. 30b)**. Repeat, spacing as specified. Lay flat on a hard surface and trim the ends.

Fig. 30a

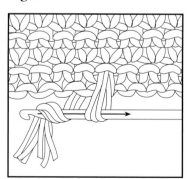

Fig. 30b

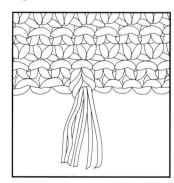

TURKEY LOOP STITCH

This stitch is composed of locked loops. Bring needle up through a stitch and back down through same stitch *(Point A)* forming a loop on **right** side of work. Bring needle up to either side of loop *(Point B)*, and back down through Point A locking stitch. Begin next stitch at Point B *(Fig. 31)*.

Fig. 31

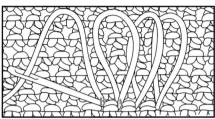

OUTLINE STITCH

Bring needle up from wrong side at 1, leaving an end to be woven in later. Holding yarn or floss **above** the needle with thumb, insert needle down at 2 and up again at 3 (halfway between 1 and 2) *(Fig. 32a)*, pull through. Insert needle down at 4 and up again at 2, making sure the yarn or floss is **above** the needle *(Fig. 32b)*, pull through. Continue in same manner.

Fig. 32a   **Fig. 32b**

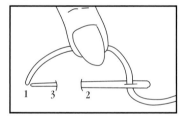   

STRAIGHT STITCH

Straight Stitch is just what the name implies, a single, straight stitch. Bring needle up at 1 and go down at 2 *(Fig. 33)*. Continue in same manner.

Fig. 33

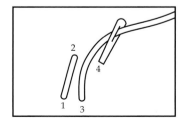

SATIN STITCH

Satin Stitch is a series of straight stitches worked side by side so they touch but do not overlap. Bring needle up at odd numbers and go down at even numbers *(Fig. 34)*.

Fig. 34

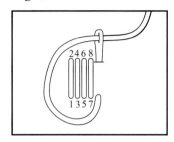

BLANKET STITCH

Bring needle up from wrong side at 1, even with edge of felt and leaving an end to be woven in later. Insert needle down at 2 and up again at 3, keeping floss below point of needle *(Fig. 35a)*. Continue in same manner, keeping stitches even *(Fig. 35b)*.

Fig. 35a   **Fig. 35b**

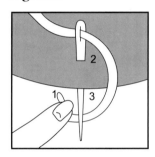   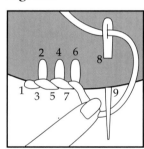

BACKSTITCH

Working from right to left, bring needle up at 1 leaving an end to be woven in later, go down at 2 and come up at 3 *(Fig. 36a)*. The second stitch is made by going down at 1 and coming up at 4 *(Fig. 36b)*. Continue in same manner.

Fig. 36a   **Fig. 36b**

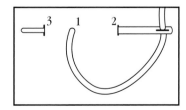   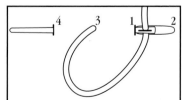

141

FRENCH KNOT

Bring needle up at 1. Wrap yarn desired number of times around needle and go down at 2, holding end of yarn with non-stitching fingers *(Fig. 37)*. Tighten knot; then pull needle through, holding yarn until it must be released.

Fig. 37

LAZY DAISY STITCH

Make all loops equal in length. Bring needle up at 1 and make a counterclockwise loop with the yarn. Go down at 1 and come up at 2, keeping the yarn below the point of the needle *(Fig. 38)*. Secure loop by bringing thread over loop and down at 3. Repeat for the desired number of petals or leaves.

Fig. 38

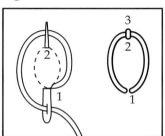

KEY

- ▪ Satin Stitch
- ◩ Lazy Daisy stitch
- ⋰ Outline stitch
- ⁄ Straight stitch
- ● French Knots
- ▮ Blue
- ▮ Dark Blue
- ▮ Green
- ▮ Pink
- ▮ Yellow

Fold

STARCHING & BLOCKING

TIPS

1. If using the same fabric stiffener for both white and colored items, starch the white items first, in case thread dye should bleed into the solution.
2. A good blocking board can make pinning easier. You can use heavy cardboard, an ironing board, ceiling board, etc.
3. Stainless steel pins with balls on the end will be easier to use and will help keep fingers from hurting. Fabric stiffener will permanently damage pins used for sewing. These can be set aside for all starching projects.
4. Fabric stiffener can be returned to the bottle after starching if it has not been contaminated with particles and dye. Clip one corner of the bag, then squeeze the bag, forcing the solution to flow into the bottle.
5. An acrylic spray can be used after starching to protect the piece from heat and humidity.

STARCHING

Read the following instructions before beginning.

1. Wash item using a mild detergent and warm water. Rinse thoroughly. Roll each piece in a clean terry towel and gently press out the excess moisture. Lay piece flat and allow to dry **completely**.
2. Pour fabric stiffener in a resealable plastic bag. Do not dilute stiffener. *Note:* This method is permanent and will not wash out.
3. Immerse dry piece in fabric stiffener, remove air, and seal the bag. Work solution thoroughly into each piece. Let soak for several hours or overnight.

BLOCKING

Good blocking techniques make a big difference in the quality of the finished piece. When pinning piece be careful not to split the threads when inserting pins between the stitches. Make sure curved parts are smooth, straight parts are straight and symmetrical components are equal. Use photo as a guide and use a generous quantity of pins to hold all of the components in place until dry.

Refer to further instructions on this page for specific projects.

SUNFLOWER BASKET

1. Remove Basket from solution and squeeze gently to remove as much excess stiffener as possible. Blot with a paper towel several times to remove excess from holes.
2. With **right** side facing, pin bottom of Basket through Rnd 11 to plastic covered blocking board, forming a 9" circle.
3. Place a 9" plastic foam ring covered with plastic wrap into Basket, or use plastic wrap to create a ring. Curve Petals upward and pin in place.
4. Allow to dry **completely**.

RUFFLED MINI TREE

1. Using heavy cardboard, form a cone that is pointed at top, 17" in height and 8½" in diameter at base. Tape along edge to secure and cover with plastic wrap.
2. Remove Tree from solution and squeeze gently to remove as much excess stiffener as possible. Blot with a paper towel several times to remove excess from holes.
3. Place Tree over cone and pin at regular intervals. Working with one Layer at a time, shape each into evenly spaced ruffles, stuffing each ruffle with plastic wrap to hold its shape; pin in place.
4. Allow to dry **completely**.
5. Apply protective coating to protect and preserve Tree after starching.

PROTECTIVE COATING

1. Remove Tree from cardboard cone. Cover cone with waxed paper.
2. Wearing gloves and using a paintbrush, apply a light coat of porcelain glaze to entire surface. Remember to check and remove drips periodically.
3. Allow to dry **completely**.

A second coat may be applied only after first coat is **completely** dry.

Note: To **wash** Tree, rinse in cool or lukewarm water, then pat dry. Tree can be reshaped if necessary by using a hair dryer and shaping after area is warm. Allow to cool before using.

credits

We extend a warm *thank you* to the generous people who allowed us to photograph some of our projects at their homes: *Wrapped Up in Afghans* — Susan Wildung, Joan Gould, Nancy Gunn Porter, and Gail Wilcox. *All Through the House* — Shirley Held. *Gifts for All* — Nancy Gunn Porter. *Hooked on Holidays* — LaJauna Hernin.

To Magna IV Color Imaging of Little Rock, Arkansas, we say thank you for the superb color reproduction and excellent pre-press preparation. We want to especially thank photographers Larry Pennington, Ken West, Karen Shirey, and Mark Mathews of Peerless Photography, Little Rock, Arkansas, and Jerry R. Davis of Jerry Davis Photography, Little Rock, Arkansas, for their time, patience, and excellent work.

A special word of thanks goes to the talented designers who created the lovely projects in this book:

Linda Bailey: *Ruffled Mini Tree*, page 124
Mary Lamb Becker: *Pretty in Peach*, page 24, and *Cheery Tree Skirt*, page 126
Dianne Bee: *Sunflower Basket*, page 67
Joan Beebe: *Darling Bubble Suits*, page 88
Rose Marie Brooks: *Downy-Soft Afghans*, page 86
Christina Romo Carlisle: *Tops for Toddlers*, page 105
Maureen Egan Emlet: *Patchwork Sampler*, page 6
Nancy Fuller: *Kid-Pleasing Plaid Afghan*, page 64
Shobha Govindan: *Pretty Pillows*, page 44; *Lacy Coaster*, page 47; *Pincushion Bonnet*, page 69; and *Cross Bookmarks*, page 112
Anne Halliday: *Snowflake Sachets*, page 128
Cindy Harris: *Four-Season Fridgies*, page 76; *Political Mascots*, page 115; and *Boo Kitty*, page 118
Jan Hatfield: *Happy Housewarming!*, page 51
Alice Heim: *Elegant Handkerchief*, page 57
Carol L. Jensen: *Feminine Scarf*, page 97
Terry Kimbrough: *Shell Jar Topper*, page 32; *Shell Basket*, page 32; *Shell Towel Edging*, page 33; *Shell Rug*, page 33; *Pansy Garden Afghan*, page 36; *Pansy Sachet*, page 39; *Petite Tissue Cover*, page 52; *Mallard Jar Topper*, page 58; and *Poppy Pot Holder*, page 75
Jennine Korejko: *Snuggly Wraps*, page 12, and *Slippers for Kids*, page 101
Tammy Kreimeyer: *Playtime Dinosaur*, page 72, and *Sweetheart Frames*, page 108

Melissa Leapman: *Building Blocks Quilt*, page 10
Jean Leffler: *Baby Brother*, page 54
Linda Luder: *For Tiny Toes*, page 85
Kay Meadors: *Delicate Cardigan*, page 94, and *Tulip Garden Sweatshirt*, page 103
Sue Penrod: *Pansy Basket Tissue Cover*, page 38, and *Haunting Magnets*, page 120
Carole Prior: *Filet Ripples*, page 18, and *Merry Afghan*, page 131
Mary Jane Protus: *Brown-Eyed Susans*, page 20, and *Handsome Stripes*, page 22
Delsie Rhoades: *Pineapple Table Topper*, page 28; *Flowerpot Lace*, page 48; *Tulip Doily*, page 60; and *Wheat Doily*, page 122
Katherine Satterfield Robert: *Frilly Napkin Ring and Place Mat Edging*, page 42
Donna Scully: *His-and-Hers Pullovers*, page 99
Rena Stevens: *Bold Appeal*, page 16
C. Strohmeyer: *Floral Ensemble Bottle Cover*, page 93
Gail Tanquary: *Country Bread Cloth*, page 62
Carole Rutter Tippett: *Lacy Hexagons*, page 14
Beth Ann Webber: *Cuddly Set*, page 80
Maggie Weldon: *Casserole Cozy*, page 42, and *Cutlery Caddy*, page 43
Margie Wicker: *Baby's Bible Cover*, page 83
Mary Workman: *Colorful Bag Rug*, page 70

We extend a sincere *thank you* to the people who assisted in making and testing the projects for this book: Janet Akins, Anitta Armstrong, Jennie Black, June Clevenger, Helga Christensen, Liz Edmondson, Lee Ellis, Patricia Funk, Linda Graves, Naomi Greening, Raymelle Greening, Jean Hall, Kathleen Hardy, Lisa Hightower, Maedean Johnson, Frances Moore-Kyle, Ruth Landon, Ruby Lee, Pat Little, Faye Morgan, Carol McElroy, Sandy Pique, Dale Potter, Hilda Rivero, Rondi Rowell, Linda Shock, Donna Soellner, Faith Stewart, Bill Tanner, Carol Thompson, and Sherry Williams.